Procedural and declarative information
in software manuals

Utrecht Studies in Language and Communication

7

Series Editors

Paul van den Hoven
Wolfgang Herrlitz

Procedural and declarative information in software manuals

Effects on information use, task performance and knowledge

Nicole Ummelen

Amsterdam - Atlanta, GA 1997

∞ The paper on which this book is printed meets the requirements of "ISO 9706:1994, Information and documentation - Paper for documents - Requirements for permanence".

ISBN: 90-420-0128-3
©Editions Rodopi B.V., Amsterdam - Atlanta, GA 1997
Printed in The Netherlands

Contents

Acknowledgements

Research is often looked upon as an isolated activity. The lonely researcher who spends years behind a desk without any contact with others is a cliché. Whilst carrying out this study and writing this dissertation, it became apparent how unjust the cliché really is. Working together with many friends and colleagues and the support they gave was of great importance to setting up, carrying out, and reporting this study. As a consequence, I had even more fun working on it. This is why I would like to take this opportunity to thank everyone concerned.

First of all, I would like to extend my thanks to my supervisor, Michaël Steehouder. When I arrived in Twente in 1992, I only associated "Steehouder" with a well-known blue textbook. Since then, Michaël has come to mean a lot more than just "Leren Communiceren" (Learning to Communicate). He was an enthusiastic supervisor, who above all stood out as discussion partner in generating ideas and conferring about papers and results. With his extensive knowledge of literature in the field of technical documentation, he was often able to supplement and improve the content of my reports, articles and the thesis. Michaël not only looked critically at my work, but also at my person and adjusted his method of supervision when necessary, even if a new approach was not quite in keeping with his own character or working method. The listening ear, the keen eye and the flexible attitude are crucial factors in supervising Ph.D. students, but sometimes difficult to realise for an experienced researcher with an own opinion. The fact that Michaël succeeded so well in this, made my time in Twente as research assistant a very pleasant one, where I was given the freedom to realise my ideas and get involved in the project. I look back with appreciation and pleasure on the contact we had, also beyond the scope of my study.

I also owe many thanks to my tutor Peter Jan Schellens. I am happy that with his help I was always able to let that one goal, i.e. to do research and write a thesis, prevail above all other goals, but I am also happy that furthermore, he gave me the opportunity to be active in other areas. During the period of writing and rewriting, I benefited from the conscientious and thorough way he read and commented on the papers. Without exception, my scribblings were returned to me with many valuable questions and suggestions. The discussions about parts of the thesis were constructive and stimulating. This enabled me to keep any stress under control during the writing period.

I would like to thank the members of the faculty of Applied Linguistics in Twente for their friendly collegiality and support. Two names should be emphasised in relation to this: Angelique Boekelder en Menno de Jong. The "peer group feedback" which is so often deployed by the faculty in education, was also active in our research room for more than three years. Our frequent discussions were not only about research, but our chairs often faced for education, day-to-day matters in the faculty, the latest gossip, the state of the world and life in general. The conclusion usually was that we would approach things quite differently. Afterwards we could peacefully get back to work again. I thoroughly enjoyed our time together in A334.

Furthermore I would like to thank several people who helped me in various ways during realisation of the research: Jacco Brok, for selflessly placing his *Keylog-*

procedure at our disposal; the 203 test persons, for their enthusiasm: after they had spent for up to two hours working intensively they usually still showed an interest and had enough energy to ask a hundred and one questions about the whys and wherefores of the experiments; Mark Kamphuis for conducting a control experiment; the secretaries of the WMW faculty at the University of Twente, in particular Ada Gieskes, Anneke Aarten, Ellen Lelyveld, Petra Bruulsema and Joan Lurvink: with them both my registration timetable for the experiments and the test persons were in good hands; Fons Maes and Hans Hoeken from the Catholic University of Brabant, for their useful comments on the first version of this dissertation; Hans Hoeken, for the many mini-courses in "Advanced Methodology and Statistics" by telephone, post, or E-mail; Kim Allwright for the quick and meticulous correction of my English; my colleagues of the Department of Applied Linguistics at the Technical University of Delft, who greatly supported me in combining a new job with the final phase of the thesis; and my family and friends, who were always prepared to listen, but also kept me involved in all kinds of things which had nothing to do with this study.

   To conclude with, there is one person to whom I owe a very special thanks. The first six months he still witnessed from a distance, but ever since we share more than just our employer, no one has been as involved in my study as he has, both in terms of content and in the supportive sense. In terms of content, because I could always rely on his technical expertise at any time of the day or night to help me in setting up and developing the click & read method. In terms of content, because he contributed his ideas and because of his uninhibited way of asking all kinds of questions about the whys and wherefores of my study. In terms of content, because even dish-washing conversations gave me new ideas. In terms of support, because of his ever-lasting readiness to deal with even the least interesting programming chores for me. In terms of support, by being able to secretly and ever so quickly fix up a temporary computer, when an old one gave problems during an experiment. In terms of support, by watching me with Argus' eyes in busy times and helping me to put things into perspective so now and then. In terms of support, because of his unremitting enthusiasm, optimism and trust. Recently, on the analogy of the word "promotor" (Dutch for tutor), he was very appropriately called the "help motor". I would like to thank my colleague, programmer and system manager Lars Boelen for his boundless and selfless commitment to my study. A commitment which is so recognisable in the result. But above all, I would like to thank him for his love and friendship. Because of him I was able to move mountains.

Delft, October 1996

To Elly, Jo, Mieke en Gerard,
because a human being is sometimes capable of so much more
than scientists expect.

Introduction

Software manuals contain a lot of procedural information: actions that software users should carry out to achieve their goals, conditions for those actions and results from those actions. Often, software manuals also contain background information about the software and its functions, such as explanations, descriptions and facts. The action information is called procedural information and the background information is called declarative information.

Technical writers do not always make clear choices with respect to these information types. It sometimes appears to be a dilemma whether or not manuals should only contain procedural information, or, in other words, whether or not declarative information should also be included. In the introduction to the Microsoft Excel/Visual Basic manual (Jacobson, 1995), the author claims for instance, that the first parts of the manual are especially designed to support doing and to teach practical skills, *not* to explain theoretical concepts. He thereby suggests that novice users will not look for theoretical explanations, whereas advanced users might be interested in explanations of underlying concepts, provided that these explanations are linked directly to actions:

> Parts 1 and 2 teach practical skills without explaining underlying theoretical concepts. Parts 3 and 4 teach theoretical concepts, but in a very hands-on, experiential way.
> (p. XIV, "Finding the best starting point for you")

However, contrary to what is mentioned, part 1 of the manual starts on page 3 with a two-page explanation about macros. First, a metaphor is used to illustrate why macros are useful and worth the investment of making them. Then, on page 4, a full page of prose text is presented to explain what macros are, what a macro recorder does, which programming language is used for the macros in Excel and what the differences are between keystroke macros and macros containing programming language. There are more explanations about underlying concepts in the first part of the manual, and in the third and fourth part, the theoretical concepts are not always linked directly to actions, either.

The introductory statement and the information that follows contradict each other and this points towards a dilemma. The author starts from the idea that leaving out declarative information makes for a more usable manual that meets the users' preferences well. Still, he decides to include declarative information in certain sections. The question is: why has the statement that no concepts would be explained not been put into effect consistently? Perhaps the author's experience or intuition told him that certain explanations are indispensable, or perhaps the results of usability tests indicated that users needed an explanation at some points.

Comments that are often made by manual users point to the same dilemma. On the one hand, software users have been reported to complain about manuals that contain too much explanatory and descriptive information, instead of information about what they should *do* (e.g. Mack et al., 1983). Because of all this unnecessary information, manuals are often considered to be *too thick*. On the other hand, users also appear to complain when the manual is *incomplete* in their eyes. Sometimes they even specifically ask for more explanations (e.g. Carroll et al., 1988).

The dilemma of whether or not to include declarative information in a manual has been the topic of scientific research. However, this research has not yet offered conclusive answers to the question of how frequently procedural and declarative information are used, nor to the question of whether or not declarative information is useful for users of software manuals. This inconclusiveness was for instance due to selection data that were not precise enough, and to experimental situations in which the manual had to be studied and memorized completely before the software itself could be used: a situation that hardly ever occurs in reality. If these problems could be solved, research results could probably give a better indication of how the practical dilemma of whether or not to include declarative information in a manual should be solved.

On behalf of this study, a new technique was developed for measuring global information selection and information use: the click & read method. This technique presented a manual on a computer screen with blurred text sections. Subjects could sharpen and read the text sections by clicking on them. The clicks were recorded in logfiles. By means of this technique, more precise data could now be recorded that indicated how often and how long procedural and declarative information were used. Moreover, the click & read method enabled users to work with the software and use the manual at the same time.

The click & read method was used to measure whether users only use procedural, or also declarative information spontaneously. Furthermore, this study offers an answer to the question of whether or not declarative information in software manuals is *useful*: it will investigate whether or not declarative information can enhance task performance, reasoning or factual knowledge. These questions will be answered in a series of experiments that also take into account simple and complex tasks, different user situations and different arrangements of procedural and declarative information.

Overview of this book

This study focuses on the questions of how frequently and how intensively procedural and declarative information are used, whether declarative information is useful and why, and what factors in the text and context affect information use.

In chapter 1, the differences between procedural and declarative information will be described. Furthermore, an overview of past research into the use and effects of procedural and declarative information will be presented. It is argued that new experiments should meet a set of requirements in order to find a precise answer to the research questions. Chapter 1 will conclude with these requirements and an overview of the research questions for this study.

The research questions will be investigated in a series of experiments. Chapter 2 will serve as a standard methodology section for all experiments. The independent and dependent variables will be described, their operationalizations will be explained, a new instrument to measure information use will be presented, and the general procedure of the experiments will be described.

The chapters 3 through 5 each focus on one research question. In chapter 3, the experiments and results concerning the use of procedural and declarative information will be described and discussed. Chapter 4 will report on the results of an experiment about the effects of declarative information. Finally, chapter 5 will deal with the possible effects of information arrangement: it will investigate how different arrangements (e.g. a different order) of procedural and declarative information in a manual can affect selection, use, performance and knowledge.

Chapter 6 will summarize the main conclusions and present practical implications, an evaluation of the experimental technique and some directions for further research. Concrete examples and illustrations of the materials that were used in the experiments can be found in Appendices 1 through 7.

Chapter 1
Procedural and declarative information

This chapter is a general introduction to the research questions concerning procedural and declarative information. Section 1.1 discusses the distinction between procedural and declarative information. Several definitions are presented along with some problems concerning those definitions. A description is given of which definitions are chosen in the context of this study with reference to the information types.

In section 1.2, an overview is presented of the past research into the use and effects of procedural and declarative information. Section 1.3 specifies five requirements for new studies into the use and effects of procedural and declarative information. Finally, the research questions are summarized in section 1.4.

1.1   The distinction between procedural and declarative information

1.1.1   Relevance of the distinction

The distinction between procedural and declarative information and the effects of these information types on user performance and knowledge are recurring topics in research literature concerning technical documentation, human computer interaction and cognitive psychology. The main reason for this attention is that procedural and declarative information are expected to meet different user needs. They are claimed to serve users who have different reading goals and to require different cognitive actions (e.g. Anderson, 1983; Charney, Reder & Wells, 1988; Alexander et al., 1991). Research has focused on the information types in order to describe what constitutes the difference and to find out why procedural and declarative information can be useful. The discussion whether or not procedural and declarative information are both useful in software manuals is the central topic of this study.

In document design literature, the need for procedural information in manuals is considered to be self-evident, but the need for including declarative information in a software manual is under discussion. Procedural information can be executed, declarative information can be understood and retained, but it is not considered to be necessary for *doing* things. As users of software manuals are expected to be primarily interested in *doing* instead of reading and understanding, procedural information is considered to be of crucial importance and declarative information is thought of as secondary. However, many technical writers also include explanations and other declarative information in their manuals. They seem to be of the opinion that a manual should be as complete as possible and they seem to make an assumption that at least part of the software users can benefit from this information.

Some research efforts have concentrated on the question of what declarative information can contribute to the user's knowledge and performance (see 1.2), but it is still difficult to draw a straightforward conclusion on the basis of the results so far.

1.1.2   Problems concerning the definitions of *procedural* and *declarative* information

Several definitions and operationalizations of procedural and declarative information are proposed in psychological and linguistic research literature. Some definitions refer to the knowledge that a user needs to perform a task, and some definitions refer to procedural and declarative information in a manual, depending on the field of research.

To illustrate this diversity, ten definitions of procedural and declarative information are presented in table 1.1 below. These have been derived from articles that report empirical research into the effects of procedural and declarative knowledge or information[1]. The articles by Alexander et al. (1991) and Mirel (1991) are research reviews. All articles relate to the knowledge or information which is necessary for solving problems or learning skills.

Table 1.1
Definitions of procedural and declarative information

	Definition referring to:	Procedural	Declarative
1. Anderson (1983)	knowledge	***Terms used***: procedural knowledge ***Implemented as***: *knowing how*; knowledge that is applied automatically and is difficult to report verbally	***Terms used***: declarative knowledge ***Implemented as***: *knowing that*; knowledge that can be reported and is not tied to a specific application
2. Kieras & Bovair (1984)	text & diagram instructions	***Terms used***: operating procedures, *how-to-do-it* instructions ***Implemented as***: a sequence of steps, not only including actions, but also conditions for actions and results from actions (pp.258 & 261)	***Terms used***: *how-it-works* information, device model ***Implemented as***: description of the components of the device, their internal working and their relation to each other; general principles underlying the system; description of the context in which it is used (pp. 258 & 266)
3. Smith & Goodman (1984)	written instructions	***Terms used***: linear instructions, *steps* ***Implemented as***: a linear sequence of steps and a general goal, with no attempt to provide readers with connections between the instructions and their prior knowledge (p.360).	***Terms used***: 1. structural instructions 2. functional instructions, *statements* ***Implemented as***: explanatory information, additional to linear instructions; 1. emphasizing the structure of the circuit ; 2. emphasizing the function (power flow) of the circuit (pp. 359 & 365)

	Definition referring to:	Procedural	Declarative
4. Reder, Charney & Morgan (1986)	text in manuals (refers to the same experiment as 5)	***Terms used***: syntax elaborations[a] ***Implemented as***: elaborations that specify how to perform a procedure (p.70); elaborations on how to issue a command, such as examples of correct commands and descriptively rich format statements (p.71).	***Terms used***: conceptual elaborations[a] ***Implemented as***: elaborations on the purpose of commands and when it was advisable to use them; elaborations on basic topics such as disk drives, subdirectories and paths (p.71).
5. Charney, Reder & Wells (1988)	text in manuals (refers to the same experiment as 4)	***Terms used***: procedural elaborations[a] ***Implemented as***: information about how to issue commands correctly: examples of correct commands, details about notational conventions etc. (p. 54).	***Terms used***: conceptual elaborations[a] ***Implemented as***: information concerning basic concepts, such as the purpose of the Rename command, or conditions for application, such as when it is advisable to rename a file (p. 54).
6. Alexander, Schallert & Hare (1991)	knowledge	***Terms used***: procedural knowledge ***Defined as***: knowledge one has of certain processes or routines; *knowing how* (p.333)	***Terms used***: 1. declarative knowledge 2. conceptual knowledge ***Defined as***: 1. Factual information; *knowing what* (p.332). 2. Knowledge of ideas, consisting of what they are, how they function or operate and the conditions under which they are used (p.332).

	Definition referring to:	Procedural	Declarative
7. Guthrie et al. (1991)	text or graphics in instructions	**Terms used**: procedural information **Defined as**: a set of separate, executable actions required of the performer. In verbal form, these are usually ordered statements (p.252)	**Terms used**: overview, statement of purpose; workspace (presented as part of a *procedural* document) **Implemented as**: Item containing information about the nature of the outcome and its organization. Permits performers to generate a conceptual model of what they are trying to accomplish (pp.251/252). The area in which the learner utilizes the procedural information, e.g. a piece of equipment (p.252).
8. Mirel (1991)	information in manuals	**Terms used**: functional information **Implemented as**: *task oriented* (p. 113 & 120).	**Terms used**: descriptive information **Implemented as**: *product oriented* information, description of the system design (p. 120).
9. Churchill (1992)	knowledge	**Terms used**: procedural knowledge **Implemented as**: *how-to-do-it* knowledge; task-related strings of actions which offer the user a "recipe" for getting the task done	**Terms used**: model-based knowledge **Implemented as**: *how-the-device-works* knowledge; knowledge about causal relationships between task-relevant, internal device components

	Definition referring to:	Procedural	Declarative
10. Donin et al. (1992)	instructions written by students	***Terms used***: procedures **Implemented as**: complex relational structures involving three types of information: goals, condition-action rules and a specification of the action structure: the action to be carried out, by whom, to what existing state, with what instruments, with what result etc. (pp.214-215)	***Terms used***: non-procedural, descriptive information (p.217 & 221) **Implemented as**: ? Results from actions are considered to be "descriptive information directly linked to procedures" (p.221). No examples are given of descriptive information that is *not* directly linked to procedures.

Notes

"Defined as" indicates that the authors give an explicit definition of the information types.
"Implemented as" indicates that an operational definition is presented in a description of (for instance) experimental materials, or can be inferred from examples.
(a) Reder et al. and Charney et al. refer to the information type in the elaborations, not to the information that is elaborated upon (see Reder et al., p.71 or Charney et al., pp.54 & 55)

Table 1.1 demonstrates that procedural information is often defined as action information or "how to do it" information; declarative information is often defined as descriptive information about "how the system works". Most of the researchers mentioned in the table make an explicit distinction between procedural and declarative information, even though they sometimes use different terms or different definitions. In contrast, Guthrie et al., who focus on procedural documents which support readers with a *reading to do* goal, discuss information in terms of procedural documents only. However, as their definitions of *overviews* and *workspace* are very similar to what is believed to be declarative (or descriptive, conceptual or explanatory) information by most other researchers, these concepts are included in the table as well, under the heading "declarative".

The definitions give a good general impression of the ways in which the concepts of procedural and declarative are interpreted. There are a lot of similarities between them, but there are also differences. In fact, it is quite difficult to judge on the basis of these definitions whether or not different researchers have investigated the same concepts: the definitions leave too much room for questions, doubts and discussion.

In a subset of the articles, manipulations in experimental manuals or instructions are demonstrated in an appendix. When analyzing these texts, it even becomes more apparent how differently the terms *procedural* and *declarative* can be interpreted (see figure 1.1 and 1.2).

Figure 1.1
Example from Charney, Reder & Wells (1988): instructions for the MS-DOS operating system for PCs[2]

Procedural elaboration
A> CHDIR B:\PROGRAMS\PASCAL <ENTER>
The first symbol in the path is a backslash (\). This means that the path to the new current directory starts with the root directory of the diskette in drive B. The path indicates that the root directory contains a subdirectory called PROGRAMS, and that PROGRAMS contains PASCAL, the directory you want to designate as the 'new' directory. As usual, the amount of location information you need to provide depends on which directory was last designated as the current directory for the drive.

Conceptual elaboration
The root directory is automatically designated as the current directory for each drive when you first start up the computer. It is useful to designate a subdirectory as the current directory when you will be working primarily on the files in that subdirectory. Then you won't have to specify the path to the subdirectory in each command you issue.

Figure 1.2
Example from Kieras & Bovair (1984): instructions for a starship control panel device

---

Operating procedures
- Turn SP switch on.
- Set ES selector to MA (or SA).
- Press button FM (or FS).
- Wait until PF indicator finishes flashing.
- Set ES selector to N.
- Turn SP off.

Device model instructions
The energy booster takes in power from the ship and boosts it to the level necessary to fire the phasers. Power that has been boosted by the energy booster is fed into the two accumulators. Both accumulators store large amounts of power ready to be discharged to the phaser bank whenever the phasers are fired.
Because the accumulators handle such large amounts of power, if they are used continuously they are liable to overload and burn out. To prevent continuous use of one accumulator, this system has two: the main accumulator (MA) and the secondary accumulator (SA).
The power coming in from the shipboard circuits is controlled by the ship's power switch (SP).
(...etc.)

What Charney et al. have included as procedural information appears to be totally different from what Kieras & Bovair have included as procedural information, and a comparison of the declarative text items leads to the same conclusion. But what exactly is it that constitutes the difference between the definitions and operationalizations? The difference between most definitions can be reduced to three issues which will be explained and illustrated with examples below.

1   Is procedural information only information at syntax level, or also at the level of computer tasks and real world tasks?
Duffy et al. (1988) refer to the distinction first made by Shneiderman (1987) between tasks at the *syntax-* (or command-, or keystroke-) level, *computer task* level and *real world task* level. Procedural information can occur at all three levels (*Press Enter; Open a file; Calculate the expenses*).

Charney et al. (1988) interpret procedural information as both action and system information at syntax level only. The example of a procedural elaboration in figure 1.1 illustrates their view. First the command is presented that tells the user what to type: an action at syntax level. Then the syntax of the command is explained. This is also part of the procedural elaboration, although the reader is not explicitly instructed to do something here. This may explain why these procedural elaborations were called "syntax elaborations" in an earlier article by Reder et al. (1986). The level of the computer task (e.g. *Changing directories*) is not specified further in their materials.

Smith & Goodman (1984) call a *general goal* in instructions, such as *Assemble this circuit* or *How to replace a flat tire* an "explanatory statement" (p.362), whereas in fact, it can also be considered to be a procedural instruction at a higher level than the level of single action steps.

Donin et al. (1991) on the other hand interpret procedural information as all the reader oriented information that is directly connected to user's actions, not only at syntax level, but also at computer task level or the level of real world tasks.

2   Are conditions and results included in procedural information, or do they belong to declarative information?
Guthrie et al. (1991) say that procedural information consists of nothing but the action sequences the user has to perform. Everything that does not fit into this category belongs to another type of information, including conditions for and results from actions. Smith & Goodman (1984) only include action sequences in their linear instructions, with no conditions or results.

The definition of procedural information by Donin et al. (1991) includes results from actions, but in the frames they present of students' texts, they call results from actions such as *light goes off* descriptive information.

According to Charney et al., conditions for applying a procedure belong to the category of conceptual information, but contrary to the other authors mentioned here, they refer to the computer task level: information that tells the user when a certain procedure is useful, and not information about the state of the system before an action step can be taken.

3   Is declarative information more than information about how-the-system-works?

Kieras & Bovair (1984) and Churchill (1992) take declarative information to be system oriented information that explains and describes how the system works and why it works that way. The focus is on elements like buttons, keys, connections and technical codes. Other researchers use a broader definition: they state that declarative information is all the information in a text, other than pure actions. Even information that has a direct link with actions is sometimes interpreted as declarative information, although it is not always explicitly labelled in that way (Guthrie et al., 1991; Charney et al., 1988).

Because of the different views on procedural and declarative information, the effects of the information types reported in one article are not directly comparable to the effects reported in another article. For reasons of comparison and interpretability, the first step in a series of investigations into the use and effects of procedural and declarative information should be the choice of an explicit and unambiguous definition for the information types.

1.1.3   Definitions chosen in this study

Similar to some of the studies described above, the goal of the current study is to investigate the use and effects of procedural and declarative information. Therefore, a description will be presented in this section of how the information types were operationalized in an experimental manual.

The concepts *procedural* and *declarative* are conceived of as *text characteristics* in this study, divided into *text content* and *text form characteristics*, as the goal of the definition is to describe how the information types will be expressed in the text of experimental manuals.

A different criterion for calling a text part procedural or declarative, which is not taken into consideration here, would be the user's interpretation of the text. A user may interpret a text for instance as procedural, even if the text characteristics are those of declarative information. This interpretation may be induced by the user's goal, by form characteristics of the text or by both. If the user's goal is *doing* something only, then he may interpret declarative information as something that has to be executed, as Carroll et al. (1986) describe (p.2). Also, if procedural text content is put in a declarative syntactic form, this may lead the user to initially interpreting it as a fact to be learned, not as a direction for an action.

Thus, not only text content, but also form characteristics of the text and users' goals should be examined in investigations into the use and effects of procedural and declarative information. The content and form characteristics of procedural and declarative text chosen in this study are described below.

Text content
In this study, procedural information consists of actions, conditions for actions and results from actions. Actions, conditions and results occur at three levels: the syntax level, the computer task level and the real world task level.

Declarative information is considered to be all (explanatory) information other than action information, referring for instance to *how the device works* and other, more specific descriptive information or facts, such as an analysis of the conventional format of commands.[3]

However, this general definition of the information types still raises questions as to how the different types should be operationalized at a more detailed text level. Therefore, an additional aid for assessing the information content was created: a set of topical questions, representative for the information types. The topical questions result from a global analysis of a small selection of software manuals.

procedural

action	*(What to do?)*
user condition	*(Which conditions have to be met by the user before carrying out an action?)*
system condition	*(Which conditions have to be met by the system before carrying out an action?)*
result	*(What will be the result of the action?)*

declarative

introduction	*(What is the topic?)*
definition	*(What is it?)*
terminology	*(What is it called?)*
description	*(What does it look like?)*
composition	*(Of which parts does it consist?)*
options	*(Which extra possibilities are there?)*
functionality	*(When is it useful?)*
analogy	*(What can it be compared with?)*
location	*(Where can it be found?)*

These topical questions were used to identify text at individual sentence or clause level. For the purpose of investigation, a procedural information block consisting of more sentences was defined as an information block containing procedural sentences only, and a declarative information block was defined as a block containing declarative sentences only. Of course, in many manuals, there are information blocks that contain *both* procedural and declarative sentences. The use and effects of these larger organizational units in manuals are however not of interest here. The question is how to *distinguish* the information types in order to investigate how software users use them and what effects they have.

The examples 1 and 2 illustrate how the topical questions were applied to classify text content.

[1]   *If you want to copy the cell to only one other cell:*
        5. Move the cursor to the cell where the copied data should
        appear and press Enter.
        If you want to copy the cell to a block of other cells:
        5. Move the cursor to a corner cell of the block where the
        copied data should appear.
        6. Type a full stop (.).
        (etc)

[2]   The concept of a block is different from the block concept in most
        other spreadsheets. A block is a group of joined cells, no matter
        whether they are marked or not. In other systems, a block is not
        called a block until it is marked.

The italic parts of [1], ("If you want to....") are user conditions for the actions 5 and 6. The user is told what to do in a certain situation. The information is thus classified as procedural information. In example [2], part of the system is compared to another system (*analogy*) and a definition is given for a block. This text element is thus categorized as declarative information.

The identification of the declarative items becomes more difficult when they answer the declarative topical questions and enable the inference of actions at the same time, as is shown in [3]:

[3]   Copying a cell to other cells using the Copy-function is especially
        useful when the cell contents are long and complicated, like in
        formulas.

[4]   Cell addresses consist of one x coordinate which refers to the
         column, one y coordinate which refers to the row and one z
         coordinate which refers to the page.

According to the topical questions, [3] deals with functionality. Literally, the
sentence tells the user why a procedure might be useful in general: it is not
necessarily related to an action. It is however possible that a user *infers* a
condition for an action here: "If I need a formula in another place in the
spreadsheet, I should use the Copy-function". In [4], cell addresses are
explained: it is a *composition* item, combined with *definitions*. Strictly
speaking, this explanation is not necessary for a user who only wants to do
something. On the other hand, it is not difficult to infer a procedure from [4].
The items described in examples [3] and [4] are still considered to be
declarative in the context of this study, as the focus is on explanations about
system elements or tasks that exceed one individual procedure. Procedural
information can only be inferred from these items.[4]

Text form
The second criterion for operationalizing procedural and declarative
information is the syntactic form. Syntactic features can signal the information
type and thus support the user's interpretation of the information. The following
syntactic form features of procedural and declarative text have been used in the
context of the current study:

Procedural	Declarative
• action verbs; imperatives	• modal verbs
• relatively short 'action' sentences	• relatively long 'fact' sentences
• step by step presentation of items	• continuous proze
• direct style	• indirect style
• if...then constructions	• modifiers

These form characteristics have been derived from several sources. Werlich
(1979) for instance distinguishes five text types: narrative, descriptive,
expository, argumentative and instructive. He outlines the prototypical syntactic
constructions that mark these information types by convention. The prototypical

constructions can be found in important parts of the text, like the first sentence of a new paragraph. Werlich's form descriptions are very clarifying, yet very detailed. An elaborate description of the syntactic form descriptions he proposes, is presented in Ummelen (1994). The form descriptions mentioned here have been generalized from Werlich's work. The same form characteristics are for instance also mentioned in Brockmann (1990) and Jansen & Steehouder (1989).

Content and form do not always match. It is possible to express an information type in variants of its prototypical form, or in the prototypical forms of another information type as Virtanen (1992) demonstrates in detail for different content types. The next example shows how a declarative syntactic form can make procedural information indirect and implicit.

[5]   The user should click the OK button.
[6]   The Edit function is a useful function to alter the data with.

The content of the information in [5] and [6] is still procedural, as the obvious goal is to tell the user what to do. Applying declarative form characteristics to procedural items may however cause procedural items to be less easily recognized by users and may therefore confuse them.

Theoretically, declarative content items can also be put in an instructive form, although this hardly ever occurs. Moreover, the only procedural form characteristic that may be applied to declarative content items is an action verb in an imperative form:

[7]   Be aware that the hidden codes in the text will be read by the printer.
[8]   You must realize that the window consists of a few icons and a pulldown menu.

To investigate the use and effects of procedural and declarative information, the content and syntactic form of the information should be matched. This is not representative for most commercial manuals, but for the purpose of operationalizing the information types unambiguously, matching content and form is the most obvious choice. The question as to what effects varying syntactic forms will have on the use and effects of procedural and declarative information falls beyond the scope of this study.

1.2   Use and effects of the information types in manuals

1.2.1   Selection and use of procedural and declarative information

It is remarkable that there are hardly any empirical data showing how software users actually select and use procedural and declarative information if both information types are available. The only data about the question of which information types are used by software users during task performance were reported in the eighties by the research group who developed the *Minimal Manual* (e.g. Mack et al., 1983; Carroll et al., 1987-1988). They had subjects to read and think out loud while reading a commercial tutorial manual and performing their tasks concurrently. Their goal was to identify and classify problems users had using the interface and the manual. One of the observations was that declarative information is often skipped by learners, whereas procedural information or information that can be interpreted as procedural information is used all the time:

> *We have found that learners are very susceptible to plunging into a procedure as soon as it is mentioned (e.g. in a preview) or of trying to execute purely expository descriptions. (....) When material is encountered that cannot be executed it is often just skipped.*
> (Carroll et al., 1986, p.2)

These results should however be interpreted with caution, as the observations were not intended to measure differences in the use information types. Still, the Minimalists were very determined in concluding that a writer should "slash the verbiage", thereby radically excluding all introductory, explanatory and descriptive information from the manual. Their solution to the users' problems of skipping and misreading is to reduce the number of different information types.

The design principle of slashing the verbiage is implemented in the Minimal Manual, together with many other design principles for tutorials[5]. The Minimal Manual repeatedly appears to work better (less training time, better performance) than the wordy commercial manuals that it is compared to. It is however not at all obvious that this success is specifically due to leaving out declarative information. In section 3.1.1, the Minimalist research will be discussed in more detail.

Some ideas about the selection and use of information in manuals in general have been reflected by Kern (1985), Wright, Creighton & Threlfall (1982), Wright (1989) and Steehouder (1994). On the basis of an observational study, Kern concludes that mechanics with much task-specific experience are less likely to consult a manual than mechanics without task-specific experience, because mechanics who have task-specific experience can find out what to do by reading the equipment. Wright et al. (1982) find that people's willingness to read instructions is much higher when the system is complex, unfamiliar and not frequently used. Wright (1989) also mentions text-internal factors that determine whether instructions will be read: people will only read and continue reading when the heading or first sentence shows that the text is relevant to their queries, when they assume they do not know the information yet, and when the text can easily be found and understood. Steehouder (1994) mentions four distinct motives for searching for information in software manuals:

(1) *impasse*: the user cannot proceed because he does not know which functions or procedures should be used. Steehouder relates this motive to a search for procedural, or *how-to* information.

(2) *error*: the user is confronted with something unexpected, an error, which urges him to look for a diagnosis and a remedy.

(3) *dis-coordination*: the user is confused by many disjointed details and fails to see any interconnection between different elements of the problem or task. According to Steehouder, he will typically look for information to get an overall picture of the program.

(4) *uncertainty*: the user is not certain as to whether or not his ideas and guesses about possible solutions are correct. He will look for information to verify his assumptions.

These studies provide general ideas about when and why people look for information in general, or for procedural and declarative information specifically. They show or suggest that information selection and use may be affected by task complexity, user's experience, the type of problem that the user encounters and the structure and signals in the manual. However, no precise information is known yet about how much information of each type is used, and for how long it is used.

1.2.2   Effects of declarative information

Several experiments have been conducted to investigate the effects of declarative information on task performance or knowledge. These experiments were conducted mainly by researchers who were either interested in investigating users' mental models of the system and the task, or in the interaction between software and users, or in the usability of manuals. Four studies are described here.

Kieras & Bovair: the effects of a device model

Kieras & Bovair (1984) conducted three experiments to investigate whether or not the process of learning to operate a simple control panel is affected by a written description and a picture of the internal mechanism of the device. This model of the control panel and the way in which it works is called a *device model* by the authors. In their first experiment, Kieras & Bovair compared two groups of subjects which both had to learn how to operate a control panel for a starship device. The first group, called the *model group*, did so by studying a device model in the form of a written text displayed on a computer screen. The device model contained a description of the control panel with all its components and the relations between those components. It put the device in a meaningful context, and the buttons and controls were also explained in terms of this fictitious set-up. In addition to the text, the subjects received a diagram of the device model on paper. Before continuing their training, subjects had to pass a test for knowledge of the model. The second studying phase consisted of a procedure training, in which the subjects were first taught a procedure and then tested, until the procedure could be performed correctly three times in a row. Then the subjects were trained for the next procedure. During the procedure training, the subjects from the model group were able to use the device model diagram.

The other group of subjects, called the *rote group*, did not receive the device model in any form. They only passed through the procedure training. The rote group had to learn the procedures by rote, and was not aware of a meaningful context or of anything that concerned the internal components or working of the device. Buttons and controls on the device were pointed to by means of abbreviations ("the SP switch", for instance, instead of "the ship's power switch"), as the meaningful terms for the switches were considered to be part of the device model information.

Both groups of subjects had to pass three different tests after the training phase. In the first test, subjects had to carry out some of the procedures they had learned before. The second test was identical, but now subjects were instructed to simplify procedures where possible: some procedures had been made deliberately inefficient. Subjects had to return after a week for the third test: the same test, but without specific instructions this time. The results showed that the model group performed better than the rote group: they needed less time for the procedure training, they achieved the correct goal more often, both immediately and after a week, they needed less time on the tests, and the proportion of efficient procedures was four times larger than in the rote group.

Kieras & Bovair conclude that presenting a device model to the learners improves their performance and retention. They suggest that the reason for this is that the knowledge of how the device works enables users to *infer* the procedures they need, even if they cannot retrieve them directly from memory. To test this hypothesis, they conducted a second experiment with the same experimental conditions: a model group and a rote group. This time, neither of the groups received a procedure training, but they were instructed to infer the procedures while thinking out loud. Thus, the rote group received no information, whereas the model group received the device model. Again, the model group performed significantly better than the rote group. They needed fewer attempts and they always explained their actions in terms of the model, contrary to the rote group.

Having confirmed the hypothesis that a device model helps users to infer procedures, Kieras & Bovair wondered what specific information in the model is responsible for this effect. They for instance distinguish the following conceptual content types: the context in which the device was placed (a space ship), general principles underlying the design of the device ("Why is an energy booster necessary?"), system topology ("What is connected to what?") and power flow ("How is the power routed through the controls to a destination?"). In a third experiment, they varied the information presented in the model. The results show that the fantasy context does not enhance the inference of procedures, but the specific information about the relation between controls and components and the power flow in the device does.

From the results by Kieras & Bovair, one may conclude that declarative information may facilitate task performance, provided that it is the specific type of declarative information that subjects can infer procedures from. With reference to the control panel device that was used here, the important information was the power flow information. It is not obvious what the comparable information in software tasks would be: probably not in the first place the power flow in the computer hardware, but a representation in any form of the internal (programming) codes and their effects. Kieras & Bovair suggest in their conclusions that there is no need for presenting a device model when the procedure is very simple or when the user can infer the device model without a written text. In accordance with this suggestion, one may also hypothesize that more meaningful procedural instructions (for instance by including the full names of the switches to be operated) will probably also enable inferences in situations that are slightly more complex.

Charney, Reder et al.: the effects of conceptual elaborations
Reder, Charney & Morgan (1986) investigated how useful elaborations in a manual are. Contrary to the subjects who participated in the experiments by

Kieras & Bovair, their subjects had to work with software and an experimental software manual.

Reder et al. prepared two versions of a PC-DOS user manual: one elaborated version, with many definitions, analogies, examples, overviews and explanations and one unelaborated version that missed all these elaboration types. Forty inexperienced computer users were instructed to study one of these manuals for 45 minutes. They were told in advance that they would have to perform some tasks on the computer afterwards. Half of the group received a specific task in advance, the other half of the group did not know exactly what tasks they would have to perform after the reading phase. Within these two groups, half of the subjects read the elaborated manual and the other half read the unelaborated manual.

When the reading time was over, the manuals were taken away and the participants were asked to perform some tasks on the computer. It was measured whether or not they could perform the tasks correctly, how much time they needed to complete all tasks and how many commands they issued to complete all tasks. The results showed that subjects with a specific task in mind used fewer commands to complete their tasks after having read the *unelaborated* manual, but subjects with a general task orientation on the other hand needed fewer commands and less time after having read the *elaborated* version of the manual. Both groups completed the same number of tasks correctly.

Charney, Reder & Wells (1988) relate these results to the ongoing discussion between the "Expounders" and the "Minimalists". The Expounders' view is that tutorial manuals should be as complete as possible. They are advocates of the elaborated manual. Minimalists, on the other hand, are convinced that manuals from which a lot of unnecessary information is omitted, work much better. Many elaborations are unnecessary in their opinion. Tests of the Minimal Manual have shown that shorter manuals indeed lead to better and faster learning. As many other design manipulations are incorporated in the Minimal Manual, it is not obvious that it is the exclusion of elaborations that yields the positive results. However, in the first instance, the success of the Minimal Manual is still interpreted as being in conflict with the Expounders' view.

The next step by Charney et al. is to find out *which* elaborations are useful for learners and which elaborations are unnecessary. In order to find an answer to that question, Charney et al. (1988, p. 54) isolate three components of learning a skill:

1   *Appreciate the meaning of novel concepts and the purpose of novel procedures*
2   *Execute the procedures correctly*
3   *Use the procedure at the approprate times*

Their assumption is that it may make a difference if a manual elaborates on all of these components, or just on one specific subset. Accordingly, the elaborations that were used in the PC-DOS manual were classified into two categories: procedural and conceptual elaborations. Conceptual elaborations concerned either basic concepts (e.g the purpose of the Rename command) or conditions for applying a procedure (when it is advisable to rename a file); conceptual elaborations relate to the first and third component of skill learning. Procedural elaborations included examples of correct commands, details about notational conventions and other elaborations that are related to the second component of skill learning.

These two types of elaborations were varied in four manuals: one with rich conceptual and rich procedural elaborations, one with sparse conceptual and sparse procedural elaborations, one with rich conceptual and sparse procedural elaborations and one with sparse conceptual and rich procedural elaborations.

In the experiment, 40 experienced and 40 inexperienced subjects participated, but none of them had ever used an IBM PC. None of them received any information about the specific tasks to perform, so every subject had a general task orientation at the time of studying the manual. After the studying phase, the subjects had to carry out the experimental tasks without being able to use the manual. The dependent measures were the time used to complete all tasks and the number of commands used to complete all tasks. The results revealed that the only elaborations that subjects profitted from were specific examples that illustrated what a correct command would look like in a specific situation. Conceptual elaborations had no effect at all. There was no difference between the experienced and the inexperienced subjects.

Smith & Goodman: the effects of structural and functional statements in instructions
Smith & Goodman (1984) investigated the role of structural and functional information in the understanding instructions for assembling an electrical circuit. They distinguish three types of instructions:

1   *Linear instructions*:
    A set of instructions that first state the general goal, followed by a sequence of executable linear steps.

Example:
General goal: "Assemble an electrical circuit".
Step: "From the underside of the console, insert a short bolt through the hole numbered 64."

2 *Structural instructions*:
   A set of linear instructions with *additional* explanatory statements about the structure of the electrical circuit to be assembled.
   Example of a structural statement that was added to the linear instructions:
   "This circuit has three major components: (1) battery, (2) switch, and (3) small lamp."

3 *Functional instructions*:
   A set of linear instructions with *additional* explanatory statements about the function and working of the electrical circuit.
   Example of a functional statement that was added to the linear instructions:
   "Current can only flow when the circuit's components are interconnected in a complete circle, each connection being made by a wire or other metal object that conducts electricity."

The additional structural and functional statements were mixed with the steps of the linear instructions. In Smith & Goodman's experiment, these three instruction types were tested. Thirty-six subjects participated in the task. The instructions were presented on a computer screen, one step at a time. After having read and understood each step, subjects pushed a button that made the text disappear, and then they could do one of three things: either they pushed another button to continue reading the next statement or step, or they actually carried out a step in the assembly of the electrical circuit, or they went back to the last part of the instructions and read it again. The reading time of the procedural steps and the execution time was recorded. Subjects also completed a multiple-choice test to measure their final understanding of the system. Finally, they were asked to recall all the instructions.

The results revealed that the reading time for the *action steps* was shorter for both structural and functional instructions than for linear ones. These advantages in reading speed even compensated for the extra time it took subjects to read the explanatory statements. The action steps from the structural and functional instructions were also recalled more accurately than those from the linear instructions. There was no difference in execution time or in the multiple-choice test.

These results were replicated in a second experiment in which only some questions in the test and the recall assignment were changed. Subjects now had to actually assemble the circuit again from memory instead of writing down the steps. The results were the same, except that the instructions did not differ on the recall test either now.

In a third experiment, Smith & Goodman included a transfer task instead of a recall test. One week after the execution of the first part, they asked subjects to assemble a similar, yet different circuit. Subjects received no procedural instructions in this transfer task, but only the same type of explanatory statements that they had used for the first task one week earlier. The linear group only received the general goal. The results of this experiment revealed that during the first task, different instruction groups did not differ with respect to reading time or execution time. Subjects who had used structural and functional instructions averaged more correct subprocedures in the transfer task than the control group, which did not perform the first task at all, and thus did not get any other instruction than to assemble the circuit that lights a lamp. The structural group also performed more subprocedures correctly than the linear group.

Smith & Goodman present their results as evidence for the claim that the inclusion of explanatory information in instructions enables users to fit the instructions better into a mental schema[6], to make better connections between the instructions and what they already know. However, the explanatory statements that they included were of a specific type, and they showed only specific effects. The different instruction types do not *always* show differences in reading time (not with skilled users and very simple tasks), they do not show any differences in the execution time (not immediately and not after a delay), nor in the questionnaires. Both types of non-linear instructions enhance verbal recall, but none of them enhance repeated execution from memory. Only structural instructions enhance performance of transfer tasks. Also, the approach by Smith & Goodman differs from for instance Kieras & Bovair in that action steps are mixed with explanatory statements instead of presenting these information types separately.

Foss et al.: the effects of conceptual information in the form of analogies and pictures

Finally, another study into the effects of declarative information is reported by Foss et al. (1987). Novice computer users were taught how to use a text editor from one of a set of manuals. They first studied the manual, and then they performed the experimental tasks on the text editor. They could use the manual during task performance, too. In addition to the manual, Foss et al. presented part of their subjects with an introduction to the concepts of the editor they were working with, in the form of analogies and pictures. Subjects who had received this information performed slightly better (faster, fewer commands) than subjects who had not, although this difference was not significant ($p < .10$).

Conclusions based on past research

The research discussed in this section seems to support the hypothesis that declarative information can be useful, but only under specific conditions. It is nevertheless difficult to determine what those conditions are in more general situations than in the experimental conditions described above and especially for the use of software manuals.

Also, the presentation of the declarative information in relation to the procedural instructions varies. Smith & Goodman present both information types in an integrated way, whereas Kieras & Bovair present them separately. Charney, Reder & Wells also mix the information types, but not at the sentence level, as Smith & Goodman do. These differences may also be responsible for different interpretations of the results.

Finally, the question should be raised if software users will actually use the declarative information if they have a choice. In the experiments described above, subjects were required to read all the instructions. Real users will however always make a selection. It would be interesting to find out whether or not this selection includes declarative information, and if so, whether or not this declarative information will have effects.

1.3   Five requirements for new experiments

The interpretation of the research reviewed in this chapter is complicated by five problems:
- *The information types have not been operationalized consistently and unambiguously.*
  Conclusions from different studies about the use and effects of procedural and declarative information do not refer to the same underlying concepts.
- *Subjects are not free to use the manual in any way they would like.*
  Subjects do not get the opportunity to use the manual while carrying out their software tasks. Instead they have to study and remember the information before they can carry out the tasks.
- *Investigations are often limited to tutorial users with a learning assignment.*
  Most studies focus on novice users in a learning context. It is not yet clear whether or not more experienced subjects without a learning intention would select and benefit from the same information.

- *The effects of task complexity are not taken into account.*
  Task complexity is not systematically varied in the studies mentioned in this section, although it may make a difference with respect to the selection and effects of the information types.
- *The set of dependent variables used to measure information effects is limited.*
  In most studies, performance measures are the important dependent variables. It would however be more informative to not only measure effects of the information types on performance, but also on aspects such as reasoning and factual knowledge (which may underly performance)

Experimental techniques to investigate the use and effects of procedural and declarative information could be improved on these aspects. A set of requirements which should be met by new experiments are presented below. In chapter 2, concrete descriptions will follow on how these requirements are met in the present study.

1.3.1   Clear   operationalizations   of   procedural   and declarative information

As was outlined in 1.1, the operationalizations of procedural and declarative information in current research vary. This makes it difficult to compare the results of different studies: it is not certain that the researchers measure effects of the same concept. Kieras & Bovair (1984) for instance measured the effects of a separate description of the system components and the system's internal working, whereas Charney, Reder & Wells (1988) for instance measured the effects of information about the usefulness of a function.

In order to enable good comparisons and interpretations of the research results, explicit, specific and unambiguous definitions of procedural and declarative information should be chosen. For the present study, these definitions were described in section 1.1.3.

1.3.2   Unrestricted selection and use of information

The experimental conditions in the studies on the effects of declarative information discussed in 1.2.2 are not representative for the reading process that a manual user is usually involved in. The subjects are forced to read *all* the information in the manual, and sometimes even to read all the information before they start doing something. In reality however, readers may skip a lot of irrelevant information. Manual users do not read everything, and quite often they do not read the text *before* they start doing something, but *while* they are carrying out tasks (Carroll et al., 1986; Carroll, 1990a).

A common way of investigating the effects of specific information in manuals is to supply subjects with different text versions. These versions differ with respect to the information types represented in them. The underlying assumption is that subjects will read and use all the information available in their text, and that differences in their task performance can thus be explained by the different information types in their texts. Subjects are sometimes even explicitly asked to study the text before they start carrying out their tasks (e.g. Charney, Reder & Wells, 1988). These data however do not account for the non-linear reading process that is common for instructional texts. By forcing subjects to read the complete instructions, it becomes impossible to find out what information they would actually look for when they can make their own decisions. Thus, the effects found in these studies do not necessarily apply to all processes of information use in manuals.

It would be a step forward if subjects could select the information they need during an experiment, and if they could use the information *when* they need it. An experimental method should enable subjects to use the manual also during task performance. Also, subjects should be able to make their own selection of the information.

For the present study, a new technique was developed to meet these requirements. This technique will be described in chapter 2.

1.3.3   More situations than just tutorial situations

Research efforts so far have mainly concentrated on learning situations and tutorials. Reder et al. (1986) reported that they also included experienced users, but their experience was not at all relevant for the tasks they had to perform. They had to work with the DOS operating system on a PC, but they had no PC experience whatsoever. Probably, their computer experience was experience with the (conceptually totally different) Macintosh system, or with a mainframe computer. Also, the experienced subjects had the same learning assignment as the totally inexperienced subjects.

Different backgrounds and different tasks may make a large difference when it comes to information use and information effects. If a user has relevant prior knowledge, he may look for other information, than a user who has no prior knowledge at all. Wright (1988, p. 632) cites results from several studies revealing that inexperienced and expert users differ with respect to the questions they ask: users in a training situation usually ask broad questions

("What do I need to know?") whereas users in a reference context tends to be more focused ("'How do I change the page number?"). Nystrand (1986) also found that high knowledge and low knowledge computer users asked different kinds of questions when using computer documentation.

Thus, there are many reasons to assume that the user situation may be a factor of influence when investigating the importance of procedural and declarative information. The studies mentioned do not take different user situations into account. In the present study, other user types will be included in the experiments, besides inexperienced users with an explicit learning intention.

1.3.4   Tasks that differ in complexity

Kieras & Bovair (1984) found some facilitating effects of declarative information in instructions, but they hypothesize that these effects may disappear when the device for which the instructions are used is very simple. Smith & Goodman (1984) failed to find a reading time advantage of instructions with explanatory statements in one of their experiments, whereas this effect was present in other experiments. In accordance with Kieras & Bovair, they attribute this lack of effect to the simplicity of the task.

However, studies into the effects of different information types did not intentionally vary the complexity of the user's task, although that might have led to different results. Moreover, if task complexity influences the effects of declarative information, it may also affect the frequency and intensity with which declarative information is used.

Wright, Creighton & Threlfall (1982) found that task complexity is one of the factors affecting people's willingness to read instructions. Many users of consumer products such as telephone systems, videotape recorders and computers fail to read the instructions that go with the device. Wright et al. listed 60 products, in categories varying from simple and non-electrical to complex and electrical. Subjects were asked to indicate for each product how much of the instructions they would read. It appeared that the product category, the assumed product complexity and the frequency with which people used the product were important determinants in their willingness to read the instructions. People are more willing to read instructions if it is an unfamiliar, complex product that they have not used frequently so far. If task complexity indeed affects information use in this way, then the possibility cannot be excluded that task complexity also makes a difference to the amount of procedural and declarative information used.

To check the preliminary assumption that task complexity partly determines whether or not declarative information is used and whether or not declarative information affects task performance and reasoning, both simple and complex tasks will be included in the present study.

1.3.5   A variety of experimental measures

The dependent variables used most frequently to measure the effects of declarative information are measures of task performance, such as performance times and the number of errors. Task performance is usually measured immediately after reading the instructions and only sometimes during the presentation of the instructions (Smith & Goodman, 1984).

There are however more possible effects of declarative information than effects on initial task performance. Measures of delayed task performance could also be included in order to find information on different types of retention or recall, for instance by letting the subjects repeat a task after a one-week delay (Kieras & Bovair, 1984; Smith & Goodman, 1984).

Besides effects on initial or delayed task performance, declarative information may also have effects on task understanding, inference making and factual knowledge. These effects can be measured by including questionnaires, transfer tasks or other tests for understanding.

Thus, a broad arsenal of experimental measures would be an additional way to refine the existing knowledge, especially about the use of declarative information. In the present study, experimental measures of both initial and delayed task performance, measures of insight into the system and the task, and measures of factual knowledge will be included.

1.4   Research questions

In the present study, the use and effects of procedural and declarative information will be investigated again, but now from a different starting point. First, the claim that non-procedural information is skipped (e.g. Carroll et al., 1987-1988) is checked in an experiment that was specially set up to record the subjects' selection behaviour and the times during which they use the information. The goal is to acquire precise and clear data about information use in a software manual, in a situation where the subjects are free to use and re-use any part of the manual during task performance.

Then, the effects of declarative information will be investigated in the same context to find out whether or not adding declarative information has any immediate or long-term effect for users of a software manual who can use the manual during task performance, and if so, whether or not these effects are comparable to the effects of declarative information that were found in the experiments mentioned in 1.2.

Finally, the possibility will be investigated of different arrangements of the instructions causing differences in the use and effects of the information types. In 1.2 it was signalled that some researchers presented procedural and declarative information in an integrated way, whereas others presented the information types in separate sessions. Also the order in which the information types are presented may make a difference.

In addition to these questions, the effects of different user situations and task complexity will be examined. The following research questions will be investigated:

1. How much procedural and declarative information do software users select and use during the performance of their tasks?
    -   Does this differ for users in different situations?
    -   Does this differ for simple and complex tasks?

2. Does declarative information affect initial and delayed task performance, reasoning and factual knowledge?
    -   Does this differ for users in different situations?
    -   Does this differ for simple and complex tasks?

3. Does the arrangement of information affect the selection, use and effects of procedural and declarative information?
    -   Does this differ for users in different situations?

Research question one about the selection and use of information will be examined in chapter 3. Chapter 4 will focus on the effects of declarative information, and chapter 5 on research question three about the influence of arrangement variables. But first, the standard methodology aspects of the experiments will be described in chapter 2.

A method for studying information use and effects in manuals

The questions raised in chapter 1 were investigated in three successive experiments. Subjects were assigned to one of three user situations (tutorial, intermediate and reference). They were asked to perform tasks with an unknown spreadsheet program, QubeCalc. A manual, consisting of procedural and declarative text blocks, was available to the subjects on a second computer screen. Subjects were stimulated to click on the text blocks when they wanted to read them, and thus, selection data and using times could be recorded in logfiles. The keystrokes in QubeCalc were recorded too. In this way, data for *information selection* and *information use* could be generated. In order to draw conclusions about the *effects* of declarative information, several performance measurements were taken. Initial task performance could be derived from the logfiles as well. Delayed task performance was measured in a separate task, without the manual and after a 20 minute delay. To measure the subjects' quality of reasoning about the software and their tasks, a special test was designed and used. Finally, the subjects' factual knowledge was measured by means of a questionnaire.

This chapter serves as a standard methodology section for all these experiments, which will be described in detail in chapters 3 through 5. The independent and dependent variables, the instrumentation and the experimental procedure are described therein.

2.1   Independent variables

2.1.1   Information type

The focus of investigation in all three experiments is on the selection, use and effects of procedural and declarative information: information type is the central independent variable. At the outset, an experimental manual was constructed in which both information types were included.

The manual presented information about a spreadsheet program: QubeCalc. (QubeCalc will be described in detail in section 2.1.4.) The manual contained all the information that subjects could need to perform any task with the spreadsheet, except for a few very advanced tasks. It was checked and pre-tested to check completeness and accuracy. Extracts from the manual are presented in appendix 1A.

Each basic user task or function, for instance *copying data* or *justifying data* was described on a separate page. In the PD-manual, which was used in all three experiments, procedural (P) and declarative (D) information about these tasks was presented in separate text blocks. Every page of the manual contained one procedural and one declarative text block, both referring to the same user task. The procedural block was positioned at the top of the page, the declarative block at the bottom[7]. The amounts of procedural and declarative information in the manual did not differ significantly.[8]

Procedural information is defined as all the reader oriented information that is directly connected to the user's actions, not only at syntax level (*Press Enter.*), but also at computer task (*Open a file.*) and real world task level (*Calculate the expenses.*) (see section 1.1.2). Not only the actions themselves are procedural, but also the concrete conditions for performing an action at a certain moment, and the result from that action (that can be a condition in itself for the next step).

Declarative information is all the information that does not fit into the categories of actions, conditions and results. Declarative information does not give the reader concrete *what-to-do* or *how-to-do-it* information, but background information (e.g *Why would anyone want to do this?*; *Where can I find this on the screen?*; *What does this icon on the screen mean?*). It does not directly support actions, but it may possibly do so indirectly (see also section 1.1.2).

Information form was operationalized according to the criteria mentioned in 1.1.3: the information was put in its prototypical syntactic form (see also Ummelen, 1994).

The headings above each text block were representative for either procedural or declarative content: the procedural headings always contained action verbs to indicate explicitly the action to be performed, while the declarative headings did not contain any action verb, but system terms and questions about the program instead. An overview of all these characteristics of procedural and declarative information in the experimental manuals is presented in table 2.1.

The visual format of the information types differed as little as possible to avoid the possibility of readers selecting a text block mainly because of visual attractiveness. For these reasons, tables and illustrations were left out. Instead of continuous prose, however, the steps in the procedural parts were enumerated, because it was possible to do so without making the visual differences between the procedural and the declarative blocks too obvious.

Table 2.1
Overview of the characteristics of procedural and declarative information as they are operationalized in the current experiments

	Procedural information blocks	*Declarative information blocks*
Content	- actions - conditions for actions - results from actions	e.g. - descriptions (What does it look like?) - analyses (Of what components does it exist?) - functionality (What is it good for?) (for a complete overview, see section 1.1.3)
Form	- action verbs - imperatives - step by step presentation of items - if...then constructions - direct style - headings: action verbs	- modal verbs - longer *fact* sentences - continuous prose - modifiers - indirect style - headings: *what/ why-* questions and system terms

2.1.2   Presence or absence of declarative information

To investigate what effects the presence or absence of declarative information has on task performance and knowledge (experiment 2), a second manual was constructed from which all declarative information was eliminated: the P-manual. The same procedural text blocks were included as in the PD-manual. The P-manual also contained two text blocks on every page. Thus, the P-manual only contained half the number of pages in the PD-manual. Details about this manual can be found in chapter 4. An extract can be found in appendix 1B.

2.1.3   Arrangement   of   procedural   and   declarative information

The arrangement of procedural and declarative information was varied in experiment 3 to investigate whether or not presenting the information types in a different order and in different sections affects the selection and use of procedural and declarative information, and whether or not these variations in the structure of the information also affect task performance and knowledge. Besides the PD-manual and the P-manual, three more versions of the manual were constructed (see overview below).

Abbreviation	Full name	Characteristics
PD	Procedural - Declarative	Procedural information at the top, declarative at the bottom of the page
DP	Declarative - Procedural	Declarative information at the top, procedural at the bottom of the page
MX	Mix	Procedural and declarative information no longer separated, but mixed over the page
HY	Hypertext	All procedural and declarative information blocks in a hypertext structure

The PD-manual was the first experimental manual. It was used in all experiments. Procedural and declarative text blocks were presented separately; procedural blocks were displayed in a block at the top of the page, while the related declarative items were displayed at the bottom of the page.

The DP-manual was the same manual as the PD-manual, but with the information blocks presented in the reversed order: declarative information at the top and procedural information at the bottom. This manual was included to investigate the effects of order.

The Mix-manual did not present the information types in separate blocks. Procedural and declarative information were broken into smaller sections and mixed, which resulted in an integrated presentation. The MX-manual was included to investigate effects of sectioning and integrating the information types.

Finally, the Hypertext-manual was an additional and more drastic variation of the arrangement variable. Contrary to the other manuals, a hypertext does not have the linear structure of a printed book. It is in fact a collection of all the procedural and declarative blocks, without a predetermined order. Users can select one block at a time on a computer screen without being able to see the related blocks at the same time. What they do see are *links* to these related blocks, in the form of underlined text parts or underlined headings of the related text blocks that are presented underneath the selected text. More details about the Mix-manual and the Hypertext-manual can be found in chapter 5.

2.1.4   Task complexity

Task complexity was expected to affect the selection and use of procedural and declarative information. Therefore, subjects had to carry out a simple and a complex task in the spreadsheet *QubeCalc*. QubeCalc is an American spreadsheet program, a so-called shareware system: it is distributed free of charge with the aim of acquiring users of the software who are willing to pay a small share if they continue using it[9]. QubeCalc runs on a PC in a MS-DOS environment. It can only be operated by keyboard, not by mouse.

QubeCalc was adequate for this study because it met two important requirements: it was unknown (none of the subjects in the three experiments had ever heard about QubeCalc before) and it differed in many respects from most well-known spreadsheets. It was necessary for the spreadsheet to be unknown to ensure that all subjects needed information during the experiments. If subjects are already very familiar with the spreadsheet, they may be able to retrieve so much information from their memories that they do not need the manual. As a consequence, it would no longer be possible to draw conclusions about the use of the manual. For the same reason, it was also necessary for the software to differ from other, well-known spreadsheets and from conventions in other widely used computer programs: these differences also ensure that all subjects need some information and will thus use the manual. The following three examples illustrate some of the uncommon features that are typical of Qubecalc:

[1]   The workspace in QubeCalc is three-dimensional. Rows, columns and pages are connected and thus form a cube which can be cross-sectioned and turned around while working with the data. Thus, the user can see the data from 6 different perspectives, but the interface does not give much feedback as to which perspective the user is working in.

[2]   Copying a block of data to another place in the spreadsheet is difficult in QubeCalc. In contrast with most other systems, users need to give the copy command first before they are able to mark a block. At the start of the procedure the cursor should be on the cell where the data have to be copied *to*. This problem is related to a different notion of the block concept in QubeCalc.

[3]   The procedures for making calculations are not self-evident. The formula syntax is intolerant: formula characters must for instance be typed in capitals.

A simple and a complex task were constructed in QubeCalc. The complexity of a user's task depends on the memory load the task imposes on the user, as well as on the type and content of knowledge that the user needs (Knowles, 1988). Memory load is high when the task consists of a large number of elements that the user has to remember, for instance long action sequences or a large number of conditions. The content of the knowledge required can cause difficulties because there may be discrepancies between the knowledge that the user already has, and the knowledge that he needs. The relevant knowledge that the user already has, for instance of the hand-performed tasks, or of a comparable software system, may differ strongly from the new knowledge that he needs, and that makes the task more difficult in the user's eyes.

Accordingly, the complex task in the experiments contained a number of subtasks with concepts that differed from the concepts in hand-performed tasks and from those in comparable spreadsheet programs. In the complex task, the datafile contained several expenses of a sporting club, spread over three years. The data for different years were entered on different pages, so that the three-dimensional idea and the perspective-function had to be used. The procedures also differed from those in hand-performed tasks and from procedures in comparable software. The action sequences to be carried out were long, with many embedded actions.

An illustration of some difficulties in the complex task
1. A calculation that has to be performed on more worksheets has to be entered only once and can then be copied to other worksheets if it refers to cells that are in a similar position. In a calculation by hand, all calculations have to be entered individually, one by one.

2. The perspective-function is a concept that does not occur in other spreadsheets. Some do have three-dimensional graphs and several worksheets overlapping eachother, but they do not enable users to make a cross-section straight through the worksheets and then give that section one or a few turns so that the user can look at the front of the cross-section.Thus, columns that were first presented one *behind* the other (so that only the first column was visible) could then for instance be looked at one *next to* the other by changing the perspective.

3. The action sequence of making a graph is long and it contains many subprocedures. A summarized version of the procedure is presented below. If the syntax level were included, there would be even more embeddings. Also, not all options in the Graph-menu are included in the procedure (e.g. defining Labels)

- Move the cursor to the relevant data.
- Go to the Main-menu and then to the Graph-menu.
    - Choose a type of graph.
        - Choose the Type- menu option.
        - Choose a graph-type.
            - If it is a Line graph, choose the type of line.
    - Choose the data that should be presented on the X-axis.
        - Choose the X- menu option.

>   - Take the cursor to the corresponding data.
>   - Define the block of data.
>   - Choose the data that should be presented on the Y-axis.
>   - Choose the A, B or C- menu option.
>   - Take the cursor to the corresponding data.
>   - Define the block of data.
>   - Repeat this if more data should be presented at the Y-axis.
>   - Choose View to present the graph on the screen.

Simple tasks, on the contrary, contained relatively familiar concepts and procedures, and relatively short and straightforward action sequences. In the simple task, subjects had to open a file containing stock data of the same sporting club. These data only took up one page in a QubeCalc file, so the perspective function was not used in this task.

Some characteristics of the simple task
1. Only basic, familiar concepts such as rows, columns and cells occurred in the simple task. Users know them from both paper applications and other spreadsheets.

2. Erasing a cell is a familiar procedure: in a calculation by hand, you would simply use a rubber eraser. It is a procedure that also occurs in all other spreadsheets

3. Inserting a column is achieved by a short and straightforward procedure:

- Take the cursor to the column that should be to the right of the column to be inserted.
- Go to the Main menu and then to the Insert menu.
- Choose Column.

The simple and the complex tasks are presented in appendix 7, and together with the experimental materials in section 3.2.2 and 4.2.2.

2.1.5   User situation

User situation was varied to determine the effects of experience and assignments on the selection and use of procedural and declarative information. It was also included to check whether or not it would affect task performance and knowledge.

The user situation is determined by a set of factors: the user's prior knowledge and experience, the user's intention (learning or doing) and the task frequency that the user expects[10]. In the experiments, three situations are defined: the tutorial situation, the reference situation and the intermediate situation.

In a *tutorial* situation, the users' intention is to learn to work with the system. Typically, they do not have much prior knowledge of and experience with the system or with similar systems. The task they perform may be a realistic task, but it is primarily relevant to the learning goal. They expect the task to occur more often, and they want to be able to perform it again, preferably without using the instructions.

In the experiments, users without spreadsheet experience and without much computer experience were assigned to the tutorial group. They were asked to learn to work with the spreadsheet, using the two tasks as study materials. They had to try to understand and learn to use the software functions and the tasks they would encounter. It was explained to them that the tasks were intended to guide them through the program, to let them practise; their assignment was to learn to work with the software and to understand it to a certain extent. Tutorial users were told in advance that they had to do a third task afterwards and to complete a questionnaire, both without the instructions. This knowledge was expected to induce a learning context.

In a *reference* situation, the users' intention is to complete a relevant task. They do not care about learning about the system, as long as they are able to do what they want to do. They have much prior knowledge and experience with computers in general, as well as with equivalents of the specific software. They do not expect the task to occur again.

In the experiments, users with much knowledge of and experience with computers and spreadsheets were assigned to the reference situation. None of these subjects had worked with QubeCalc, the experimental spreadsheet, before, but they did have much experience with other spreadsheets, such as LOTUS 1-2-3, Quattro Pro or Microsoft Excel. Subjects in the reference situation were told that they had to focus on the two tasks in the experiment, and that they had to carry them out as fast as they could. At the outset, they were NOT told that they would have to perform a third task as well. They assumed they would be ready after two tasks. This assignment was expected to induce a reference context.

Intermediate users find themselves somewhere in between tutorial and reference users. They have a basic knowledge of computers and the relevant software, and they have a relevant task to perform. Though they do not really intend to learn, they are aware that their task will occur more often in the future.

In the experiments, users with some elementary knowledge of and experience with computers or spreadsheets were assigned to the intermediate situation. Just like the reference users, they had to perform the two tasks as fast as possible. Contrary to the subjects in the reference situation, however, they were told in advance that there would be a third task afterwards, a similar task that contained elements they had seen before in the first two tasks. They were also told they could use the instructions in all three tasks, so they were unaware that the instructions would be unavailable during the test task.

The subjects' prior knowledge and experience were determined before the experiment started. They were asked to specify how often they worked with computers, with what software, and for which real world tasks. The precise profiles of the three user situations with respect to knowledge and experience are described below. Subjects were assigned to the category that matched their profile best.

Tutorial
- subjects who had never worked with a spreadsheet before, or subjects who had worked with a spreadsheet on less than 5 occasions in total
- subjects who had used a maximum of only one specific spreadsheet program before
- subjects who had only used the spreadsheet "to see what it is" or for single, elementary tutorial sessions in the past
- subjects who only seldom used the computer, for a maximum of two different software applications (a word processor was for instance a standard application that almost all subjects used sometimes)

Intermediate
- subjects who incidentally worked with spreadsheets (a maximum of 5 sessions per year)
- subjects who had used one specific spreadsheet program before
- subjects who had used the spreadsheet for real, relevant, though simple tasks (e.g. administering telephone bills in their student homes)
- subjects who use the computer on a regular basis, though not very frequently, and who use it for more than two applications.

Reference
- subjects who often and regularly worked with spreadsheets (twice a month or more)
- subjects who had used two or more specific spreadsheet programs
- subjects who performed real, relevant and high level tasks with the spreadsheets they knew
- subjects who used the computer very frequently, for all types of applications (at least three different applications)

Experience versus situational aspects
All three experiments started from the assumption that it was the *combination* of advance knowledge and experience on the one hand and situational aspects such as the user's assignment on the other hand that affected information use and effects. These two components of the user situation were not tested separately in the main experiments. To check whether the components *experience* and *assignment* also had separate effects on information selection and information use, a control experiment was conducted in which experience and assignment were separate factors. The results will be reported in section 3.5.2.

2.2   Dependent variables

The experiments were designed to measure the effects of the independent variables on information selection and use, and on task performance and knowledge.

2.2.1   Information selection and information use

The dependent variables for information selection and use were the following:

Information selection
- The number of occasions subjects select a procedural or a declarative information block
- The information type that subjects begin with when they start looking for information

Information use
- The amount of time (in seconds) that subjects spend using procedural and declarative information

It is important to note that *using information* is not intended to be synonymous to *reading time* in the experiments. It implies reading the information, but also thinking about it and applying it to a task while the information is still active. Reading time was not considered to be the most relevant measure, because the subjects do not stop using the information once they stop looking at the text. The time users spend on reading, thinking and trying to translate and apply the information is the relevant information using time in the context of the research questions.

On the other hand, measuring reading times may be interesting in some specific cases. It would for instance be possible that some text characteristics, such as the syntactic form of the information, only affect the reading times, but not the planning or thinking stage that immediately follows reading (see for instance Wright & Wilcox, 1978). However, this research question falls beyond the scope of this study.

The observation technique should allow for precise observations of which information subjects select and use, when they select it and how long they use it. How the dependent variables of information selection and use are operationalized in the experiments is explained in section 2.3 about the instrumentation.

2.2.2 Performance, reasoning and knowledge

To test the effects of declarative information and the arrangement of the two information types, dependent variables were included of initial task performance, delayed task performance, reasoning and factual knowledge. The distinction between these categories is based on research by Young (1983, p. 37; see also chapter 4), who proposes that a user's mental model should support three aspects of the use of a system: *performance, learning* and *reasoning*. The user's mental model should contain enough and relevant knowledge to support the user's choice of procedure: it should for instance contain details of the performance *(performance)*. Also, the user's mental model should enable generalizations and long-term retention *(learning)*. Furthermore the mental model should enable the user to predict the system's response, to invent methods and to explain the system's behaviour *(reasoning)*. To check whether or not the manuals contribute to good mental models, dependent variables were included that yield information about all these aspects.

Initial task performance
Initial task performance was the subjects' performance on the simple and complex QubeCalc tasks, that were carried out with the support of the manual. For initial task performance, the relevant variables were:

- Task performance time (seconds)
- Number of incorrectly performed subtasks
- Number of inefficiently performed subtasks
- Number of attempts to complete a subtask

These variables could be derived from logfiles in which all the subjects' keystrokes were recorded. *Keylog[11]* was the program that logged the keystrokes and times and wrote them to a file. Keylog was run parallel to QubeCalc, but it did not affect the spreadsheet at all. Subjects were unaware that their keystrokes were registered: there was no indication of the logging procedure on the screen and Keylog did not make the spreadsheet react slower.

The *performance time* for a subtask is the time in seconds from subtask boundary to subtask boundary. During initial task performance, this variable not only consisted of the time subjects actually spent on carrying out the task, but also of the reading time, as they are an integral part of task performance in the chosen setting. The seconds that were lost due to computer breakdowns or other distractions were subtracted from the performance time.

A subtask was marked *correct* if the subject's result was the same as the intended result, which was formulated in advance. For instance, if the assignment was to copy a block of data to a specific place, the subtask scored correct if the intended block of data was indeed copied to the intended place, no matter how the subjects did this. This information could be derived from the processed logfiles. In case of doubt, an extra check consisted of viewing the saved files that the subjects had edited and viewing videotapes of the experimental session.

The correctness variable does not reflect how subjects reached their results. If there were more ways to achieve the intended result, the procedure that the subjects had chosen was marked for *efficiency*. Suppose a subject did not use the *Copy* menu option to perform the copy subtask, but instead retyped all the information in the intended place. Then the subtask was still marked as being correctly performed, but for the efficiency variable as inefficiently performed.[12]

For almost all subtasks in the experiments there were more possible ways to carry them out correctly. However, there was always one procedure which was the most efficient. *Efficient* means the shortest and most straightforward way to reach an intended goal. However, in QubeCalc, the most efficient way to solve a problem is not always the easiest for the users. A good example is the calculation of an average. The most efficient procedure is using a formula and using the function key F3 to define the block of data to be averaged. For a lot of users it is however easier to enter all the numbers with a + sign in between, put this string in brackets, and divide it by the total amount of numbers, which they count themselves. This procedure is not only inefficient because it takes more time and thinking by the user, but also because it may make subsequent parts of the user task more laborious: the resulting string cannot be copied to another place in the file. If the most efficient procedure is used, the spreadsheet will automatically adapt to different cell addresses and calculate a new average when the string is copied to another cell.

The *number of attempts* to complete a subtask was also counted. In advance, criteria were formulated for the start of a new attempt. The logfiles generally contained clear indications of new attempts being started. The most obvious example was the *Escape* button, followed by a repetition of the first steps of the procedure. There were also procedures that did not need to be restarted, but that could be retried half way. This type of repeated attempts also counted. Repeated attempts were however only counted if they represented a complete procedure or procedure part. A correction of typing errors was for instance not counted as an attempt, whereas entering different cell addresses did count as an attempt. The minimum number of attempts was always 1, unless the subtask had not been performed.

Delayed task performance
In experiments 2 and 3, the effects of different manual versions on task performance after a delay were investigated. If the subjects scored well on

delayed task performance, this was interpreted as an indication of long-term retention of strategies and procedures.

A 20-minute complex distractor task (see appendix 2) was constructed, which subjects had to carry out after completion of the simple and complex tasks. After the distractor task, subjects were again asked to perform a new complex task with QubeCalc. This task was similar to one of the subtasks they had already encountered during the initial task performance phase, but now they used a different datafile and they could not use the manual. The keystrokes were again logged.

The performance measurements were the same as those for initial task performance:

- Task performance time (seconds)
- Correctness of the solution
- Efficiency of the solution
- Number of attempts

These variables could also be derived from the QubeCalc logfiles, similar to the measurements of initial task performance[13].

Reasoning
The reasoning variable represents the insight users have into the software and the task, the ability to reason about it, to explain things that happen on the screen, to predict things that will happen and to invent strategies to solve real-world problems. To investigate effects on reasoning, an interactive test was constructed in which the experimenter carried out a task and simultaneously tested the subjects according to a standard procedure. The manual could not be used during this test.

The reasoning test contained four subvariables, which are specified below. Each subvariable was represented in 4 or 5 items in the test. The number of items that were performed correctly were counted. The subvariables were:

1 Efficiency	Recognizing that a more efficient procedure or strategy would be appropriate
2 Error handling	Detecting, diagnosing and recovering from errors
3 Explaining	Explaining why something happens on the screen
4 Applied insight	Inventing strategies or procedures to achieve a certain goal

1   During the test, the experimenter deliberately carried out some procedures in an inefficient way. Subjects were asked to signal any inefficiencies and tell the experimenter how the action could be performed more efficiently.

> *Situation:* The experimenter says that she is going to format a large block of numbers to one decimal place. She starts doing so cell by cell. If the subject does not indicate that it could be done faster, she continues to format the whole block cell by cell.
> *Action by the subjects:* Subjects have to indicate that the formatting can be done faster if it is done for the whole block at once. They also have to tell the experimenter *how* this should be done, to check if they really know the alternative, or just speculate because the cell-by-cell method takes so long.

This *efficiency* measure is based on the same idea as the efficiency variable in the performance test. The performance test examines whether or not subjects actually work efficiently, whereas in the reasoning test, the subjects' awareness of more efficient ways to carry out a certain subtask is tested, and their ability to judge a procedure by efficiency. The items in the test that were intended to measure efficiency scored a "+" if the subjects had indicated during the test that there were more efficient ways to solve a problem and if they had shown that their remarks were not based on guessing. If subjects did not make remarks about efficiency, the experimenter continued to carry out the inefficient procedure, and the item scored a "-".

2   During the test, the experimenter deliberately performed some actions incorrectly. Subjects were asked to signal this. Subsequently they were asked why the indicated action was not correct and what should be the correct solution instead.

> *Situation:* The experimenter tells the subject that she is going to change the existing numbers to numbers with 1 decimal place. Then she incorrectly selects the menu option *Justify* instead of *Format*. (This is less trivial than it may seem, because the tasks were stated in Dutch, whereas QubeCalc's interface is all English, and Justify is not a well-known English word to Dutch students.)
> *Action by the subjects:* Subjects should indicate that Justify is not correct (detection), why it is not correct (background) and how the task should be performed instead (recovery). If subjects do not immediately indicate that *Justify* is wrong, then the experimenter waits a second and asks the subject which menu item should be chosen next (*Right*, *Left* or *Center*). If the subjects mention one of these menu options as the next step, then the score for error detection is "-". If they still signal the error, the score is

"+". If subjects do not notice the error, the task performance will get stuck in the end, as Justify does not do anything to the data. Errors only count as being detected if subjects signal it before the Justify menu and its submenus are passed through.

In these items for measuring *error handling*, subjects were actually tested for three subvariables: detection, background and recovery. Subjects received a "+" for detection if they signalled an error made by the experimenter. If the error was detected, the subjects were asked *why* they thought it was an error, what was wrong with it. Subjects were supposed to indicate what the problem was, but they did not necessarily have to give the correct solution immediately. They could for instance say that the actions performed by the experimenter would have a different effect than the intended effect, without mentioning what the correct procedure would be (background). Finally, subjects were asked to tell the experimenter how the error could be corrected (recovery).

In experiment 2 (chapter 4), detection, background and recovery were not yet given a separate score. *Error handling* scored a "+" when the error was detected and properly corrected. Subjects were asked for the background of the error, but they did not receive a separate score for it. In experiment 3, all three components of error handling were given a separate score.

3   At some points during the test, subjects were asked by the experimenter to explain what was happening on the screen and why it was happening.

> *Situation:* The screen is empty because an empty page has appeared after changing the perspective. If you don't understand what the perspective function does, it looks as if all the data are lost.
> *Question by the experimenter:* "Why is the screen empty?"

If subjects gave the correct explanation, the answer scored a "+", if they gave the wrong explanation, the answer scored a "-". In case of doubt, the experimenter asked non-directive questions to let the subjects specify their answers (e.g. *What do you mean exactly?*).

4   At some moments during the test, the experimenter indicated that she wanted to achieve a certain goal. The subjects were then asked what strategy should be followed (what actions were necessary) to achieve that goal.

> *Task:* "See to it that all the averages are listed on one separate screen."
> *Question by the experimenter:* "How would you do this?"

These items, representing the *applied insight* variable were intended to test if subjects were able to translate their insight into the spreadsheet system and tasks by inventing solutions for a certain problem. The typical question for these items is *How would you do this?* or, incidentally, *How do you know that?*, if an explanation or a solution can be deduced from information on the screen. Subjects were supposed to give the most efficient solutions for a problem. If they had understood the situation and the spreadsheet tasks, it was possible for them to formulate an efficient solution. Thus, mentioning a possible solution was not enough here. Correct answers scored a "+", incorrect answers a "-".

Efficiency and error handling were part of the reasoning task, although they could also be interpreted as performance measures. However, as this test task was not performed by the subjects themselves but by the experimenter, these measures were of a different kind than the other performance measures. Subjects only watched what was happening and commented on it. They translated their knowledge of performing tasks into an explicit explanation of why a different strategy would be better, or why a certain action was wrong and how it could be corrected. The focus here is not on what they do, but on what they *know*. That is why all four measures are called reasoning measures here.

Factual knowledge
Factual knowledge is part of the user's mental representation which may be a basis for performance and reasoning. In the tests for performance and reasoning, it is difficult to measure factual knowledge separately. Therefore, a questionnaire to measure factual knowledge was added. The questionnaire was completed by subjects after they had finished all other tasks. It contained 9 to 12 open questions about QubeCalc facts (the number of questions differed over the experiments). The complete questionnaires are presented in appendix 3.

Examples
- Which information can be found on the status line?
- Mention three different types of data in Qubecalc.

Both the manual and the spreadsheet could not be used during completion. Subjects could only get the answers by retrieving them from their memories, or by guessing.

The questionnaires were marked by hand for correctness of the answers. When the questionnaire was designed, an answering model was also made. The answers given by the subjects were compared to the model answers, and were marked accordingly as correct, incorrect, partly correct, or *don't know*. Correct answers scored 1, incorrect answers scored 0. Partly correct answers and *don't know* answers were given a separate score at the outset. In the analysis, partly correct answers were counted as correct, and *don't know* answers were counted as incorrect.

2.3   Instrumentation

2.3.1   Requirements

To be able to answer research questions about the selection and use of information, a technique was needed that enabled relevant observations and measurements of information use in software manuals. The technique should meet three types of requirements: requirements of reliability, external validity and feasibility.

Reliability
The instrumentation should enable accurate registration and count *what* information subjects select, *when* they select certain information and *how long* subjects use this information. It should also enable accurate registration of the actions performed with the software (QubeCalc). Finally, it should be possible to make the selection moments visible in relation to the stage of task performance.

Validity
The technique should approach a natural situation as closely as possible. The subjects should be enabled to work with the software and the manual at the same time. The interaction of the subjects with the software and the manual should not be obstructed or interrupted, in order to create a situation that approaches a realistic setting as much as possible in an experimental context. Subjects should be free to use the manual whenever they want and they should also be free to select and use from the manual what they want (see section 1.3.2). Also, the recorded data should only represent the interest variable: there should be no interference with other variables.

Feasibility
The research technique should enable data collection for a relatively large number of subjects within a reasonable amount of time and money.

2.3.2   An evaluation of available techniques

Available methods for measuring reading behaviour and text comprehension often originate in other contexts than software manual research. Three available methods for measuring reading behaviour have been considered, of which the third has also been applied to manuals:

1   Recording reading times for studying the comprehension of individual sentences
2   Eye movement registration
3   Thinking and reading aloud

1   Recording reading time for studying the comprehension of individual sentences

Methods for measuring reading and text comprehension at the word and sentence level have often been applied in psycholinguistic studies: comprehension is for instance measured by presenting a text on a computer screen, word by word or sentence by sentence. Subjects have to press a button as soon as they have understood what they have read. Pressing the button causes the next word or sentence to appear on the screen. The subjects' reaction times are the relevant data for inferring what cognitive processes take place during reading.

This method does not meet all requirements of external validity mentioned in section 2.3.1, as the subjects' freedom to select and use information is restricted in four related ways. First of all, subjects are not at all able to select any information at the start of their search. They see isolated details from the text which have already been selected for them and which are presented in a predetermined order. When reading a paper manual in a natural situation, readers see at least two pages of text, or a contents page, from which they can make their own selection.

Secondly, in this technique readers are more or less forced to read the complete text, from the beginning to the end. As they cannot skip certain parts of the manual during reading, the most they can do is ignore some of the information and continue to the next part. However, they will not easily do that because they cannot go back to the ignored text parts when they need them later on. When using a paper manual in real life, readers usually read only a part of the information. Whole parts of the manual remain unread if the user does not consider those parts useful or necessary (Wright, 1989).

Thirdly, the method determines the order of reading information: a linear order. Readers cannot change this order, contrary to a manual in book form, where users themselves determine the order of reading information in a realistic context.

Finally, subjects cannot re-read information. Information that has been read disappears from the screen and has to be remembered. When using a paper manual in a natural situation, readers can decide to re-read text parts as often as they want.

2 Eye movement registration

A second method that may be applicable for measuring reading behaviour in instructions is eye movement registration. Eye movements and fixations are measured by a system which beams a small spot of light on the subject's cornea and captures the reflection (e.g. Just & Carpenter, 1980). In that way it is possible to register the exact location the reader is looking at in the text.

Until now, eye movement registration methods in reading research have mainly been applied to words or locations within sentence boundaries. In these settings, subjects often need to wear a helmet. As a result they can hardly move their heads, which seriously obstructs them in working with software at the same time. Also, micro-eye movement registration is a method that is expensive and requires specialized experience.

However, the most important objection against these techniques is that they do not allow for recording macro eye movements; the technique which should be chosen for this purpose should be applicable to larger text passages. Subjects should be able to jump from one part of a manual page to another, no matter how far the parts are apart. Moreover, their eyes will not only be focused on the manual, but also on the computer screen which displays the software. Schumacher & Waller (1985) mention three techniques for recording macro eye movements. These techniques are more applicable than the micro eye movement techniques, but they have different difficulties with respect to ecological validity. For one of the techniques, (i.e. a light pen attached to a joystick), a semi-darkened room is required. In other instances, subjects have to point to all the sentences they read. Currently, there are even more modern techniques, which for instance use infra-red light. It is not certain yet whether these registration techniques would be possible and accurate.

Thus, as eye movement registration did not meet the requirements of external validity and feasibility, this technique was also abandoned for the goals of this study.

3 Thinking and reading aloud

A third method to be considered for measuring information use is the thinking and reading aloud method. According to the thinking aloud method, subjects try to solve problems and use the manual as they would normally do, but they are required to read everything out loud and to think aloud about everything that comes to mind. The experimenter prompts the subjects in a non-directive way to think out loud if they forget to do so. The resulting protocols are analyzed in order to find answers to the research questions.

The advantages of the thinking aloud method may be obvious: subjects are completely free to determine their own strategies and select the text parts they think useful. The experimenter is able to mark what has been read, and he can also see and mark what subjects do with the software.

The thinking aloud method however has also been abandoned for the current research questions, because it did not meet the requirements of validity for measuring reading time (1), the requirements of feasibility (2) and possibly the requirements of validity for other measures (such as selection) (3), although the third objection is still under discussion.

1   The method is not valid when it comes to measuring reading times. The thinking aloud method certainly enables the experimenter to see and record *what* information subjects select, but when it comes to recording *when* subjects select information and *how long* they use the information, the procedure becomes inaccurate. The experimenter would have to time everything manually, using either a stopwatch or a video clock. This requires continuous concentration by the experimenter if the selected information is marked during the experiment, or a lot of extra time if audio or videotapes have to be analyzed. Moreover, the recorded times may not be valid for measuring reading time, because of the extra time it takes for subjects to do everything while reading out loud and verbalizing their thoughts. This delay is probably not the same for all subjects.

2   The method is too laborious for the current research questions.
    If there are large numbers of subjects to be tested and precise data to be recorded, the thinking aloud method is very time-consuming, as all the subjects' verbalizations have to be typed out into protocols and analyzed. As a result, either the number of subjects is small, or the analysis is more or less global in most thinking aloud studies.

3   There is a risk of interference in the method with the experimental tasks and the selection behaviour. Ericsson (1988) compares thinking aloud methods to the methods used in traditional reading research (measuring reading times and eye-fixations) and concludes that those traditional methods are informative in a given type of process, such as an easy text which can be read linearly for general comprehension, whereas thinking aloud is more informative in difficult texts where the reader has to actively link text parts and his advance knowledge. Ericsson sums up empirical evidence which shows that reading aloud does not interfere with normal text comprehension.

At most the reading times are longer. However, the empirical evidence underlying Ericsson's conclusions does not include instructional texts. The aspect of using a text when working with a device outside the text at the same time is not present in the studies he discusses, although the risk of interference between the thinking aloud method and problem solving processes or information selection may be different from the risk of interference between thinking aloud and text comprehension in other text types.

Although the thinking aloud technique has often been applied to software manuals, for instance in the research by Carroll et al. (e.g Carroll, 1990a) and in the context of usability testing (e.g Schriver, 1984), the discussion about a possible interference of the thinking aloud method with the processes of selecting and understanding information and the process of problem solving is not yet based on sufficient empirical evidence. Yet, many researchers have warned against the risk of the thinking aloud method influencing problem solving processes. Norman (1983) warns against the risk of subjects becoming aware of irrational decisions just because they need to verbalize their thoughts. He has seen subjects rationalizing their decisions verbally afterwards. If Norman is right, subjects may also use the manual more often than they would normally do in such situations. Sasse (1989) warns that the need for thinking and reading aloud and the encouragemements of the experimenter if subjects forget to do so make thinking aloud highly artificial behaviour which may interfere with the other tasks the subjects have to perform. This may well include information selection. In summary: it is not certain that the thinking aloud method indeed interferes with information selection and information use, but serious doubts have been raised.

2.3.3   An alternative technique: the click & read method

As the disadvantages of the available methods were considered to be too serious, an attempt was made to develop a new method that would meet all requirements. The result of this attempt was called the *click & read method*. This new method was intended to enable a precise recording of all selection moments and using time in the process of a software user using the manual while working with a software program. The aim was to simulate a real book and a real reading situation as closely as possible, without losing sight of a precise registration of the important data. This section will elaborate on several aspects of the click & read method: how it looks and works, its initial development, an improved variant of the method, hardware constraints during the development, and the preparation and calculation of the recorded data.

2.3.3.1   A description of the click & read method

In the click & read method, a photograph of a printed manual was displayed on a computer screen (see appendix 4A). The layout of the manual was that of a printed book: two pages at a time. The pages could be turned by clicking on buttons at the bottom left and right of every page. Subjects could also go directly to the contents page from every page in the manual by clicking on a *Contents* button.

Each page contained two blocks of verbal information, but the information blocks were not immediately readable: they were purposely blurred. Subjects could enlarge and sharpen the information by clicking on it. Those clicks were recorded in a logfile, along with the moment of clicking: in that way, the important data were recorded.

Subjects could select information on the basis of the headings above the information blocks. Contrary to the text blocks, those headings were always sharp and well legible. They were indicative of the content of the information. The blurring technique left as much text visible as was possible without eliminating its purpose: the incentive to click on the information. Subjects could not actually read the information without clicking it, but they could get a rough impression of what was there. Their main source of information however, were the headings.

The contents page displayed the headings of all information blocks in the manual. Subjects could select information by clicking on a title or heading that matched their interest and were then taken directly to the pages where the selected information was. On those pages, the information was still blurred: subjects had to look for the appropriate information block and click on it again to sharpen and enlarge it.

Once a text block was enlarged, it partly covered the blurred pages that it came from (see appendix 4B). These pages were still visible in the background. If the subjects had finished using the information, they could click on a *Return to full page* button under the enlarged text block. That button took them back to the blurred page, from which the subjects could make another selection. It was not possible to turn pages or go to the contents page before clicking the *Return to full page* button.

This method was used in experiments 1 and 2. For experiment 3, the method had to be slightly adapted to new research questions. The main principle of selecting information that is at first blurred and later sharpened stayed the same, but the information blocks did not cover the rest of the text anymore and the *Return to full page* button was eliminated. When subjects clicked on an information block, the block was only sharpened and slightly enlarged, but it remained in the same page position leaving the other text blocks visible and clickable.

The information blocks that were not selected stayed blurred. When subjects had finished using the information, they could click directly on another text block to sharpen it. The block that was clicked before would then become blurred again. It was also possible to turn pages or go to the contents page directly from a sharpened information block. The new pages that would then appear on the screen would only show blurred information again.

2.3.3.2   Initial technical development

The object oriented programming language *Visual Basic 3.0* (Microsoft) was used to create an interface that contained the typical characteristics of a book. Then the experimental manuals were adapted in *PhotoStyler 2.0* (Aldus) to fit the interface. Finally, a procedure was written in Visual Basic to record mouse clicks and times. The programming details will not be specified any further. The result of this initial development phase was the click & read method as it was applied in both the first and the second experiment.[14]

The interface constructed in Visual Basic consisted of a transparent *form* with clickable buttons and frames on it. Different backgrounds could be placed behind the form: i.e. the pages of the experimental manual, that were scanned and loaded as pictures. The frames on the form, which were also transparent, were matched to fit the information blocks in the background. When subjects clicked on an information block, they actually clicked on an invisible frame. The forms, the invisible frames and the buttons all had names or numbers. The names of the forms shown on the screen were written to the logfiles when subjects clicked on them.

The programming code behind a frame unloaded the current and loaded the next, enlarged picture. Subjects could also click on buttons at the bottom of the page (see appendix 4A). By clicking on the buttons on the bottom left and the bottom right they could turn the pages, in backward and forward direction respectively. By clicking on the *Contents* button, they could go to the contents page, which was constructed in the same way as the rest of the manual, except for the larger number and smaller size of the invisible frames. The frames on the contents page took subjects directly to the intended page.

Separate forms were made for the enlarged and sharpened blocks (see appendix 4B). The background picture was the page where the selected information came from. On top of this picture, the enlarged and sharpened information block was shown. Once an information block was selected and enlarged, the only way for subjects to continue was to go back to the full page by clicking the *Return to full page* button.

The experimental manuals were first printed on paper. The prints were scanned as black and white photos in a compressed format. In the scanning process, a high resolution and good contrast and brightness settings were chosen. This was necessary, because it directly affects the quality of the text on the screen. A Hewlett Packard Scanjet IIP was used.

Each scanned picture showed one page from the manual. The scanned pictures were edited step by step in PhotoStyler 2.0. First, the pictures were loaded and resized to fit exactly one half of a 17" screen. The resized pictures were subsequently pasted either into the right or the left side of an empty PhotoStyler file that was exactly the size of *two* pictures or pages next to each other. The process was continued by resizing the next picture and pasting it next to the first picture, in the correct page order.

Next, the information in the pictures was blurred, except for the headings and the contents page. Blurring was just one of many ways to make the information illegible. Other ways for instance were changing the contrast, *motion blur*, *mosaic* screening, and adding noise to the picture. A relatively light blurring effect yielded the best results however. The information was unsharp, but it was still recognizable as text. If subjects looked closely at it, they might even be able to read it. Thus, subjects were provoked to click on the information, but they already knew where they were going because of the sharp headings and the vague text that they saw before the click. The resulting pictures were saved as bitmaps.

Finally, the enlarged information blocks were created. The blocks were cut out of the scanned pictures and resized to cover approximately 75% of the screen. Then they were saved as bitmaps, too.

2.3.3.3   An improved variant of the click & read method

In the third experiment, the arrangement of procedural and declarative information was varied (see 2.1.3). The Mix-manual, in which procedural information was interrupted in several places by different blocks of declarative information, caused a need for improving the original click & read method.

Subjects would still have to be able to select a complete block of procedural information, not just part of it. So, after clicking on part of the procedure, the whole procedure should become readable. At the same time, subjects should be able to see the blurred declarative blocks that interrupted the procedure, and they should be able to select those blocks. If the text blocks were enlarged the way they had been in the first and the second experiment, then there would be no room left for inserting the blurred declarative parts. Also, the original click & read method always required the subjects to go back to the full page first.

As a consequence, the click & read method was adapted. The level of the enlarged text blocks was eliminated. Instead of loading the enlarged pictures, the invisible frames on the blurred pages now loaded the picture of the same full page again, but now with the selected text block sharpened. It was not enlarged, and it stayed in its original place. The surrounding text blocks remained blurred. For the subjects, it appeared as if the picture stayed the same, and the text block they had selected became sharp (see appendix 4C).

Because of these changes, the construction of the manual types for the third experiment was slightly different. As the selected text blocks were not enlarged but only sharpened, the pictures for the enlarged text blocks were no longer necessary. Instead, separate pictures were made of the full pages, one with all text blocks blurred and the others each with one different text block sharpened.

A complication of this new approach was that the characters in the sharpened information on the 17" screen were very small without the enlargement. To enhance the legibility, a compromise was chosen: the sharpened information was put in a slightly larger typeface, and as a result, the blurred information had to be put in a slightly smaller typeface than the original one. With a 21" screen, this extra operation is not necessary.

2.3.3.4 Hardware constraints in the development of the click & read method

As the hardware constraints that were met at the time this research was conducted are probably not real constraints anymore when this dissertation is published, it may be clarifying to mention the limitations at the time of the three experiments. There are constraints with respect to processor type, screen size, internal memory and hard disk.

Processor type
At the time this research started, the standard PC was a 486DX33. The first experiment was however conducted on a 486DX2/66, as the standard computers were too slow: subjects had to wait several seconds for the newly clicked text blocks to build up on the screen. All the experiments were conducted on a 486DX2/66, as this processor type appeared to be fast enough to run the method. The selected text blocks appeared on the screen without delays. More perfect results however would now be obtained with new processor types.

Screen size

The click & read method requires at least a 17" screen. This screen size was used in all three experiments. It is not possible to use smaller screens because the text on the screen would become too small for the headings to be readable. A 21" screen size would be even better, because it makes the need to reduce the size of the Photostyler bitmaps redundant. Thus, a lot of labour would be saved, and the quality of the screen text would drastically improve. Unfortunately, 21" screens are still very expensive.

Internal memory

The click & read method works best with at least 16 megabytes of internal memory. It does however also work with 8 MB. The first two experiments with the click & read method were conducted with 8 MB of internal memory, under Windows 3.1. The disadvantages were however obvious: the machine made too much noise because of the constant swapping of data between internal memory and the hard disk. Fortunately, the subjects in experiments 1 and 2 claimed that they had not been distracted by the noise. However, a more quiet environment is still preferable for carrying out complex tasks. 8 MB of memory is even more annoying in the construction phase: it makes the editing of PhotoStyler pictures a very slow process.

In the third experiment, there were more pictures and a new version of Windows (3.11). 8 MB of internal memory was no longer sufficient then. Memory was added to a total of 16 MB. That solved both the problems of the swapping noise and the PhotoStyler editing.

Hard disk

Each page from the manual, and each enlarged text block has its own bitmap picture. The pictures require a lot of disk space. For the third experiment (that contained far more pictures than the other two), an 800 MB hard disk was necessary to scan and edit the pictures. Once the pictures are resized and ready, they take up less space, and the 800 MB disk space is not necessary anymore. Using a 21" screen however requires a large hard disk during the whole experiment, because the pictures are not resized anymore and thus take up more disk space.

2.3.3.5   Data preparation and calculation of the dependent variables

In the click & read method, all mouseclicks on procedural and declarative information along with the clicking time were recorded in a logfile. The actions performed on the QubeCalc computer were recorded in a second logfile. The logfiles had to be processed to prepare the data for statistical analysis. This processing and the details for calculating the dependent variables for information selection and information use are presented below.

Processing the logfiles

The processing of the logfiles was a three-stage process. First the two logfiles were "zipped" into one large, integrated logfile, which was automatically simplified to make it adequate for calculations and qualitative analysis. Then, the simplified logfiles were printed on paper, and the second part of the analysis was done by hand: the boundaries between different tasks and subtasks were marked and the task performance measures were given a score. In the third stage of the logfile processing, the task boundaries and the other data marked by hand were entered as codes in the raw integrated logfiles. The selection data and the using time were then calculated automatically, and a SPSS-file was generated.

Phase 1: integrating and simplifying the logfiles

A TurboPascal program "zipped" the logfiles of the manual and the QubeCalc-logfiles into one raw logfile that showed the QubeCalc actions and the reading actions in the right order on a time basis. An example of such an integrated file can be found in appendix 5A. The time settings on the two computers were synchronized to enable this step. At the start of the experiments, the experimenter pressed keys on both computers at the same time. If the time was not synchronous already, a computer program recalculated the time in the logfiles on the basis of this synchronization moment and the time lapse.

The integrated files were however too voluminous and too untransparent to localize task boundaries and to check whether a subtask was carried out correctly, because every single keystroke was listed together on a separate line with the accompanying time. Therefore, the integrated files were simplified (see appendices 5B and 5C).

First, *strings of data* that subjects had entered in the spreadsheet were summarized on one line: all subsequent numbers and characters were put on the same line, with the time of the first and the time of the last character. Words and numbers were much more recognizable in that way.

Secondly, all *arrow keys* were put on one line with the time of the first and the last keystroke. Sixteen times <Up> listed in a column was for instance summarized as "16 x <Up>" on one line in the logfile. If there were four <Right>s between the <Up>s, it was summarized as 16 x <Up>, 4 x <Right>. Moreover, the summarized (net) cursor movement was put at the end of the line between brackets. In this case, that would be (4, 16). At "8 x <Left>, 2 x <Down>" the net cursor movement is (-8, -2).

Thirdly, the *menu options* that the subjects had chosen were explicitly added to the logfiles. Subjects choose an item from the menu by using the arrow keys, but arrow keys are also used frequently for different things. However, as menu options in QubeCalc always followed a forward slash (/), it was possible to generate the names of the chosen menu options automatically.

Phase 2: marking task boundaries and giving scores to subtasks for correctness
In the simplified logfiles, the boundaries between different subtasks were marked by hand, and subsequently entered in the original integrated computer files. In case of doubt, the videotapes were used to verify if the subject had indeed finished a subtask at a certain time.

Also, each subtask was given a score for correctness and efficiency according to the standards that were formulated in advance, and the number of attempts were counted. These scores were also entered in the integrated file.

Finally, computer breakdowns and recovery actions by the experimenter were noted, so that those times could be subtracted from the subject's using time. The same procedure was applied for other interruptions of the tasks. All marks were entered in the integrated logfile.

Phase 3: counting clicks and calculating information using time
All the dependent variables could now automatically be calculated (e.g. times) or counted (e.g. clicks, number of incorrect subtasks) from the integrated logfile with the added information. Subsequently, an input file for statistical analysis was created. The input file was generated automatically in the format of an SPSS datafile.

Calculation of selection data
With respect to information selection, three variables could be derived from the logfiles:
- the number of clicks (on procedural information, on declarative information and total)[15];
- the percentages of clicks on procedural and declarative information (in relation to the total number of clicks);
- the number of first clicks on procedural information and the number of first clicks on declarative information in a subtask.

Only the clicks that fell within the boundaries of the task and that brought the subject to a readable part of the information were counted. Thus, the clicks to and from the contents page were for instance not counted, as it was not obvious at that time which information the subjects were looking for. The clicks on the page-turn buttons were not counted either, for the same reason. In experiment 3, these clicks did become relevant for calculating the using time.

The computer registered to which specific information block the subjects were taken at a click. The information blocks were numbered for this purpose. Procedural blocks had odd numbers whereas declarative blocks had even numbers. As a result, it was possible to count the number of procedural and declarative clicks automatically.

The total number of clicks was the sum of all procedural and declarative clicks, and the percentages of clicks on procedural and declarative information were also calculated.

A special program checked and registered the information type of the first click in each subtask. If the first block had an odd number, it was counted as a procedural block. If it had an even number, it was counted as a declarative block. The number of first clicks on procedural information were eventually compared to the number of first clicks on declarative information.

Calculation of using time
There were two measures of information use:
- using time (of procedural and declarative information, and the total information using time)
- percentage of procedural and declarative using time (in relation to the total using time)

Measuring the times during which the subjects actually used the instructions was more complicated than measuring information selection, because they had to be calculated, whereas clicks could be counted. The using time was defined as the time that the information blocks were actually visible on the screen within the boundaries of one QubeCalc-task, minus the time that subjects were obviously distracted by other things than the experimental tasks. More precisely, the time during which subjects used a certain text block was calculated as follows:

1 from the moment that subjects clicked on a text block to the time of the next click. In experiments 1 and 2, the next click was a *Return to full page* click. In experiment 3, with the adapted click & read method, this was a click on another text block.
2 from the moment that subjects clicked the text block to the time of the subtask-boundary, if the end of the subtask came before the next click. Subtask boundaries were included in the logfiles during the preparation of the data for statistical analysis (see 2.3.3.5). The idea behind this criterion is that subjects stop using the information as soon as they have finished the

task for which they originally clicked the information. A control for this assumption was the first sequence of keystrokes or clicks after the task boundary; after a break (in which subjects read the new subtask assignment) the first thing they did was either to click a new item, or start solving the new task, without using the instructions. The information that was still on the screen was not being used at that time. The tasks were chosen in such a way that the information blocks that subjects would need were not the same in subsequent tasks.

The time during which subjects were engaged in other activities had to be subtracted from these basic times. Subjects' other activities could fall into two categories:

1   actions to recover from technical problems such as a computer breakdown
2   other distractions, such as tying shoe laces and blowing one's nose

It is assumed that subjects do not use the displayed information in these situations. These data and times could either be derived from the QubeCalc-logfiles, or they were kept manually. During the experiment, the experimenter took notes of the distractor activity and the approximate time. A videocamera that was placed behind the subjects registered the activities in the category of *other distractions* as an additional check. After the experiment, the tapes were played back to record the number of seconds the distraction lasted. Those times were subtracted from the relevant tasks and subtasks.

The total using time was the sum of all the using time for procedural and declarative information. The percentages of time spent on procedural and declarative information were calculated.

This operationalization of using time worked well, except for two specific situations. Incidentally, subjects carried out actions while the relevant information was not on screen anymore. This would happen when subjects selected a text block, read it, closed it, thought about what they read and then applied it. However, both pilot studies and experimental data show that the text blocks selected to solve a problem, generally stay open until the problem has been solved. Subjects hardly ever decided to memorize what they had read and closed the manual before having solved their problem. This is not very surprising, as there was no need at all for the subjects to try to remember the information. It was much easier to leave the selected information on screen and switch from one screen to the other if necessary.

Also, subjects sometimes carried out actions after having already read the relevant information in an earlier subtask. They remembered the relevant information and did not need to look it up again. In those instances, the knowledge has been internalized in the subjects' memories, and they do not need the information directly from the manual anymore. The information using time is calculated in the subtask in which the information was used. The occurrence of this phenomenon is restricted by the construction of the subtasks, which were all different and did not contain any overlapping actions.

2.4   Procedure

The experimental setting
Two computers were positioned at an angle of 90° in relation to each other (see figure 2.1). The subject sat at the QubeCalc screen, and the other screen with the manual was on a separate table to his right. Left-handed subjects could easily turn their revolving office chair and use their left hand if necessary. The QubeCalc screen only had a keyboard, and the screen that displayed the manual only had a mouse for the subjects to work with. The other parts of the computer were hidden behind or underneath the tables. The experimenter was seated on the other side of the room, behind the subjects' back. A videocamera was also positioned behind the subject's back on the other side of the room.

Figure 2.1
Experimental setting

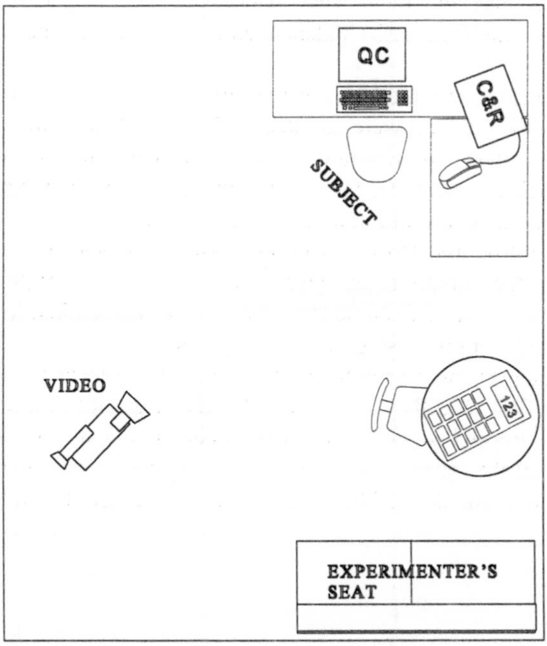

In the second and third experiment, which contained an interim task between the initial task performance and the reasoning test, a table and a chair were put against the wall in a corner of the test room. There was a four function calculator on the table, which was necessary for subjects to perform the interim task. A whiteboard was hung in front of the table, with the instructions for the interim task attached to it with magnets. The extra table was put in the room to let the subjects get away from the computers and the QubeCalc task; the intention was to distract them from the computer tasks as well as possible.

Introduction to the experiment

During the recruitment, subjects had been told that the experiment was about spreadsheets. After the subjects had entered the experimental room, they took a seat at the computers. They were first asked a set of questions to determine their age, education and their experience with computers and spreadsheets. Then a verbal explanation was given of what was expected of them. Subjects read the same explanation on a sheet of paper (see appendix 6) and were given the opportunity to ask questions about the experiment. After the spreadsheet, the manual and the videocamera were started, subjects could practise the click & read technique by clicking on a page from a cookery book. Once they indicated that they had understood the procedure, the experiment started.

Initial task performance

The tasks that the subjects had to carry out had been given to them in the form of a ready-made datafile, which was available on the PC's hard disk, and an instruction sheet that told them what to do with the file and the data in it. Subjects carried out their tasks independently while using the click & read manual.

The experimenter was present, but did not answer any questions about the experimental tasks. Subjects were not observed systematically; the experimenter was engaged in other activities during the experiment, and the subjects were informed about this in advance. There were two reasons for the experimenter to be present during the phase of initial task performance:

1 Subjects could be assisted if QubeCalc crashed; the subject would then be returned to the situation in which he was working right before the breakdown occurred. Of course this type of help was marked in the logfiles, and subtracted from the task performance times.
2 The experimenter could keep track of the time. If subjects needed too much time for the first task, they were warned and asked not to forget the second task. In the tutorial situation, the experimenter added that there was no hurry, but that the second task also contained some subtasks that the subject might want to learn about. The reason for this timekeeping was to avoid the

risk of subjects getting stuck in one single subtask and spending all their time on that task. A lot of interesting data would otherwise get lost.
When the subjects had finished their tasks, they indicated that they were ready.

Interim task
In experiments 2 and 3 (chapter 4 and 5), the initial tasks were followed by an interim task, which distracted the subjects from the QubeCalc tasks and filled the gap between the initial task performance and the delayed task performance. The interim task was not related to QubeCalc. It was carried out on paper, away from the QubeCalc computer and it lasted approximately 20 minutes (see appendix 2).

Delayed task performance
When the subjects had finished the interim task in experiment 2 and 3, they carried out the delayed task. They were asked to carry out a subtask on their own, without the manual. This subtask was the first subtask of the task used in the reasoning test.

Reasoning test
The reasoning test was then initiated by the experimenter who simultaneously tested the subjects. The performance of the test task was a standard performance that was practiced many times by the experimenter before the experiments started. Everything was planned: the errors that the subjects had to detect, the inefficient ways to perform actions, and the questions for the subjects. A script was made for as many reactions and answers by the subjects as could be foreseen.

The reasoning test yielded relevant results, and for the subjects it was a fairly natural situation. One disadvantage of this technique however is that the possibility of the experimenter having an influence on the subjects can never be excluded. An effort was made to minimize that risk in two ways: there was only one experimenter who worked with all subjects, and there were so many practising sessions that the performance of the test became a routine performance. Moreover, if there still was an influence, it is likely that it occurred with all subjects.

The reasoning tests were videotaped, as the involvement of the experimenter did not allow for simultaneous marking of the answers that the subjects had given to the questions in the test.

Factual knowledge test
The last part of the experiment was the questionnaire. Subjects completed it on paper. Neither the manual nor the spreadsheet could be used during completion. The experimenter did not answer questions about the questionnaire.

Explanation of the experiment
When all experimental tasks were finished, the subjects received a verbal explanation of the experiments and the tasks. They were asked a few additional questions and they received a financial reward.

The following three chapters will describe in more detail how the selection and use of procedural and declarative information are investigated using the click & read method. Chapter 4 focuses specifically on measuring effects of declarative information, thereby reporting the results on the different effect measures. In chapter 5, both information use and effects are measured for four different arrangements of procedural and declarative information.

Chapter 3

The use of procedural and declarative information in software manuals

This chapter describes an experiment that was designed to investigate the use of procedural and declarative information in both simple and complex tasks, and in three user situations: tutorial, intermediate and reference. Two replications of this experiment will also be discussed.

3.1   Introduction

3.1.1   Previous research: declarative information is skipped

Hardly any research has been reported so far that specifically focuses on the question of how software users select and use procedural and declarative information. However, the research underlying the development of the Minimal Manual (e.g Mack et al., 1983; Carroll et al., 1986; Carroll, 1990a) gives some insight into the question of what information is selected and skipped in standard commercial manuals.

Mack et al. (1983) observed ten subjects while they were using commercial self-study training materials for word processors. The goal of the researchers was to identify, taxonomize and analyze problems that new users encountered when learning to work with a new program: not only problems concerning training manuals, but also problems in the interface. The subjects had to think out loud while they were carrying out their tasks. The analysis of the thinking aloud protocols yielded a broad range of user problems, which are classified into eight categories. The goal of this analysis was exploratory, in that the frequencies of particular problems were not counted and the criteria for problem categories were not specified.

The main conclusion by Mack et al. is that users are active. They prefer to learn a new system while being actively engaged in carrying out relevant tasks, instead of learning by reading. However, the standard self-study manuals which were available at the time did not support active learning. Carroll et al. (1986; 1987-1988) for instance describe how subjects had trouble finding the procedural information in the standard manual that supported their tasks. They either tried to execute non-procedural information or they skipped crucial material that was not directly executable.

In subsequent studies, the results and observations were used to develop training materials that did support an active learning process. Carroll et al. (1988) developed "Guided Exploration Cards", a set of instructional cards which met four criteria based on the requirements of an active user:

1   Task-orientation
As users are interested in carrying out relevant tasks, each card addressed a goal that was considered to be relevant for the user (for instance: *Typing something*, or *Underlining something*).

2   Incompleteness of procedures
The cards intentionally did not provide the user with step-by-step specifications of the procedures. Wherever possible, hints were presented that were intended to let the learner try things by himself. The incompleteness was intended to keep the user focused on the learning task and to prevent him from following directions as an end in itself, without knowing what happens at each step.

3   Modularity
The cards were not ordered. The cards did not contain references to other cards, so the learners could use them in any order: modularity was intended to support self-initiated problem solving (p.109). Also, the internal organization of the cards was modular: each card consisted of four fixed elements that were graphically blocked off.

4   Addressing error recognition and recovery
Procedures to recover from errors were included to give the learners the feeling that they always had a way out, no matter what error they made. In this way, the risk of active learning is restricted.

The Guided Exploration Cards were compared to the standard self-study manuals that had also been used in prior experiments. They contained the same contents as the standard manual, but were much briefer: the information was presented in a less detailed way.

Twelve subjects were observed in a simulation of an office setting. Half of them had to carry out the tasks with the Guided Exploration Cards, the other half with the standard manual. All subjects had to think out loud during the learning process. In addition, time and performance measurements were taken. After the learning phase, subjects had to complete a post-test.

The results showed that users of the Guided Exploration Cards spent less time learning and performed better (with less failures) on the post-test than users of the standard manual. The researchers take this as preliminary evidence for the claim that *less can be more* (p. 121): minimal materials work better for active learners. In spite of these positive results, subjects also encountered problems while using the cards. One problem is specifically relevant to the questions concerning procedural and declarative information:

> The cards provided very little explanatory material, and some learners expressed a wish for more. Such material could be made available as optional information on the cards for learners who wanted more than simply a procedure. This might help reduce the problems of gaps in learners' understanding which we observed can result in inefficient procedures. (p.124)

The next step was the development of a manual for active learners: the Minimal Manual. Carroll et al. (1987-1988) describe how their previous work led to the conctruction of the Minimal Manual. Apart from the principles underlying the Guided Exploration Cards, an additional principle is made explicit here: *slashing the verbiage*. It means that all information that is not strictly necessary is left out of the manual to prevent learners from misreading and skipping crucial information. The information in the manual is presented briefly and only once. In Carroll (1990b) the minimalisation of the information in the manual is summarized as follows:

> The ever-present sales-pitch should be cut (the user has already bought the system), section overviews, previews and reviews should be drastically cut (users often try to execute them), far less how-it-works information should be presented (new users don't have to know details of magnetic recording to use diskettes). (p. 212)

In spite of the remarks by the subjects in the Guided Exploration Cards-experiment, the Minimal Manual does not follow a different approach when it comes to explanatory information. The Minimal Manual that is enclosed as an appendix to Carroll et al. (1986) indeed shows that hardly any explanatory information is included.

Comparative tests of the Minimal Manual and standard commercial manuals revealed that the minimalist method yielded much better results: learners who used the Minimal Manual for instance made fewer errors, got started faster and worked more efficiently. These results in favour of the Minimal Manual have been reconfirmed in several experiments and also in replications by other investigators (e.g. Lazonder & Van der Meij, 1993).

In spite of the fact that the results probably arise from more than one manipulation in the Minimalist text design, the principle of drastically cutting down on the amount of information is often interpreted as the main feature that distinguishes the Minimal Manual from other manuals, although Carroll & Van der Meij (1996) warn against the short-sightedness of seeing *brevity* and

Minimal Manual as synonymous. The recommendation to cut down on information has been emphasized in many publications about Minimalist design principles, and this recommendation usually refers to non-procedural information (e.g. Charney, Reder & Wells, 1988).

3.1.2   Current approach

In the following experiment, the principle of leaving out declarative information is put to the test. During observations of subjects using standard self-study manuals (Mack et al., 1983), it appeared that subjects tended to skip everything that was "just information". As a result, much information was left out of the Guided Exploration Cards. However, after the experiment, the Guided Exploration-subjects expressed their desire for *more* explanatory information. This was not incorporated in the Minimal Manual.

The contradiction of subjects skipping explanatory information in the standard manuals and subjects wanting more explanatory information in the Guided Exploration Cards may be caused by the fact that the design of the standard manuals does not allow users to select relevant information, nor to easily skip irrelevant information. This results in comments such as "I want to do something, not learn how to do everything." and in subjects flipping pages in a manual while saying "This is just information" (Carroll et al., 1987-1988, pp. 126-127). The design of both the Guided Exploration Cards and the Minimal Manual do provide the learner with a structure that makes skipping and selecting information easier, but the declarative information is mostly absent.

In the following experiment, a manual is tested which contains both procedural and declarative information. Declarative information is made easily recognizable and it is incorporated in a text structure that enables easy information selection and skipping. Thus, the decision of what information is useful and what information is not useful is not made for the users, but they can decide about the relevance of information themselves. The experiment is intended to yield more specific information about how frequently learners use different information types when they have a free choice.

The experiment differs from Carroll's method in more ways:

* The concepts of procedural and declarative have been explicitly defined and operationalized, whereas Carroll does not define declarative information explicitly.
* Instead of the thinking aloud method, the click & read method is used.

* Apart from the learners in a tutorial situation, two other user situations are included to check whether or not more experienced users or different assignments affect the selection and use of information.
* Task complexity was systematically varied to check if complex tasks cause the users to select different information than simple tasks.
* Subjects worked with a spreadsheet instead of a word processor. Carroll et al. (1987-1988) suggest that applying the Minimalist instruction model to other domains than word processing may make a difference (p.150).

If Carroll's observations for the standard manuals also apply to other manual types in which declarative information is included, then the hypothesis should be that subjects hardly use any declarative information and, if they do, it is because they interpret it as procedural information. However, if procedural and declarative information are easily recognizable and findable, subjects may be able to select and use the declarative information when they need it and skip it when they do not need it. Regarding the remarks about a lack of explanatory information made by the subjects who used the Guided Exploration Cards, one would then expect that users do look for declarative information. It is however uncertain in what proportions they then select procedural and declarative information. Furthermore it is uncertain whether or not software users other than first-time learners select and use the same information, and whether or not task complexity makes a difference in the selection and use of information types. The answers to the following research questions should bring more clarity:

1   How much procedural and how much declarative information do users select and how long do they use the information types?
2   Do text-external factors such as user situation and task complexity affect the selection and use of procedural and declarative information in a software manual?

These research questions have been investigated in three successive experiments. The first experiment focused on questions about information use only. The second and the third experiment focused primarily on effects of declarative information and on the influence of information structure, but, as the text version constructed for experiment 1 was also included in the other two experiments, these experiments also contained replication data to check the outcome of the first experiment with respect to information use. Experiment 1 and the replications in experiment 2 and 3 are reported in this chapter.

3.2   Experiment 1

The primary goal of experiment 1 was to find out how much procedural and declarative information users in different situations and with different tasks will actually use if it is totally up to them to decide what to read and what to skip.

A secondary goal of this experiment was to test the click & read-method and evaluate whether or not it is an adequate instrument for measuring information use in software manuals. The conclusions with respect to the secondary goal will be drawn in chapter 6.

3.2.1   Design

To investigate the research questions, a mixed design was chosen with four independent variables: user situation, information type, task complexity and task order.

Both task complexity and information type were within-subjects variables. Every subject had to perform one complex and one simple task with QubeCalc. The order in which the complex and the simple tasks were performed was counterbalanced across the user situations. Also, every subject had access to a manual with both procedural and declarative information about the spreadsheet and the tasks.

User situation was a between-subjects variable: each subject was assigned to one single situation for the whole experiment. Three user situations were defined: the tutorial situation, the reference situation and the intermediate situation (see 2.1.5).

Task order was also a between-subjects variable. The order of execution of the simple and the complex task was systematically alternated in the experimental groups. However, as task order was assumed to affect the results, it was analyzed as a separate factor in order to monitor its influence.

The selection and use of procedural and declarative information were the important dependent variables in this study. Selection was measured by recording the number of times the subjects selected each of the information types, and information use was measured by recording the time that subjects actually spent using the information types. In section 2.3.3.5, the calculation of the dependent variables was described in detail.

3.2.2   Materials

Software and tasks
Subjects worked with the spreadsheet QubeCalc (see 2.1.4). A complex and a simple task were given to them in the form of a ready-made QubeCalc datafile and an instruction paper, which told them what to do with the data (see appendix 7A).

The complex task contained 8 subtasks. The subjects had to:
- open the file they needed
- edit a part of the data
- change the perspective
- define a graph and display it on screen
- go back to the original perspective
- calculate an average number and copy that to other spreadsheet-pages
- copy a block of data to a different position on the same page
- save the file

The simple task also contained 8 subtasks. The subjects had to:
- open the relevant file
- delete a row of data
- enter new data
- change the number of decimals for part of the data
- multiply two cells
- add up a column
- insert a column
- save the file

Manual
Every subject received the same text, with procedural information in a block at the top of the page, and declarative information in a block at the bottom[16] (the PD-manual). The information types were operationalized according to the criteria discussed in 2.1.1 with respect to content and form.

The manual was presented on a second screen, according to the click & read-method, in the format and structure of a printed book. Subjects had to click on the information they needed. The selected information and the time subjects spent using this information were recorded in logfiles.

Test task and questionnaire
The phase of working with the spreadsheet and the manual in experiment 1 was followed by a post-test and a questionnaire, even though measuring information

effects was not one of the goals of the first experiment. The subjects were still confronted with the post-test and the questionnaire for three reasons:

1   Subjects in the tutorial and the intermediate situations were promised a third task.
2   The test and the questionnaire served as pilot materials for subsequent experiments, where the measurement of information effects was one of the main goals.
3   The interpretation of the data concerning information use may be facilitated by the availability of performance data. The questionnaire was analyzed, as the scores may relate to the amount of information that was read by the subjects. The post-test could however not be analyzed, because subjects skipped all subtasks they thought they could not solve. As a result, the number of subtasks that were actually performed varied greatly. As the materials were used as pilot materials, subjects were also asked to explain their problems aloud, and the experimenter intervened when necessary. These restrictions were not applicable to the questionnaire.

Subjects had to perform the test task and complete the questionnaire, both without being able to use the manual. The test task was similar to the tasks that the subjects had performed in the first phase of the experiment, but in this case, the subjects had to create a file on their own by entering data according to an example on paper. The questionnaire contained 9 questions about QubeCalc facts. All those facts had been presented in the manual in the first phase of the experiment.

3.2.3   Procedure

At the time of recruitment, subjects were not told that the study they would participate in, was about instructions. They knew they would have to work with a spreadsheet program, and they were told that the study was set up to investigate how people with varying amounts of knowledge and experience would work with the software concerned.

The experiment took about an hour and a half. The subjects were asked to take a seat at the QubeCalc computer. The experimenter then explained that one screen would display the spreadsheet, while the manual could be read on the other screen.

Before the subjects were assigned to an experimental task, they had to answer a few questions about their computer experience and their spreadsheet experience in particular. Depending on their answers, the subjects were assigned to the user situaton that matched their profile best. Inexperienced subjects were assigned to the tutorial situation, experts were assigned to the reference situation and subjects with an intermediate level of spreadsheet experience were assigned to the intermediate group (see section 2.1.5).

The assignment was then explained by the experimenter. In addition, all subjects had to read the written instructions for the experiment to see if they still had any questions (appendix 6). In the meantime, the software and the videocamera were started.

After the subjects had declared that they had read and understood their assignment, they could practice clicking text blocks on a page copied from a cookery book. They were asked to answer four questions about ingredients and preparing the recipe to practice the process of information seeking. After this practice task, the subject could click on *Ready, start experiment*. The contents page of the experimental manual appeared on the screen and subjects could start carrying out the experimental tasks.

When a subject had finished the second task and indicated that he was ready, the manual was closed and the text disappeared from the screen. In the subsequent phase of the experiment, subjects had to complete the questionnaire and the performance test without the manual. Half of the subjects in each group were presented with the post test first. The other half of the subjects had to complete the questionnaire first, away from the QubeCalc screen.

After the experiment, subjects were paid DFL. 15 compensation fee. The experimenter explained to them what the experiment was about and answered their questions. Finally, the subjects answered two more questions about how they usually use manuals when working with software, and about problems they might have encountered when working with the experimental manual.

3.2.4   Subjects

Fifty-two subjects participated in the experiment: 16 women and 36 men. The average age of the subjects was 20.8 years. Twenty subjects were assigned to the tutorial situation, 18 to the intermediate situation and 14 to the reference situation. All subjects were 2nd and 3rd year students of the School of Management Studies at the University of Twente. One subject in the tutorial situation misunderstood the experimental procedure. These data were left out of the analysis.

3.2.5   Results

A four-way analysis of variance[17] was conducted to analyze the data, with information type, task complexity, user situation and task order as independent variables. Task complexity and information type contained repeated measurements. Tukey' s HSD range tests at the 5% level were used for posthoc comparisons of user situations[18].

The results are presented in three categories: information selection, information use and performance. Performance results are not presented as effect measures yet, but they are included to make the results for information selection and information use more interpretable. Effects of task order are also discussed separately, as task order is not a factor of primary interest.

Gender was not expected to affect the results and therefore it was not included as a separate independent variable in the analysis. However, as one of the conditions contained equal numbers of men and women, a separate analysis was carried out to test this assumption. The results are presented at the end of this section.

Information selection
The first measure for information selection is the number of clicks. The mean numbers of clicks in the three user situations and in the simple and complex tasks are presented in table 3.1.

Procedural information is selected more often than declarative information ($F(1,45) = 78.36$, $p < .001$). On average, 61.4% of the clicks are clicks on procedural information, whereas 38.6% of the clicks are clicks on declarative information.

There is a main effect of user situation on the number of clicks ($F(2,45) = 6.68$, $p < .01$). Tukey's HSD test reveals that subjects in the tutorial situation select more information than subjects in the reference and the intermediate situation. This difference between the user situations does not vary with task complexity: the interaction between task complexity and situation is not significant ($F(2,45) < 1$).

The interaction between information type and user situation is not significant either ($F(2,45) = 2.96$, $p = .06$). One-way analyses of variance, with user situation as a factor and the number of procedural and the number of declarative clicks as separate dependent variables, show that the user situations differ with respect to both the number of procedural and declarative clicks ($F(2,48) = 8.30$, $p < .001$; $F(2,48) = 3.84$, $p < .05$). Tukey's HSD tests reveal that tutorial users select both more procedural and more declarative information than users in the reference situation. The intermediate situation does not differ from either of the other two situations.

Thus, the selection of both procedural and declarative information contributes to the main effect of situation. As a result, the proportions of procedural and declarative clicks are equal in all three situations: the mean percentages of procedural and declarative clicks in the three user situations are all close to a 60% - 40% relation.

The subjects selected more information in the complex task than they did in the simple task ($F(1,45) = 23.01$, $p <.001$). The interaction between task complexity and information type is not significant ($F(1,45) = 2.56$, $p = .11$), indicating that task complexity has an effect on both procedural and declarative information. Separate tests affirm that in the complex task, procedural and declarative information are both selected more often than in the simple task ($F(1,50) = 11.13$, $p < .01$; $F(1,50) = 9.43$, $p < .01$) As a result, the proportions of procedural and declarative information are very similar, both in the simple task (62.1% - 37.9%) and the complex task (61.5% - 38.5%).

There was no interaction between user situation and task complexity ($F(2,45) < 1$). A trend was found toward a three-way interaction between user situation, information type and task complexity ($F(2,45) = 2.59$, $p = .09$). The means in table 3.1 suggest that the reference situation deviates slightly from the other two user situations. Separate analyses for the user situations and the simple and the complex tasks however show that procedural information is always selected more often than declarative information. Only one thing is remarkable: by way of exception, in the reference situation in combination with the complex task, the difference between procedural and declarative clicks only just reached significance ($F(1,13) = 4.82$, $p = .047$).

Table 3.1
Information selection, experiment 1:
*Mean numbers and mean percentages[19] of procedural and declarative clicks in three user
situations and in simple and complex tasks*

User situation/ Tasks	Procedural clicks	Information type (%)	Declarative clicks	(%)	Total clicks
Tutorial *(n=19)*					
Simple	8.1	62.7	5.4	37.3	13.5
Complex	13.7	63.3	8.4	36.7	22.1
Overall	21.8	62.4	13.8	37.6	35.6
Intermediate *(n=18)*					
Simple	6.5	59.0	3.9	41.0	10.4
Complex	9.6	60.8	6.3	39.2	15.9
Overall	16.1	61.5	10.2	38.5	26.3
Reference *(n=14)*					
Simple	4.6	66.5	2.4	33.5	7.0
Complex	7.4	56.3	5.6	43.6	13.0
Overall	12.0	59.9	8.1	40.1	20.1
All situations *(n=51)*					
Simple	6.6	62.1	4.0	37.9	10.6
Complex	10.5	61.5	6.9	38.5	17.4
Overall	17.1	61.4	10.9	38.6	28.0

A different aspect of information selection is the order in which the subjects
select procedural and declarative information. The underlying question is: do
subjects select procedural information first before they start looking for
declarative information, do they click on declarative information first, or is their
first click equally as often procedural or declarative? This aspect of information
selection is represented by the number of first clicks on procedural information
and the number of first clicks on declarative information in different subtasks of
a task. The mean numbers of first clicks on procedural and declarative
information are presented in table 3.2. When interpreting the table, one should
bear in mind that the total number of first clicks is not always equal to the total
number of subtasks (16) as the subjects were free to determine whether they
wanted to use the manual or not. As a consequence, the manual is not used in
every subtask.

Table 3.2
Information selection, experiment1:
Mean number of procedural and declarative first clicks in three user situations
and simple and complex tasks (16 subtasks)

User situation/ Tasks	Information type		
	Procedural	Declarative	Total
Tutorial *(n=19)*			
Simple	2.5	1.0	3.5
Complex	3.8	1.4	5.2
Overall	6.3	2.4	8.7
Intermediate *(n=18)*			
Simple	2.6	0.6	3.2
Complex	3.1	1.2	4.3
Overall	5.7	1.8	7.5
Reference *(n=14)*			
Simple	1.8	0.3	2.1
Complex	2.1	1.3	3.4
Overall	3.9	1.6	5.5
All situations *(n=51)*			
Simple	2.4	0.7	3.1
Complex	3.0	1.2	4.2
Overall	5.4	1.9	7.3

There are more first clicks on procedural information than on declarative information ($F(1,45) = 88.61$, $p < .001$), which shows that subjects more often start with selecting procedural information than with selecting declarative information, as becomes obvious when looking at the means in table 3.2. This result should however be interpreted with reserve, because procedural information is always positioned at the top of a page. It is possible that especially the first click in a subtask is affected by information order on the pages in the manual. Experiment 3 tests this effect (see chapter 5).

There is a main effect of user situation on the total number of first clicks ($F(2,45) = 11.39$, $p < .001$), which means that the number of subtasks in which users select any information differs significantly for the user situations. (If there is no first click, then subjects have not selected any information at all.) Post hoc comparisons show that users in the tutorial situation select information in a wider range of subtasks than users in the other two situations.

Finally, task complexity has a significant main effect on the number of first clicks ($F(1,45) = 31.23$, $p < .001$), showing that in the complex task, subjects select information in more subtasks than they do in the simple task. In other words: in the simple task, they can carry out more subtasks without using any information at all. No interactions between the variables were found.

Information use

Information use is represented by the mean using time in seconds for procedural and declarative information (see 2.2.1). These means are presented in table 3.3.

Overall, procedural information is used longer than declarative information $(F(1,45) = 62.18, p < .001)$. On average, procedural information is used in 68.6% of the total information using time, and declarative information is used in 31.4% of the time.

There is also a main effect of situation on the using times $(F(2,45) = 9.96, p < .001)$. Post hoc comparisons reveal that users in the tutorial situation use information longer than users in the other two situations.

There is a significant interaction between user situation and information type $(F(2,45) = 10.44, p < .001)$. One-way ANOVAs followed by post hoc comparisons show that tutorial users use *procedural* information longer than users in the other two situations $(F(2,48) = 17.48, p < .001)$, but there appears to be no significant difference in the using time of *declarative* information for the user situations $(F(2,48) = 1.01, p = .37)$. This causes a relative difference in the ratio of procedural to declarative information for the total information using time, which is illustrated by the percentages in table 3.3. These percentages also differ significantly: users in the tutorial situation use relatively more procedural and less declarative information than users in the intermediate situation $(F(2,48) = 2.96, p = .06$, with Tukey's HSD showing a difference at the 5% level between the two indicated groups.).

In the complex task, the information in the manual was used longer than in the simple task $(F(1,45) = 42.58, p < .001)$. There is no interaction between situation and task complexity $(F(2,45) <1)$.

The interaction between task complexity and information type is significant $(F(1,45) = 4.64, p < .05)$, which suggests that the proportional use of the information types also depends on task complexity.

These two-way interactions are qualified by a significant three-way interaction between user situation, task complexity and information type $(F(2,45) = 3.58, p < .05)$. The means in table 3.3 indicate how these interactions should be interpreted. Overall, procedural information seems to be used relatively shorter and declarative information relatively longer in the complex task, but the percentages do not differ by much. However, in the reference situation, the relative difference between information use in the simple and in the complex task is obvious. It is the reference situation which is sensitive to task complexity and therefore primarily responsible for the significant three-way interaction. The effect of information type disappears in the reference situation and the complex tasks $(F(1,13) = 1.88, p = .19)$: procedural and declarative information are used equally as long there. In all other combinations of user situation and task complexity, procedural information is used significantly longer than declarative information.

Table 3.3
Information use, experiment 1:
Mean times (seconds) and mean percentages[20] of using procedural and declarative information in three user situations and in simple and complex tasks

User situation/ Tasks	Information type				
	Procedural	(%)	Declarative	(%)	Total
Tutorial *(n=19)*					
Simple	590	75.2	214	24.8	804
Complex	1166	75.9	375	24.1	1541
Overall	1756	75.3	589	24.7	2345
Intermediate *(n=18)*					
Simple	369	62.2	186	37.8	555
Complex	697	62.3	470	37.7	1167
Overall	1066	62.2	656	37.8	1722
Reference *(n=14)*					
Simple	251	77.8	64	22.2	315
Complex	571	61.1	385	38.9	956
Overall	822	67.5	450	32.5	1272
All situations *(n=51)*					
Simple	419	70.9	163	29.1	582
Complex	837	67.0	411	33.0	1248
Overall	1256	68.6	574	31.4	1830

Performance data
The performance data in this experiment are primarily used to get an impression of the subjects' achievements. The performance data consist of the number of incorrectly performed subtasks, the total time needed to carry out the 16 subtasks and the number of errors and *don't knows* in the questionnaire. The means are presented in table 3.4.

Table 3.4
Experiment 1: Mean performance data for three user situations and simple and complex tasks

User situation/ Tasks	# Incorrect subtasks	Performance time (min)	# Errors in questionnaire
Tutorial *(n=19)*			
Simple	0.4	24.09	
Complex	1.9	40.49	
Overall	2.3	64.58	3.4
Intermediate *(n=18)*			
Simple	0.4	17.17	
Complex	1.6	34.83	
Overall	2.1	52.00	3.6
Reference *(n=14)*			
Simple	0.5	13.58	
Complex	1.8	32.94	
Overall	2.3	46.52	2.4
All situations *(n=51)*			
Simple	0.4	18.76	
Complex	1.8	36.42	
Overall	2.2	55.19	3.2

There was no significant difference between the situations with respect to the number of incorrect subtasks ($F(2,45) < 1$). In the complex task, more subtasks were carried out incorrectly than in the simple task ($F(1,45) = 45.81, p < .001$). There was no interaction between user situation and task complexity ($F(2,45) < 1$).

There was a main effect of user situation on the performance time ($F(2,45) = 8.45, p < .001$). Tukey's HSD test showed that the subjects in the tutorial group needed significantly more time than subjects in the other two groups. Task complexity also affected the performance time: the complex task took the subjects longer than the simple task did ($F(1,45) = 87.21, p < .001$). No interaction between user situation and task complexity was found ($F(2,45) < 1$).

User situation did not affect the number of errors in the questionnaire ($F(2,48) = 2.72, p = .08$).

Effects of task order
The order in which the simple and the complex task were presented to the subjects was expected to have an effect on the data: a complex task is relatively easier if you have to do it after the simple task, and relatively more difficult if

you have to start with it. The simple task is very simple if you have done the complex task first, whereas it is less simple if you start with it.

Therefore, the order was counterbalanced: in each user situation, half of the subjects started with the simple task and continued with the complex task, and the other half of the subjects carried out the tasks in the opposite order. To test for order effects, task order was included as a between-subjects factor in the data analysis. The data are presented in table 3.5.

Table 3.5

Experiment 1:Effects of task order on using procedural and declarative information in three user situations and simple and complex tasks

Order/ User situation/ Tasks	Number of clicks			Using times (sec)			Number of first clicks		
	Proc	Decl	Tot	Proc	Decl	Tot	Proc	Decl	Tot
Simple task first									
Tutorial									
Simple	11.3	7.7	19.0	931	354	1284	3.6	1.2	4.8
Complex	8.2	5.0	13.2	827	283	1111	2.9	1.4	4.3
Intermediate									
Simple	10.0	5.7	15.7	559	219	778	3.4	0.6	4.0
Complex	7.1	4.0	11.1	522	319	840	2.7	1.2	3.9
Reference									
Simple	6.3	2.7	9.0	391	60	451	2.9	0.0	2.9
Complex	3.9	3.4	7.3	285	422	708	1.4	1.1	2.6
Complex task first									
Tutorial									
Simple	5.1	3.4	8.5	284	88	372	1.6	0.8	2.4
Complex	18.7	11.4	30.1	1471	457	1928	4.6	1.2	5.8
Intermediate									
Simple	3.0	2.1	5.1	178	153	331	1.8	0.7	2.4
Complex	12.0	8.7	20.7	873	621	1494	3.4	1.1	4.6
Reference									
Simple	3.0	2.1	5.1	112	68	180	0.9	0.6	1.4
Complex	10.9	7.8	18.7	856	349	1205	2.7	1.4	4.1

There were no main effects of task order (*number of clicks*: $F(1,45) = 1.58$, $p = .22$; *using time*: $F(1,45) < 1$; *number of first clicks*: $F(1,45) = 1.08$, $p = .30$). Thus, the amount of information that is selected and the time that is spent using the information in both tasks does not depend on the order in which the tasks are carried out.

Task order interacts systematically with task complexity (*number of clicks*: $F(1,45) = 60.60$, $p < .001$; *using time*: $F(1,45) = 36.45$, $p < .001$; *number of first clicks*: $F(1,45) = 47.09$, $p < .001$), which confirms the assumed effect of task order: there are more clicks ($t = 8.98$, $df = 25$, $p < .001$), more first clicks ($t = 7.86$, $df = 25$, $p < .001$) and longer using time ($t = 11.46$, $df = 25$, $p < .001$) in the complex task when the complex task is carried out first. When the simple task is carried out first, the difference between the simple and the complex task disappears with respect to using time and the number of first clicks ($t = 0.21$, $df = 24$, $p = .84$; $t = 1.13$, $df = 24$, $p < .27$). There are even more clicks in the simple task than in the complex task when the simple task is carried out first ($t = 2.29$, $df = 24$, $p < .05$).

The two-way interaction between task order and task complexity is qualified by a three-way interaction between task order, task complexity and information type (*number of clicks*: $F(1,45) = 19.93$, $p < .001$; *using time*: $F(1,45) = 28.21$, $p < .001$; *number of first clicks*: $F(1,45)$, $= 28.64$, $p < .001$). Separate paired t-tests reveal that the interaction effect of task complexity and task order is different for procedural and declarative information. The selection and use of procedural information is more sensitive to the effects of task order and complexity than the selection and use of declarative information.

When the *complex* task is carried out first, subjects select both more procedural ($t = 9.68$, $df = 25$, $p < .001$) and more declarative information ($t = 6.68$, $df = 25$, $p < .001$) in the complex task than they do in the simple task. When the *simple* task is carried out first, subjects click procedural information more often in the simple task, than in the complex task ($t = 2.98$, $df = 24$, $p < .01$) and they make an equal number of selections on declarative information ($t = 1.33$, $df = 24$, $p = .20$) in the simple and the complex task.

Similar results are obtained for the number of first clicks. When the complex task is carried out first, the number of first clicks is larger in the complex task than in the simple task for both procedural and declarative information ($t = 6.33$, $df = 25$, $p < .001$; $t = 2.90$, $df = 25$, $p < .01$). When the simple task is carried out first, the results differ for procedural and declarative first clicks. The number of first clicks on procedural information is larger in the simple task than in the complex task ($t = 3.26$, $df = 24$, $p < .01$), but the number of first clicks on declarative information is still larger in the complex task than in the simple task ($t = 3.22$, $df = 24$, $p < .01$).

The using time shows that both procedural and declarative information are used longer in the complex task, when the complex task is carried out first ($t = 10.28$, $df = 25$, $p < .001$; $t = 5.02$, $df = 25$, $p < .001$). When the simple task is carried out first, the differences between the simple and the complex task for both procedural and declarative using time disappears ($t = 0.94$, $df = 24$, $p = .36$; $t = 1.17$, $df = 24$, $p = .25$). What is striking however, is that the means for procedural using time are higher in the simple task whereas the means for declarative using time are still higher in the complex task.

In summary, the effects of task complexity depend on the order in which the simple and the complex task are presented. When the complex task comes first, the difference in information selection and use for the simple and the complex task is larger than when the complex task comes second. When the complex task comes second, these differences sometimes even disappear or turn out to be significant in the reverse direction: in the simple task, there are more clicks than in the complex task.

What is more surprising, is the finding that the interaction effect of task order is different for procedural and declarative information. The selection and use of procedural information is more sensitive to the effects of task order and complexity, than the selection and use of declarative information. When the complex task comes first, subjects select and use more information in the complex task. This applies to both procedural and declarative information. When the simple task comes first, subjects select and use more procedural information in the simple task than they do in the complex task, but they still select and use more declarative information in the complex task.

Gender effects
In the tutorial situation, enough female subjects participated to enable an analysis for gender effects. Such an analysis is not a specific goal of this study. It only serves as a control, because the male subjects by far outnumbered the female subjects in the experiment.

The 11 men and 8 women in the tutorial situation were compared on all the dependent variables. No gender effects were found, neither for information selection or use, nor for performance measures, with only one exception: on average, it took female subjects longer to complete the tasks ($F(1,17) = 5.19$, $p < .05$). Female subjects in the tutorial situation on average needed 70.7 minutes, whereas male subjects only needed 60.1 minutes. On the basis of these results, the data were collapsed over the gender factor in the subsequent experiments.

3.2.6 Summary

The results of the first experiment are summarized in this section. In the subsequent sections of this chapter, two replications of this experiment will be reported. The consistent results and the differences will be discussed in 3.5.

- Procedural information is selected more often and used longer than declarative information. Overall, subjects select 61.4% procedural and

38.6% declarative information. Procedural information is used in 68.6% of the total information using time, declarative information in 31.4% of the total information using time.

-   The first click in a subtask is more often on procedural than on declarative information.
-   Subjects in the tutorial group select more procedural and more declarative information than subjects in the intermediate and reference situations.
-   Subjects in the tutorial group spend more time using information than subjects in the intermediate and the reference groups. This is due to the fact that they spend more time using *procedural* information; declarative information is used equally as long in all three situations. Therefore, the time ratio for the two information types differs for the user situations: the tutorial group uses procedural information relatively longer and declarative information shorter.
-   In the complex task, subjects select more information and they use it longer than in the simple task.
-   There is a small indication that the ratio of procedural to declarative information in the using time differs for the simple and the complex task. In the complex task, declarative information may be used relatively longer. This is due to the reference situation.
-   The use of information types interacts with both task complexity and user situation. Reference subjects who carried out the complex task used procedural and declarative information equally long.
-   The difference between the simple and the complex task with respect to information selection and use depends on the order of the simple and the complex task. When the simple task is carried out first, subjects no longer select and use more procedural information in the complex task.

3.3   Replication 1

Experiment 2 was designed to investigate the effects of declarative information on task performance, delayed task performance and reasoning. As the first part of the study was identical to the first part of experiment 1, and as half of the subjects worked with exactly the same manual as in experiment 1, the data of these subjects could be used for a replication. In this chapter, only the replication data are discussed. The complete experiment is described in chapter 4.

3.3.1   Design

The independent variables in the replication were again information type, task complexity, user situation and task order. Information type and task complexity were within-subjects variables: every subjects had access to procedural as well as declarative information, and every subject had to carry out a simple and a complex task. User situation and task order were between-subjects variables: every subject was assigned to one of the three user situations for the duration of the whole experiment (the tutorial, the intermediate or the reference situation), and every subject carried out the simple and the complex task in one of the two possible orders.

The dependent variables for information use were the same as those in the first experiment: the number of procedural and declarative clicks were measures of information selection, and the using time represented the time users spent using procedural and declarative information.

3.3.2   Materials

Software and tasks
Subjects again had to perform two tasks with the spreadsheet QubeCalc, a simple and a complex task. Also, they had ready-made datafiles at their disposal again. The contexts of the tasks presented to subjects were the same as those presented in the first experiment.

In this replication, each task contained only 6 subtasks instead of 8 subtasks (see appendix 7B). In the complex task, subjects had to:
- open the relevant datafile
- change the perspective
- calculate an average number on three different pages in the spreadsheet
- change the perspective back to the original perspective
- copy a block of data to a different position on the same page
- save the file

In the simple task, subjects had to:
- open the relevant datafile
- enter new data
- erase data in a single cell
- change the number of decimals in a column of data,
- insert a column
- save the file

It was not just the number of subtasks that was different in this replication. The two collections of subtasks also sharpened the contrast between the simple and the complex task with respect to the first study. The most difficult subtasks of the simple task were deleted, and so were the least difficult subtasks of the complex task. So, the simple task was made simpler, whereas the complex task was made more complex. The simple task no longer contained any calculations, not even a relatively simple multiplication. In the complex task, subjects no longer had to edit existing data. The construction of a graph was also deleted from the complex task, but for other reasons: the spreadsheet contained a bug that threw subjects out of the program after a certain combination of keystrokes when creating graphs.

Manual
Apart from a few small changes at the sentence or word level, the text version that contained both procedural and declarative information was the same as the text version that was used in the first experiment. The manual was again presented according to the click & read method.

Test and questionnaire
Performance tests and a questionnaire were important parts of the experiment of which this replication was a part: the actual objective of the complete experiment was to measure the effects of declarative information (see chapter 4). Only the initial performance data and the questionnaire scores of this replication will be reported. The questionnaire only differed slightly from the questionnaire in experiment 1: it now contained 12 questions about QubeCalc facts instead of 9.

3.3.3   Procedure

The procedure of the replication was almost identical to the procedure described in detail in 3.2.3, with the only difference being that subjects had to carry out an interim task between the two experimental tasks and the questionnaire phase (see chapter 4). The interim task had no relation to Qubecalc.

The complete experiment took over two hours. The first part took one hour approximately. Subjects were paid DFL. 30.

3.3.4   Subjects

Twenty-five subjects worked with the text version that contained both procedural and declarative information, 17 men and 8 women. One subject in the tutorial situation forgot to carry out the simple task. His data were eliminated from the analysis. The subjects were second and third-year students from the University of Twente. Their average age was 21.6 years.

3.3.5   Results

Information selection

Information selection is represented by the mean number of procedural and declarative clicks in the three user situations and in the two tasks. These means are presented in table 3.6.

Procedural information was selected more often than declarative information ($F(1,18) = 58.19$, $p < .001$). Overall, subjects selected 62.5 % procedural information and 37.5% declarative information on average.

A main effect of user situation ($F(2,18) = 9.39$, $p < .01$) indicates that the total amount of selected information differs for the user situations. Post hoc tests reveal that users in the tutorial situation select more information than users in the reference situation. The mean number of clicks in the intermediate situation is half way between the numbers in the tutorial and the reference situation, but the differences are not significant.

A significant interaction effect of user situation and information type ($F(2,18) = 14.82$, $p < .001$), shows that the effect of user situation is different for the two information types. Separate analyses indeed show that the number of declarative clicks does not differ significantly over the situations ($F(2, 22) = 2.11$, $p = .15$) whereas the number of procedural clicks does ($F(2,22) = 6.92$, $p < .01$). Tukey's HSD test shows that users in the tutorial situation select more procedural information than users in the reference situation. The intermediate situation does not differ significantly from the other situations. This two-way interaction of user situation and information type is qualified by a three-way interaction of user situation, information type and *task order*. This three-way interaction will be interpreted separately below, together with other task order effects.

Finally, there is a main effect of task complexity on the number of clicks ($F(1,18) = 64.23$, $p < .001$): subjects select more information in the complex task than they do in the simple task. Unlike the complexity variable in experiment 1, task complexity does not interact with information type ($F(1,18)$

< 1), nor with user situation (F(2,18) < 1). No three-way interaction was found between user situation, information type and task complexity (F(2,18) < 1).

Table 3.6
Information selection, replication 1:
Mean numbers and mean percentages[21] of procedural and declarative clicks in three user situations and in simple and complex tasks

User situation/ Tasks	Procedural clicks	(%)	Declarative clicks	(%)	Total clicks
			Information type		
Tutorial *(n = 7)*					
Simple	6.7	*74.1*	3.1	*25.9*	9.9
Complex	14.4	*61.0*	9.7	*39.0*	24.1
Overall	21.1	*61.6*	12.9	*38.4*	34.0
Intermediate *(n = 8)*					
Simple	3.6	*89.6*	0.4	*10.4*	4.0
Complex	11.3	*65.2*	7.0	*34.8*	18.3
Overall	14.9	*69.2*	7.4	*30.8*	22.3
Reference *(n = 9)*					
Simple	0.8	*91.7*	0.1	*8.3*	0.9
Complex	6.8	*55.6*	7.2	*44.4*	14.0
Overall	7.6	*57.3*	7.3	*42.7*	14.9
All situations *(n = 24)*					
Simple	3.5	*83.2*	1.1	*16.8*	4.5
Complex	10.5	*60.4*	7.8	*39.6*	18.4
Overall	14.0	*62.5*	9.0	*37.5*	22.9

The number of first clicks on procedural or declarative information in a subtask is an indication for the order of information selection. The means are presented in table 3.7.

There were more first clicks on procedural blocks than on declarative blocks (F(1,18) = 20.61, p < .001). This effect did not depend on task complexity nor on user situation: the interactions between information type and complexity and between information type and user situation are not significant (F(1,18) = 3.31, p = .09); F(2,18) = 1.94, p = .17).

There was a main effect of situation on the total number of first clicks (F(2,18) = 17.97, p < .001). Post hoc tests showed that there are more first clicks in the tutorial group than in the two other groups. Thus, the users in the tutorial group select information in a wider variety of subtasks than users in the reference and intermediate situations.

There were more first clicks in the complex task than in the simple task ($F(1,18) = 17.21$, $p <.01$), which indicates that in the complex task, there are more subtasks in which people select information than in the simple task.

There was a significant interaction between task complexity and user situation ($F(2,18) = 10.79$, $p < .01$), suggesting that the effect of task complexity differs for user situations. Separate tests indeed show that task complexity has an obvious impact on users in the reference situation ($F(1,8) = 38.47$, $p < .001$): it causes subjects to select information in more subtasks than in the simple task. In the other two user situations, there is no significant effect of complexity (Tutorial: $F(1,6) = 2.88$, $p = .14$; Intermediate: $F(1,7) = 2.54$, $p = .16$).

No three-way interaction was found between user situation, information type and task complexity ($F(2,18) = 2.12$, $p = .15$).

Table 3.7
Information selection, replication1:
Mean number of procedural and declarative first clicks in three user situations and
simple and complex tasks (12 subtasks)

| User situation/ | Information type | | |
Tasks	Procedural	Declarative	Total
Tutorial *(n=7)*			
Simple	3.7	1.0	4.7
Complex	2.6	1.4	4.0
Overall	6.3	2.4	8.7
Intermediate *(n=8)*			
Simple	2.1	0.3	2.3
Complex	2.3	1.0	3.3
Overall	4.4	1.3	5.6
Reference *(n=9)*			
Simple	0.4	0.0	0.4
Complex	1.8	1.2	3.0
Overall	2.2	1.2	3.4
All situations *(n=24)*			
Simple	2.0	0.4	2.4
Complex	2.2	1.2	3.4
Overall	4.1	1.6	5.8

Information use
The replication data for information use are presented in table 3.8.

There is a main effect of information type on using time, which means that overall, procedural information is used longer than declarative information ($F(1,18) = 9.39, p < .01$).

There is also a main effect of user situation on using time ($F(2,18) = 4.32, p < .05$). Post hoc tests show that subjects in the tutorial situation spend more time using information than subjects in the reference situation. The time in the intermediate situation does not differ significantly from that in the other two situations.

Again, the interaction between information type and user situation is significant ($F(2,18) = 6.28, p < .01$). Separate tests for the procedural and declarative using time revealed that the user situations differ significantly with respect to the time spent on using procedural information ($F(2,18) = 10.38, p < .001$; the only significant difference was the one between the tutorial and the reference situation). The user situations do not however differ with respect to the using time of *declarative* information ($F(2,18) <1$). This effect is noticeable in the percentages in table 3.8: the ratios in the reference situation deviate from those in the other two situations.

A trend towards a three-way interaction between situation, information type and task complexity ($F(2,18) = 3.12, p = .07$) qualifies the two-way interaction between information type and user situation. Separate tests revealed that subjects in both the reference and the intermediate situation no longer spent more time using procedural information: procedural and declarative information are used equally long (*reference & simple task*: $F(1,8) = 2.18, p = .18$; *reference & complex task*: $F(1,8) = 2.51, p = .15$; *intermediate & complex task*: $F(1,7) = 2.55, p = .15$. The difference between procedural and declarative using time remains specific to the tutorial situation, however (*simple task*: ($F(1,6) = 21.78, p < .01$; *complex task* ($F(1,6) = 6.89, p < .05$), and there is a tendency towards significance in the intermediate situation and the simple task ($F(1,7) = 3.71, p = .09$).

This is similar to the results of experiment 1, although the three-way interaction was significant there, and the only situation in which there was no difference between procedural and declarative using time was the reference situation in combination with the complex task. In this replication, the difference also disappears in the simple task in the reference situation and the complex task in the intermediate situation. This may be due to the possibility of intermediate subjects behaving more like reference subjects here, and to the fact that the simple task in the replication was far more simple than the simple task in experiment 1: reference subjects in particular could often do this simple task without clicking any information at all, which yields a slightly distorted view.

Finally, a main effect of task complexity on the using time ($F(1,18) = 60.85$, $p < .001$) again shows that in the complex task, information is used longer than in the simple task.

No further interactions were found.

Table 3.8

Information use, replication 1:

Mean times (seconds) and mean percentages[21] of using procedural or declarative information in three user situations and simple and complex tasks

User situation/ Tasks	Information type				
	Procedural	(%)	Declarative	(%)	Total
Tutorial *(n=7)*					
Simple	329	*84.9*	82	*15.1*	411
Complex	916	*65.2*	454	*34.8*	1370
Overall	1204	*66.8*	525	*33.2*	1729
Intermediate *(n=8)*					
Simple	142	*88.7*	10	*11.3*	152
Complex	678	*64.7*	437	*35.3*	1115
Overall	820	*66.4*	447	*33.6*	1267
Reference *(n=9)*					
Simple	27	*98.6*	0.4	*1.4*	27
Complex	345	*48.9*	533	*51.1*	878
Overall	372	*50.9*	533	*49.1*	905
All situations *(n=24)*					
Simple	154	*88.9*	27	*11.1*	181
Complex	634	*59.2*	477	*40.8*	1111
Overall	782	*61.0*	503	*39.0*	1285

Performance data

The performance results in this replication were primarily used to get an impression of the subjects' achievements. Similar to experiment 1, the performance data consist of the number of incorrect subtasks (i.e. the subtasks for which subjects were not able to find the correct strategy and the correct solution), the total time needed to carry out the 12 subtasks and the number of errors and *don't knows* in the questionnaire. The means are presented in table 3.9.

Table 3.9

Replication 1: Mean performance data for three user situations and simple and complex tasks

User situation/ Tasks	# Incorrect subtasks	Performance time (min)	# Errors in questionnaire
Tutorial *(n=7)*			
Simple	0.14	10.96	
Complex	1.14	35.78	
Overall	1.29	46.74	4.87
Intermediate *(n=8)*			
Simple	0.38	5.57	
Complex	0.25	29.20	
Overall	0.63	34.76	3.63
Reference *(n=9)*			
Simple	0.33	3.36	
Complex	0.67	32.06	
Overall	1.00	35.42	3.78
All situations *(n=24)*			
Simple	0.29	6.32	
Complex	0.67	32.19	
Overall	0.96	38.50	4.08

There were no significant differences between the situations with respect to the number of incorrect subtasks ($F(2,21) < 1$). No main effect of task complexity on the number of incorrect subtasks was found either, although there was a trend towards a higher number of incorrect subtasks in the complex task ($F(1,21) = 3.88$, $p = .06$). There was no interaction between user situation and task complexity ($F(2,45) = 2.39$, $p = .12$).

There was no main effect of user situation on the performance times ($F(2,21) = 1.93$, $p = .17$). Task complexity however did affect the performance times: the complex task took the subjects longer than the simple task did ($F(1,21) = 98.18$, $p < .001$). No interaction between user situation and task complexity was found ($F(2,21) < 1$).

User situation did not affect the number of errors in the questionnaire ($F(2,21) = 1.11$, $p = .35$).

Effects of task order
To test for order effects, task order was again included as a between-subjects factor in the data analysis (see table 3.10). The following results should however be interpreted with great caution as the number of subjects is very small: it varies from 3 to 5 subjects per cell.

Table 3.10

Replication1: Effects of task order on using procedural and declarative information in three user situations and simple and complex tasks

Order/ User situation / Tasks	Number of clicks			Using time (sec)			Number of first clicks		
	Proc	Decl	Tot	Proc	Decl	Tot	Proc	Decl	Tot
Simple task first									
Tutorial									
Simple	7.0	4.0	11.0	358	94	452	3.8	1.0	4.8
Complex	11.0	8.2	19.2	913	422	1335	2.6	1.0	3.6
Intermediate									
Simple	3.8	0.2	4.0	164	5	170	2.4	0.0	2.4
Complex	9.8	5.0	14.8	615	473	1089	2.0	1.0	3.0
Reference									
Simple	1.3	0.3	1.5	60	1	61	0.8	0.0	0.8
Complex	5.8	5.3	11.0	194	445	639	1.5	0.8	2.3
Complex task first									
Tutorial									
Simple	6.0	1.0	7.0	258	51	309	3.5	1.0	4.5
Complex	17.3	10.3	27.7	922	506	1428	2.3	2.3	4.7
Intermediate									
Simple	3.3	0.7	4.0	105	17	122	1.7	0.7	2.3
Complex	13.7	10.3	24.0	782	376	1159	2.7	1.0	3.7
Reference									
Simple	0.4	0.0	0.4	1	0	1	0.2	0.0	0.2
Complex	7.6	8.8	16.4	466	602	1069	2.0	1.6	3.6

There were no main effects of task order on the using times and the number of first clicks (*using times*: $F(1,18) < 1$; *number of first clicks*: $F(1,18) = 1.24, p = .28$). However, task order did affect the number of clicks ($F(1,18) = 4.67, p < .05$): subjects clicked more often when the complex task was carried out first.

Similar to the results from experiment 1, task order appears to interact with task complexity for the number of clicks ($F(1,18) = 9.95, p < .01$) and the number of first clicks ($F(1,18) = 8.59, p < .01$). However, on this occasion there was no two-way interaction between task order and task complexity for the using time ($F(1,18) = 2.50, p = .13$). Paired t-tests show that there are more first clicks ($t = 4.30, df = 9, p < .01$) in the complex task than in the simple task when the complex task is carried out first. Or, in other words: in the complex task, subjects selected information in a wider variety of subtasks than in the simple task as long as the complex task came first. However, when the *simple* task was carried out first, there were equal numbers of first clicks in the simple and the complex task ($t = 0.51$, $df = 13$, $p < .62$). For the number of clicks, paired t-tests show that in any task order, subjects select more clicks in the complex task than they do in the simple task (*simple task first*: $t = 4.10$, $df = 13$, $p < .01$; *complex task first*: $t = 6.79$, $df = 9$ $p < .001$), but a separate one-way ANOVA shows that the difference is significantly smaller when the simple task is carried out first ($F(1,22) = 7.94$, $p < .05$).

A significant three-way interaction effect of task order, information type and user situation on the number of clicks ($F(2,18) = 5.05$, $p < .05$) qualifies the two-way interaction that was found between user situation and information type (see 3.3.5 *Information selection*) . Separate analyses for the two task orders showed that in any task order, simple task first or complex task first, there is a significant main effect of user situation on the number of procedural clicks. In both cases, the tutorial group selected more procedural text blocks than the reference group (*complex task first*: ($F(2,7) = 5.82$, $p < .05$; *simple task first*:($F(2,11) = 9.20$, $p < .01$). The intermediate group did not differ significantly from the other groups. Subjects in the tutorial situation also selected more declarative clicks when the simple task came first ($F(2,11) = 4.84$, $p < .05$) (again with the only significant difference being the difference between the tutorial and the intermediate situation), but subjects in all three user situations selected an equal number of declarative clicks when the complex task came first ($F(2,7) < 1$).

The three-way interaction between task order, task complexity and information type that was found in experiment 1 is not found at all in this replication (*number of clicks*: $F(1,18) < 1$; *number of first clicks*: $F(1,18) < 1$; *using times*: $F(1,18) = 1.63$, $p = .22$). No further effects were found.

3.3.6   **Summary**

The results of this replication are very similar to the results of experiment 1. The main results are summarized below.

- In accordance with experiment 1, procedural information is selected more often and used longer than declarative information. Overall, subjects select 62.5% procedural and 37.5% declarative information. Procedural information is used 61% of the total using time, declarative information 39% of the total using time.
- Again in accordance with experiment 1, the first click in a subtask is more often on procedural than on declarative information.
- Subjects in the tutorial group selected more information than subjects in the reference group. Contrary to experiment 1, in this replication this effect only

occurs for procedural information, but not for declarative information: tutorial subjects click more often on procedural information than subjects in the other two groups, but declarative information is clicked equally as often in all three user situations. This leads to a shift in the percentages of procedural and declarative in information selection. In experiment 1, both procedural and declarative information was clicked more often.

- Subjects in the tutorial group spent more time using information than subjects in the reference group. Again, this effect only occurs for procedural, but not for declarative information: tutorial subjects use procedural information longer than subjects in the other two groups, but declarative information is used equally as long in all three user situations. This effect also occurred in experiment 1. It results in a relative shift in the time proportions: the tutorial group uses procedural information relatively longer and declarative information shorter.
- In accordance with experiment 1, subjects select more information in the complex task than in the simple task and they use it longer in the complex task as well.
- The ratio of procedural to declarative information in the information using time does not differ for the simple and the complex tasks, contrary to experiment 1.
- Again, the use of information types appears to interact with task complexity and user situation. Subjects in the reference situation with the simple or the complex task and subjects in the intermediate situation with the complex task use procedural and declarative information equally long. In experiment 1, the using time for both information types was only the same for reference subjects with a complex task: other subjects used procedural information longer. Also, the three-way interaction was significant in experiment 1, whereas it was only a tendency in the replication.
- The difference between the simple and the complex task with respect to information selection and use does not depend on the sequence of the simple and the complex task, as was found in experiment one. Instead, another effect of task order was found. When the order of the tasks was *complex-simple*, subjects in the three user situations clicked on an equal number of declarative blocks, while the number of clicks on procedural information differed for the situations.
- Subjects in the reference situation select information in fewer subtasks in the simple task than they do in the complex task, contrary to other subjects. This effect did not occur in experiment 1.

3.4   Replication 2

The second replication was part of a third experiment, which was designed to investigate the influence of text structure on information selection, information use and information effects. This experiment differed from its two predecessors in two respects: task complexity was no longer varied and the click & read method had undergone a few changes. The version of the manual that was included in the first and the second experiment was still the same in the third experiment, however: it was one of four manual versions there. The first phase of the experiment was again identical to the first phase of the other experiments, except for the variation in task complexity.

In this chapter, the focus is on the second replication of experiment 1, and more specifically on the subjects who worked with the PD-manual, which had also been used in the other experiments. The complete third experiment and the results with respect to information structure are described in detail in chapter 5.

3.4.1   Design

Again, a mixed design was chosen, this time with one within-subjects and one between-subjects variable. Information type was the within-subjects variable: the manual that was used to carry out the experimental task contained procedural and declarative information. In experiment 1 and in replication 1, task complexity was the other within-subjects variable, but this variable was no longer included in replication 2. Thus, subjects received only one spreadsheet task, and task order was no longer a relevant variable either. User situation was the between-subjects variable. Each subject was assigned to one of the three user situations (see 2.5).

The dependent variables did not differ from those used in the previous two experiments. Information selection was measured by recording the number of procedural and declarative clicks, information use was measured by calculating the using time of procedural and declarative information.

3.4.2   Materials

Software and tasks
The subjects received 8 subtasks together in one task, which they were to carry out in a ready-made datafile in QubeCalc (see appendix 7C). Two subtasks came from the former simple task and the other four subtasks were originally

included in the complex task. The context presented to subjects was the same as the context provided for the complex tasks in experiment 1 and replication 1. The subjects had to:
- open the relevant file
- change the number of decimals
- change the perspective
- calculate an average number
- change the perspective back to the original perspective
- insert a column
- copy a block of information to a different page in the spreadsheet
- save the file

Manual
The text version that was used for this replication was exactly the same as the text versions used in experiment 1 and replication 1. The presentation of the text differed, however, due to an adaptation of the click & read method.

In the first and the second experiment, the information that was selected by the subjects was not only sharpened, but also enlarged against the background of the blurred page. Thus, after the mouse click, the text partly covered the rest of the information. The reader had to go back to the full page before being able to select new information. In the third experiment, the selected information was also sharpened, but only slightly enlarged and it did not cover the rest of the text. On the contrary: the text was displayed in the exact same place as the blurred text before the mouse click. At the same time, the other (blurred) information blocks were still visible and clickable, so the step back to the full page was not necessary anymore. Background and details about this adaptation of the method can be found in 2.3.3.3.

Although this adaptation had some small technical consequences for the calculation of the using time, it was not expected to cause differences in the selection and use of the information compared to the first and the second experiment. The only difference is that the end of the using time was now signalled by a click on another text block, a click on the contents button or a click on a *next page* button, whereas they were previously always signalled by the *Return to full page* button. The new click & read method could possibly reduce the time between two successive block selections, but it was not expected to affect information use in itself.

Questionnaire
Performance tests and a questionnaire were important parts of the experiment of which replication 2 was a part. Only the initial performance data and the questionnaire scores will be reported for this replication. The questionnaire

differed only slightly from the former questionnaires. It contained 12 questions about QubeCalc facts. Further details can be found in chapter 5.

3.4.3   Procedure

The procedure of the replication is identical to the procedure of replication 1. Subjects again had to carry out an interim task between the experimental task and the questionnaire phase (see chapter 5). The interim task had no relation to Qubecalc.
The complete experiment took almost two hours. The first part took approximately one hour. Subjects were paid DFL. 20.

3.4.4   Subjects

Twenty-one subjects worked with the text version that was also used in experiment 1 and replication 1. There were fourteen male and seven female subjects, who were all university students. Their average age was 22.6 years.

3.4.5   Results

Information selection
The results for information selection are presented in table 3.11. Again, procedural information was selected significantly more often than declarative information ($F(1,18) = 57.05$, $p < .001$). Furthermore, a main effect of user situation on the number of clicks was found ($F(2,18) = 4.70$, $p < .05$). Post hoc tests showed that the tutorial group selected more information than the reference group. The intermediate group did not differ from the other two groups.

There was no significant interaction between user situation and information type ($F(2,18) = 1.95$, $p = .17$), as is illustrated by the percentages in table 3.11.

Table 3.11
Information selection, replication 2:
Mean numbers and mean percentages of procedural or declarative clicks in three user situations

User situation	Procedural	(%)	Declarative	(%)	Total
		Information type			
Tutorial *(n=7)*	26.4	*60.5*	18.4	*39.5*	44.8
Intermediate *(n=6)*	19.5	*59.9*	13.3	*40.1*	32.8
Reference *(n=8)*	14.6	*59.0*	10.4	*41.0*	25.0
All situations *(n=21)*	20.0	*59.8*	13.9	*40.2*	33.9

The first clicks in the subtasks are presented in table 3.12. There are more first clicks on procedural than on declarative information ($F(2,18) = 44.80$, $p < .001$). There is also a main effect of user situation on the number of first clicks in the task ($F(2,18) = 6.50$, $p < .01$). Post hoc tests showed only a significant difference between the tutorial and the reference group; subjects in the tutorial group selected more first clicks, or in other words: they selected information in a wider variety of subtasks.

There is a significant interaction between user situation and information type ($F(2,18) = 4.56$, $p < .05$). Separate tests showed that the tutorial and the intermediate groups selected more procedural than declarative first clicks ($F(1,6) = 32.81$, $p < .01$; $F(1,5) = 13.91$, $p < .05$), but in the reference group, this difference was no longer significant ($F(1,7) = 5.12$, $p = .06$). This result was not found in experiment 1 and replication 1.

Table 3.12
Information selection, replication 2:
Mean numbers of first clicks on procedural and declarative information in 8 subtasks

User situation	Procedural	Declarative	Total
	Information type		
Tutorial *(n=7)*	5.9	0.9	6.8
Intermediate *(n=6)*	4.3	1.7	6.0
Reference *(n=8)*	3.4	1.6	5.0
All situations *(n=21)*	4.5	1.4	5.9

Information use
The data for information use are presented in table 3.13. Procedural information is used longer than declarative information ($F(1,18) = 33.71, p < .001$). There is also a main effect of user situation on the using time ($F(2,18) = 12.92, p < .001$). Tukey's HSD tests indicate that the tutorial group spent more time using information, than both the reference and the intermediate groups.

The interaction between information type and user situation is again significant ($F(2,18) = 6.15, p < .01$). Separate analyses revealed once again that the time span during which subjects use declarative information remains almost constant for the different situations ($F(2,18) = 1.64, p = .22$), whereas the times for procedural information differ significantly ($F(2,18) = 13.09, p < .001$). The percentages in table 3.13 illustrate this phenomenon.

Table 3.13
Information use, replication 2:
Mean times (seconds) and mean percentages of using procedural and declarative information in three user situations

| User situaton | Information type | | | | Total |
	Procedural	(%)	Declarative	(%)	
Tutorial *(n=7)*	1798	70.7	732	29.3	2530
Intermediate *(n=6)*	1184	68.8	526	31.2	1710
Reference *(n=8)*	680	57.7	493	42.3	1173
All situations *(n=21)*	1197	65.2	582	34.8	1779

Performance data
The performance results in this second replication are again used to get an impression of the subjects' achievements. Similar to experiment 1 and replication 1, the (initial) performance data consist of the number of incorrect subtasks (i.e. the subtasks for which subjects were not able to find the correct strategy and the correct solution), the total time needed to carry out the 16 subtasks and the number of errors and *don't knows* in the questionnaire. The means are presented in table 3.14.

In the third experiment in which this replication was included, more elaborated performance results were used as effect measures. These will be reported in chapter 5.

Table 3.14

Replication 2: Mean performance data in three user situations

User situation	# Incorrect subtasks	Performance time (min)	# Errors in questionnaire
Tutorial *(n=7)*	1.29	55.92	7.00
Intermediate *(n=8)*	0.17	41.24	6.33
Reference *(n=9)*	0.25	31.42	2.83
All situations *(n=24)*	0.57	42.39	4.55

There was a main effect of user situation on the number of incorrect subtasks ($F(2,18) =6.24, p < .01$). Tukey's HSD test indicated that subjects in the tutorial group finished with more incorrect subtasks than subjects in the reference and intermediate groups.

There was also a main effect of user situation on the performance times ($F(2,18) = 8.98, p < .01$). Tukey's HSD test showed that the subjects in the tutorial group needed significantly more time than subjects in the reference group. The intermediate group did not differ from the other two groups.

Finally, user situation also affected the number of errors in the questionnaire ($F(2,8) = 11.62, p < .01$). Tukey's HSD test showed that users in both the tutorial and the intermediate groups made more errors in the questionnaire than users in the reference group. However, this result should be interpreted with great reserve, as the number of subjects who actually completed the questionnaires in this second replication was too small (Tutorial: n=2; Intermediate: n=3 ; Reference: n=6).

3.4.6   Summary

The results in this replication are in agreement with the results obtained in experiment 1 and replication 1. The main results are summarized below.

- Overall, procedural information was again selected more often and used longer than declarative information. Overall, subjects selected 59.8% procedural and 40.2% declarative information. Procedural information was used in 65.2% of the total information using time, declarative information in 34.8% of the total information using time.
  Contrary to experiment 1 and replication 1, the difference between the information types for the number of clicks is not significant anymore in the

reference situation, although there is still an obvious trend in the same direction.

- The first click in a subtask was more often procedural than declarative.
- Subjects in the tutorial group selected more information than subjects in the reference group.
- Subjects in the tutorial group used information longer than subjects in the reference group. The effect of user situation on the using time only occurred for procedural, but not for declarative information. Thus, tutorial subjects use procedural information longer than subjects in the other two groups, but declarative information is used equally as long in all three user situations. This results in a relative shift in the time ratios: the tutorial group uses procedural information relatively longer and declarative information shorter.

3.5   Discussion and conclusions

3.5.1   Selection and use of procedural and declarative information

The main conclusion in all three experiments is that procedural information is selected more often than declarative information, and that procedural information is used longer than declarative information. However, declarative information is still selected in 30 to 40 % of the clicks, and 30 to 40% of the time spent on using information is spent on declarative information.

These results at least partly contradict the findings of the Minimalists, who reported that learners consistently skip declarative text and who recommend that declarative information should be left out as much as possible. Although procedural information seems to be the most important information type for QubeCalc users (which confirms that users are task oriented), the results clearly do not support the claim that declarative information is skipped in the processes of information selection and information use.

There may be many reasons why the results in this experiment differ from Carroll's results. Perhaps the differences are caused by the presentation of the text on a computer screen; it may be possible that the click & read method induces a different selection behaviour than the thinking aloud method applied to paper materials. However, it seems very unlikely that the click & read method causes subjects to use so much declarative information if they are actually not at all interested in this information.

The different results could also be caused by different observation techniques. In the thinking-aloud method, people say out loud that they are not interested in a certain part of the manual, whereas they may already have used it. Unless *everything* is read out loud, the investigator does not know precisely what information has been used, like with the click & read method.

The use of a spreadsheet system instead of a word processor may also contribute to the difference in results. The spreadsheet is a fairly complex system in the user's eyes. The real world problems that have to be solved may be more complex than those in learning how to use a word processor. On the other hand: in the eighties, when Carroll and his colleagues conducted their research into the Minimal Manual, a word processor was also a completely new device for most people and it may have caused the same conceptual problems as spreadsheets (still) do nowadays. Moreover, task complexity does not seem to influence the use of declarative information any more than it influences the use of procedural information.

A more plausible explanation would be that the text in the experimental manual differs in many respects from the text in the traditional manuals that were used by Carroll and his colleagues. If it is true that the text design in the experimental click & read manual enabled subjects to recognize the information types, distinguish between them and select them at the right moment, and if it is true that the traditional manuals used by Carroll did *not* enable the subjects to easily recognize and find the information types, then the difference in text design seems to be the main cause for the different results. Consequently, one may draw the conclusion that declarative information is used by all user types, as long as it can be found and clearly distinguished from action information.

3.5.2 Effects of user situation on selection and use

All three experiments show that the selection and use of procedural and declarative information depend partly on the user situation. In general, subjects in the tutorial group select more information than subjects in the reference group and sometimes also more than subjects in the intermediate group. This is not surprising, as subjects in the tutorial group have no spreadsheet experience and only moderate general computer experience. It is highly probable that their need for information is generally bigger than the more experienced users' need for information in the other two situations. Inexperienced users have to look up even the most basic procedures or explanations, whereas more experienced users are able to apply things that they already know. Moreover, the users in the tutorial condition were told to take their time to learn to work with the spreadsheet, whereas the subjects in the other two user situations were assigned to work as fast as possible.

For the information selection data (the number of clicks), the difference between the tutorial situation and the other situations is based on differences in the selection of both procedural and declarative information: both information types are selected more often by subjects in the tutorial situation. Thus, the proportions procedural-declarative are approximately the same in all three user situations as far as the number of clicks is concerned.

For the using time, the difference is only based on different time spent on procedural information. Declarative information is used equally as long in all three user situations. This results in a shift in the percentages of procedural and declarative using time: the tutorial group for instance uses a higher percentage of procedural information and a lower percentage of declarative information as far as the using time is concerned.

The difference in the using time for *procedural* information is in agreement with the difference in the number of clicks. An obvious explanation would be that users in a tutorial situation are primarily interested in *doing* things. They lack prior knowledge and experience, so they use a lot of procedural information. Users in a reference situation can do many things on the basis of their prior knowledge, and thus do not need to use all the procedural information that users in the tutorial group do.

The lack of difference in the using time for *declarative* information raises two questions:

1   Why don't users in a tutorial situation use declarative information longer?
Users in the tutorial situation clicked more often on declarative blocks than users in the reference situation: on that basis, one would expect that the using time for declarative information would also be longer than that in the reference situation. It is not, which means that the average using time per click is lower (see table 3.15).

Table 3.15
Average time (seconds) for using declarative information blocks

Task	Tutorial	User situation Intermediate	Reference
Simple task			
exp. 1	36.77	53.51	21.20
repl. 1	26.08	26.00	4.0
Complex task			
exp. 1	51.95	75.63	69.67
repl. 1	61.95	77.92	68.96
Overall			
exp. 1	42.80	68.26	59.65
repl. 1	46.75	77.68	68.45
repl. 2	45.02	44.01	50.26

The explanation for this phenomenon is probably that tutorial users do not yet have a mental model that is advanced enough to attach declarative information to. They probably select it because they feel they should learn as much as possible about Qubecalc, or because they have problems carrying out a difficult procedure and expect to find additional information there: these experiments do not yield specific information about the subjects' motivations for selecting information. Once the tutorial subjects have selected a declarative block, they read it for a relatively short time and then continue their task or their search for information. This short time is either caused by the feeling that the selected information was not what they needed, or by the feeling that they do not understand it completely. If the first cause is true, then this would be in agreement with the results by Carroll and his colleagues, whose subjects indicated by thinking aloud that they thought they did not need information that was not directly related to doing. However, the fact remains that the subjects still spent time on the declarative blocks, and it is therefore also possible that this will yield better task performance and insight. Of course, these experiments do not yet answer this question. Chapter 4 will deal with this question.

2   *Why don't users in a reference situation spend less time using declarative information?*
An alternative explanation for the constant using time of declarative information in the three user situations focuses on the question of why reference users spend less time using declarative information. This may be related to the applicability of prior knowledge and experience in a new situation. Perhaps procedures are the elements in the user's prior knowledge that can easily be applied to a new

situation, whereas declarative knowledge is more tied to a specific system and less easy to transfer. In this line of reasoning, reference users can profit from their prior procedural knowledge and skills, but they cannot use the declarative knowledge they already have. Therefore, they spent less time on procedural information than other users, but the same amount of time on using declarative information.

The two variables manipulated in the user situations: experience and assignment

The conclusions with respect to the effects that user situation has on the selection and use of procedural and declarative information show that information use by tutorial users is not identical to information use by users in the reference group. However, the results that have been found for the three user situations may be obscured by the fact that two variables are confounded: the user's experience and the nature of the experimental assignment. Specific combinations of these variables were used to define the tutorial, the intermediate and the reference situations. In order to get a more precise idea of the critical factors causing the differences between the situations, a small control experiment was conducted[22].

The user situation variable was split into two separate variables, each with two values: the variable *experience* (novices and experts) and the variable *assignment* (a learning assignment and an assignment that was aimed at fast completion of the task). This resulted in a 2 x 2 factorial design. The combination of novice users and a learning assignment was similar to the tutorial user situation, and the combination of expert users and the fast completion assignment was similar to the reference situation.

Thirty-three subjects were assigned to the *novice* or the *expert* conditions according to their level of experience. They received either a *learning* or a *fast doing* assignment. They carried out one QubeCalc task, consisting of eight subtasks. Half of the subtasks were simple, the other half were complex subtasks. They could use the PD-manual, presented according to the click & read method in experiment 3 (see sections 2.3.3.3 for a description of this variant of the click & read method).

The control experiment did not include an interim test, a reasoning test or a questionnaire; only phase one of the previous experiments was repeated. The dependent measures were the number of clicks, the number of first clicks, the using time and the task performance time. Besides experience and assignment, information type was analyzed as an additional independent variable containing repeated measurements. The data are presented in table 3.16.

Table 3.16
Effects of experience and assignment on information selection, information use and task performance

Experience/ Assignment	# Clicks proc	decl	Using time (s) proc	decl	# First clicks proc	decl	Performance time
Novices							
Learn[1]	17.3	11.9	1111	559	3.6	2.0	2159
Fast	12.6	8.6	641	392	4.1	1.4	1509
Experts							
Learn	12.7	9.4	643	342	3.3	1.7	1531
Fast[2]	9.4	6.6	389	458	3.6	0.9	1321

1 = tutorial situation
2 = reference situation

First of all, the user situations as previously defined, were analyzed separately in the same way as in the previous experiments, to check whether or not the same results would be obtained. The group of novice users with a learning assignment (tutorial situation) was compared to the group of expert users with a fast completion assignment (reference situation). The results were indeed similar to those found in experiment 1 and the two replications. The user situations differed on the number of clicks ($F(1,14) = 5.51$, $p < .05$), on the using time ($F(1,14) = 5.11$, $p < .05$), on the number of first clicks ($F(1,14) = 5.97$, $p < .05$) and on the task performance time ($F(1,14) = 4.63$, $p < .05$). The tutorial users clicked more often than the reference users, they spent more time using information and carrying out the task and they selected information in a wider variety of subtasks. For the using time, the interaction between user situation and information type was again significant ($F(1,14) = 6.33$, $p < .05$); again, the using time for procedural information differed ($F(1,14) = 8.75$, $p < .01$), whereas the using times for declarative information did not ($F(1,14) < 1$). The user situations, as previously defined, before thus yielded the same effects as in the previous experiments.

The different combinations of experience and assignment were then analyzed by means of a three-way analysis of variance with the factors experience, assignment and information type. The variable information type contained repeated measurements. The results show no significant effects of experience, nor of assignment on the *number of clicks*, although there is a trend towards an effect of assignment. (*experience:* $F(1,29) = 2.67$, $p = .11$; *assignment:* $F(1,29) = 3.48$, $p = .07$). For the *using time*, both separate variables show trends towards significance (*experience:* $F(1,29) = 4.18$, $p =$

.05; *assignment:* $F(1,29) = 3.31$, $p = .08$). For the *performance time*, there is only a trend towards a significant effect of assignment (*experience:* $F(1,29) = 2.81$, $p = .11$; *assignment:* $F(1,29) = 3.13$, $p = .09$). For *the number of first clicks* (or: the number of different subtasks in which subjects selected information) the results clearly show that experience is the variable affecting the number of subtasks in which subjects select information. Assignment does not have any effect on the number of first clicks (*experience:* $F(1,29) = 4.94$, $p < .05$; *assignment:* $F(1,29) < 1$). No interactions were found between experience and assignment for any of the dependent variables, indicating that possible effects of experience and assignment occur independently from one another.

As was to be expected on the basis of the previous experiments, there was a main effect of information type for the number of clicks ($F(1,29) = 52.64$, $p < .001$), the using time ($F(1,29) = 11.37$, $p < .01$) and the number of first clicks ($F(1,29) = 36.34$, $p < .001$); procedural information was selected more often in general and as a first click and it was used longer. There were no interactions between information type, experience and assignment.

It is remarkable that there are no significant effects of experience, nor of assignment on any of the dependent measures. The trends towards significance point to combined effects of the two variables. The difference between the tutorial situation and the reference situation may be the result of the variables *experience* and *assignment* reinforcing eachother. The situation is clear only for the number of first clicks: experience is the only variable to cause differences with respect to the number of subtasks in which information is selected.

3.5.3   Effects of task complexity on selection and use

In both experiment 1 and replication 1, subjects selected more information in the complex task than in the simple task and they also used it longer. This result only seems to confirm that the complex task is indeed complex and the simple task simple, or at least less complex. It is not surprising that subjects select more information to solve complex problems, nor that they spend more time using this information. In replication 1, another result points in the same direction: users in the reference situation selected information in fewer subtasks for the simple task than they did for the complex task. This difference did not occur in other situations. This is probably due to the fact that the simple task is simple enough for reference users to carry it out without using much information, whereas it still contains a few difficulties for the users in the other situations. The effect probably did not occur in experiment 1 because the simple task was relatively more difficult than the simple task in the replication.

In general, the ratio of procedural to declarative information for the total number of clicks and for the total using time does not vary with task complexity. The combination of task complexity and user situation *does* however cause a change in the using time of information types. In the first experiment, reference users with a complex task spent equal time using procedural and declarative information. In the first replication, the difference in time spent on procedural and declarative information not only disappears in the reference situation and the complex task, but also in the reference situation and the simple task, and in the intermediate situation and the complex task.

This suggests that the more experience users have, the more they tend to use relatively less procedural and relatively more declarative information than users with less experience. Possible explanations for this phenomenon have been presented in 3.5.2. What was not explained there is the fact that this effect especially occurs when the task is complex. Increasing task complexity apparently causes reference and intermediate subjects to attach a higher degree of importance to declarative information than in the simple tasks. The simple task does not trigger questions and curiosity, but in the complex task, they probably feel the need to understand what they are doing and to understand the consequences of their actions, whereas tutorial subjects take more for granted and are already satisfied when they have succeeded in completing their tasks successfully.

3.5.4   The order of clicking procedural and declarative information

In all three experiments, the first click in a subtask was more often procedural than declarative. It suggests that procedural information is usually used first in the process of carrying out a task, and declarative information second. That is in agreement with the findings of the Minimalists: the first thing that users want to do is act.

However, the fact that procedural information was always positioned at the top of the page in the experimental manual makes this conclusion a questionable one at this stage. It may be possible that the subject's first click is not consciously a selection on a procedural block, but just an automatic selection of information at the top of a page. If this result is to be taken as an indication for the order of information use, then the reverse information order on a page should first be tested to see if the first click in a subtask is still more often on procedural than declarative information. The tests on reverse order, with declarative information consistently at the top of the page, will be reported on in chapter 5.

This effect of procedural information being selected before declarative information does not depend on task complexity, and only replication 2 shows a relation to user situation: in the reference situation, subjects selected as much procedural as declarative information equal to the first click in a subtask. Although this result matches the results for the using time (the preference for procedural information disappears in the reference situation), it is unclear why it only occurs in replication 2. The most obvious difference, in comparison with the former two experiments, was the adapted click & read method. However, it is not obvious how this difference could have led to an interaction of user situation and information type. Perhaps, the adapted click & read method allows subjects to select information more accurately, but it remains unclear how this happens: the first click in a subtask often started from a new blurred page, which looked the same as a blurred page in experiment 1 and replication 1. The differences are not really noticeable until *after* the first click on a page. Another explanation may be found in the collection of subtasks: although most of the subtasks were not new, it is possible that precisely this combination of subtasks causes the reference users to begin with declarative information more often.

3.5.5   Effects of task order

Task order does not in itself affect the amount of selected information or the using time: subjects select equal amounts of information and they spend equal amounts of time using it, irrespective of the order in which the simple and the complex task are carried out.

Task order does affect the differences between the simple and the complex task. Overall, subjects select more information in the complex task than they do in the simple task. However, when the simple task is carried out first, these differences often disappear. In experiment 1, the number of clicks was even higher in the simple task than in the complex task when the simple task came first. This was expected: when the simple task is carried out first, the complex task is less complex than it would be if the complex task was carried out first. In replication 1, the differences between the simple and the complex tasks remained for the using time, but that may be explained by the fact that the simple task was far more simple there than in experiment 1 and thus less adequate preparation for the complex task.

A more precise view of this task order effect emerges from experiment 1: the differences between the simple and the complex task disappear mainly for procedural information, but not for declarative information. Overall, more procedural *and* more declarative information is selected in the complex task than in the simple task. Also, both information types are used longer in the complex task. When the simple task comes first, declarative information is still selected more often in the complex task, but procedural information is selected more often in the *simple* task than in the complex task. The using time for both procedural and declarative information is the same in both tasks.

Thus, the need for procedural information seems to be induced primarily by order: when subjects get started, they need to know what to do, no matter whether they have a simple or a complex task. This is again in agreement with the findings of the Minimalists: users are active and interested in doing. They often start acting before they really understand the task.

The need for declarative information is induced primarily by task complexity: declarative information is generally used more often and longer in the complex task than in the simple task, no matter whether this task comes first or second.

These results are however not confirmed by the results of replication 1. In the replication, procedural and declarative information are selected more and used longer in the complex task, no matter whether this task is carried out first or second. This may be due to the sharper contrast between the simple and the complex task: the simple task was made so simple that the need for selecting any information there was far less than in experiment 1. Thus, the facilitating effect of the simple task on the complex task is strongly reduced.

Replication 1 reveals yet another effect of task order, which in turn did not occur in experiment 1. In replication 1, the number of clicks on procedural information differed for the three user situations. The number of clicks on declarative information did not differ, but the equal number of declarative clicks in the three user situations only occurred when the complex task was carried out first. When the complex task came first, the equal number of declarative clicks resulted from the tutorial subjects clicking less on declarative blocks and the reference subjects clicking more on declarative blocks than in the opposite task order.

Several explanations are possible here. When the simple task is carried out first, the reference subjects rush through it, because they were assigned to do so and because they have the experience to do so. They hardly read anything. When the complex task comes second, they select a certain amount of declarative information, probably because the task complexity and the software itself raise questions. The tutorial subjects, on the other hand, were assigned to learn about their tasks and about QubeCalc and they had less prior knowledge: it was not unlikely that they already selected declarative blocks in the simple task. However, the complex task that came next was so complex that they needed to select a lot of declarative information again (either because they wanted to understand, or because they wanted additional information when they did not succeed in completing their tasks). Together, they selected more declarative blocks than the reference subjects. When the complex task is carried out first, the simple task also becomes more simple for the tutorial subjects, who selected less declarative information there: they have already learned a lot from the complex task.

3.5.6   Conclusions

Declarative information is a substantial part of the information that subjects select and use while they carry out a task, although procedural information is selected more often and used longer. Users tend to start their information search in a new (sub)task with procedural information, although this may depend on the order of the information types in the manual.

The use of information types depends on the user situations, especially in combination with task complexity. Reference users spend relatively less time on procedural and more time on declarative information than tutorial users. Complex tasks in combination with a lot of user experience and insufficient time cause users to spend the same amounts of time on procedural and declarative information.

On the basis of these conclusions, one may not recommend leaving declarative information out of software manuals. On the contrary: users seem to have a very consistent need for declarative information. Whether this information need results in effects on task performance and knowledge will be discussed in the next chapter.

Chapter 4
Effects of declarative information on task performance, reasoning and knowledge

This chapter focuses on the question whether or not declarative information in a software manual is useful for software users. It describes an experiment that was designed to investigate the effects of declarative information on initial and delayed task performance, reasoning and the knowledge of facts about the software and the tasks.

4.1   Introduction

The usefulness of procedural information in a software manual does not seem disputable; both advisory and research literature agrees that action information is relevant and necessary for computer users (Brockmann, 1990; Horn, 1985; Hartley, 1994; Carroll, 1990a). In experiment 1 and in both replications of that experiment, procedural information turned out to be the information type that subjects use most.

However, experiment 1 and its replications also revealed that declarative information is certainly not ignored during task performance. On the contrary, the proportion of declarative information in the total information selection and use is substantial and fairly constant. Apparently, subjects perceive the declarative information blocks as useful information as well. But, in spite of the subjects' selection behaviour, it is not yet certain whether selecting declarative information really helps them in any way. Does it affect task performance? Do subjects get a better understanding of their tasks? Do they know more about the system afterwards? In the next experiment, not only information selection and use is investigated, but also the effects of declarative information on performance, reasoning and knowledge measures.

4.1.1   Contradictions and problems in previous research

The studies by Charney, Reder & Wells (1988) and Kieras & Bovair (1984) about the effects of declarative information are often cited in document design literature (see section 1.2.2). Charney et al. investigated whether or not software users in a learning context could benefit from procedural and declarative elaborations in a computer manual. Subjects studied one of four manual versions with varying amounts of procedural and conceptual elaborations, before they were asked to carry out a spreadsheet task. The subjects had to remember the information they studied: once they started their task, they could no longer use the manual. Charney et al. measured performance times and they counted how many commands subjects issued during their first and only attempt to carry out the task. Their conclusion was that conceptual elaborations did not help users to perform their tasks more accurately or more efficiently. Procedural elaborations, and particularly situational examples, on the contrary did help.

Kieras & Bovair (1984) tested whether how-it-works information would help subjects to learn how to operate a fantasy control panel. How-it-works information contained specific descriptions of the controls and their path relations to the internal components, contextual information, details about the nature of components and general principles about how the system worked. All subjects completed a learning phase first, in which they were trained to carry out the procedures until they knew them by heart. In addition, half of the subjects could study the internal working of the device from the how-it-works information that was presented to them in the form of a text and a picture. Subjects were pre-tested to see how well they remembered the procedures and facts. If they did not remember enough, they had to study the procedures or the how-it-works information again, until they did.

After this training phase, the subjects carried out the experimental tasks without any instructions. The procedures that they had to carry out did not differ from those in the training phase. Then subjects were sent home, and asked to come back after one week for an additional test. This was the same test as the one that the subjects had performed after the training phase. Kieras & Bovair recorded training times, the amount of correctly remembered procedures, the proportion of *short-cuts* (more efficient procedures where possible) and execution times of retained procedures. They found that how-it-works information could help subjects to get better results on all measures, than subjects who had not used this information. Their explanation of this advantage was that subjects were able to infer procedures from the how-it-works information. In a subsequent experiment (which is discussed in more detail in section 1.2.2), Kieras & Bovair identified the information that specifically enabled these inferences: information about system elements and the way they are connected, and information about how the power flows through the system.

The studies by Kieras & Bovair and by Charney et al. seem to be in contradiction: Kieras & Bovair find results in favour of declarative information whereas Charney et al. do not find any results to show that declarative information has a positive influence. There may be several reasons for this difference.

First, the operationalizations of procedural and declarative information are different. Perhaps the type of declarative information defined by Kieras & Bovair (a representation of the internal working of the device) has different effects to the declarative information defined by Charney et al. (for instance: information about new concepts and the purpose of procedures). If Kieras & Bovair are right, Charney et al. may not have included information that enables subjects to infer procedures in their conceptual elaborations.

Another difference that may have led to different results is the device with which subjects had to work: Kieras & Bovair used a fantasy control panel device whereas Charney et al. use an existing computer operating system. Perhaps, subjects who worked with the non-existing device had more need for declarative information because the device was completely new, whereas the subjects who worked with the operating system already may have had preliminary ideas of how computer programs generally work. Also, there may be a difference in complexity between a fantasy control panel and a computer operating system which may lead to different effects of declarative information.

Thirdly, the subjects in Kieras & Bovair's experiment received hands-on procedure training, whereas the subjects in the experiment by Charney et al. learned both procedural and declarative information from the book. If the supposition is true that declarative information cannot be effective until subjects have some knowledge of, or experience with the procedures, then it may explain why Kieras & Bovair find effects and Charney et al. do not.

Thus, drawing concrete conclusions about the effects of declarative information for software users in more or less realistic situations is still difficult. Drawing these conclusions is not only complicated by the differences mentioned above, but also by a few aspects of the experimental procedure used by Kieras & Bovair and Charney et al.: the restriction of using the manual before the task performance phase; the lack of freedom the users have to decide which information they want to use; and the dependent variables being restricted to measurements of initial and delayed task performance.

Restriction of using the manual before the task performance phase
In the approach by Charney et al., subjects studied the manual and were tested afterwards. In the approach by Kieras & Bovair, subjects studied the declarative information and they received a hands-on training to carry out the procedures, also before they were tested. However, if software users have a choice, they are known to start carrying out tasks immediately. They only use information when

they need it, while carrying out their tasks (e.g. Carroll, 1990a). They will usually not study any relevant information *before* trying to carry out their task for the first time.

Lack of freedom to select and skip information

The studies by Kieras & Bovair and Charney et al. started from a situation in which every subject had studied *all* the information that was available. In the experiments by Kieras & Bovair, subjects were even tested to check whether or not they remembered the information. However, software users will usually not read all the information that is available to them if they have a free choice: software users have been reported to make selections of what information they need and to skip irrelevant information (Carroll, 1990a).

Restriction to initial and delayed task performance

Contrary to Charney et al., Kieras & Bovair not only measured task performance immediately after the studying phase, but also after a one-week delay. As it is possible that declarative information may have long-term effects, without effects on initial task performance, the results by Kieras & Bovair are more informative. However, it is possible that declarative information has more effects that are relevant for software users: it would be even more informative to include yet other effect measurement than initial and delayed task performance measurements.

In this study, a starting-point for investigating various effects of declarative information is found in Young's (1983) theory about mental models. Young proposes three categories of criteria for good users' mental models, which support a wide range of tasks: criteria of *performance*, *learning* and *reasoning*. If a mental model meets the performance criteria, it supports for instance the choice of a method and details of performance. If a mental model is in agreement with the learning criteria, it supports generalizations and retention. If a mental model meets the reasoning criteria, it supports the invention of new methods and explanations of the system's behaviour.

Young explores two types of mental models and tests them against these criteria: *Surrogate models* and *Task/action mapping* models. Surrogate models are representations of the internal components and the working of a device. Task/action mapping models are performance oriented representations of a task to be performed and the actions that must be taken to do so. On the basis of several analyses of pocket calculators and their underlying models, Young states that surrogate models are "clearly biased towards reasoning criteria" (Young, 1981, p. 50): a surrogate mental model (knowledge of the internal working of the device) enables a user for instance to predict how the system will respond to a certain input, to explain the system's behaviour and to invent strategies for problem solving, but it does not meet performance and learning criteria. Task/action mappings on the other hand deal with the connection between the structure of the task and an action sequence, and thus address the performance criteria, but their relevance to both learning and reasoning criteria is restricted.

When Young's theoretical claims are translated into the importance of declarative information in manuals, they predict effects of declarative information (surrogate model) on reasoning tasks. To test this assumption, separate reasoning tasks should be included as experimental measures. Of course, the effects of declarative information on reasoning may also be the underlying cause for long-term task performance improvement, but this cannot be made visible by measuring task performance only. Moreover, there is also a possibility that declarative information may affect insight and knowledge, without affecting task performance. Therefore, effect measures to test the quality of reasoning in isolation may be a valuable supplement.

A final and fairly straightforward assumption is that declarative information may affect the user's factual knowledge about the system, just like declarative information that is studied from text books enlarges the reader's factual knowledge. Of course, manuals are used in a different way than text books, and more factual knowledge may not be of direct use for the software user. But explicitly testing for effects on factual knowledge may help to specify or explain any effects of declarative information in more detail.

4.1.2   Current approach

In the next experiment, the effects of declarative information are investigated again, but with a different approach than that chosen by Kieras & Bovair (1984) and Charney, Reder & Wells (1988). The click & read method already used in experiment 1 (see chapters 2 and 3) is used to present the manuals and to record data about information selection and use. The click & read method was chosen to overcome some of the problems that were mentioned above. It enables the subjects to determine themselves when they use the information: contrary to the experiments by Kieras & Bovair and Charney et al., subjects are able to carry out their task and concurrently use information from the manual. They are not required to study and remember information. Furthermore, the click & read method lets subjects free in their choice of what to read and what to skip; they are not required to study the complete manual.

Effects of declarative information are not only measured at initial task performance level, but also at three other levels: delayed task performance, reasoning and factual knowledge. Delayed task performance is measured in a post-test after a 20-minute interval. A reasoning task and a questionnaire are also included after this delay.

The concepts of procedural and declarative information were operationalized according to the criteria specified in 2.1.1: the same criteria as were met in the manual in experiment 1 (chapter 3). The operationalization of declarative information differs in some ways from that by Kieras & Bovair and Charney et al. (see chapter 1), but the information that they consider to be *how-it-works* or *conceptual* is included in the operationalization of declarative information in the next experiment.

Three user situations were again included: a tutorial situation, an intermediate situation and a reference situation (see 2.1.5). Kieras & Bovair included only novices in their experiments, who received a learning task. Charney et al. tested 40 novice and 40 experienced subjects, who all received the same learning task. Charney et al. did not find any differences between novice and experienced users.

Also task complexity was again included as a variable. Kieras & Bovair suggest in their conclusions that providing users with how-it-works information may not be necessary when the device that they have to operate is very simple. On the basis of this suggestion, task complexity was again varied in the following experiment.

Hypotheses
The hypotheses concerning initial task performance are tendentious, since there are no reports yet of any effects having been recorded while subjects concurrently carry out their task and use information from a manual. Moreover, the results that are available are in contradiction. On the basis of the study by Charney et al (1988), one might expect that declarative information does not have any effects on initial task performance, but on the basis of the results by Kieras & Bovair, one would expect that subjects who have used declarative information perform their tasks more accurately, more efficiently and faster.

On the basis of the results reported by Kieras & Bovair (1984), it is furthermore hypothesized that declarative information has a positive effect on delayed task performance. Also, declarative information is expected to positively affect reasoning (Young, 1983) and factual knowledge about the system and the tasks.

4.2   Experiment 2

Subjects in three different user situations worked with a simple and a complex spreadsheet task and a version of the click & read manual that either did or did not contain declarative information. Information effects were measured in several ways. The task performance of subjects with the P-manual (procedural information only) was compared with the task performance of subjects with the PD-manual (both procedural and declarative information). Then, after an interim task, subjects performed a test to measure delayed task performance and reasoning. Finally, factual knowledge was tested.

4.2.1   Design

For investigating the effects of declarative information on initial task performance, a mixed design was chosen with four independent variables: *task complexity, task order, user situation* and *manual version*. Each subject had tasks of varying complexity: every subject had to perform a simple as well as a complex one. The order in which they had to perform the tasks was counterbalanced over the conditions. Task order was included as a between-subjects variable to test for sequence effects. Task complexity was operationalized by varying the familiarity of concepts and procedures, the length of required action sequences, and the embedding in action sequences (see 2.1.4).

User situation was another between-subjects variable. Subjects were assigned to one of the three user situations: the tutorial situation, the intermediate situation, or the reference situation (see section 2.1.5 for details of this procedure).

Manual version was the third between-subjects variable. During the experiment, subjects received one of two manual versions: either a manual containing both procedural and declarative information, or a manual with procedural information only. The manuals were randomly spread over the conditions.

In order to answer the research questions about the effects of declarative information on delayed task performance, reasoning and factual knowledge, the within-subjects factor task complexity was left out of the design as it was no longer relevant: during delayed performance, the reasoning test and the questionnaire, no distinction was made between simple and complex tasks anymore. The order in which subjects had performed the simple and the complex task in the first phase of the experiment may still affect delayed task performance, reasoning and factual knowledge. Therefore, task order was still included as a between subjects variable. User situation and manual version were again included as between-subjects variables.

Both initial and delayed task performance were operationalized by recording task performance time, the number of incorrectly performed subtasks, the number of inefficiently performed subtasks and the number of attempts participants needed to complete the subtasks.

Reasoning was operationalized by means of a test that required subjects to predict and explain aspects of the task and the system, to initiate strategies to solve a problem, to detect, diagnose and recover from errors and to signal inefficient strategies for carrying out a task (see section 2.2.2).

Factual knowledge was operationalized by means of a 12-item questionnaire containing questions about QubeCalc facts (see appendix 3).

4.2.2   Materials

Software and tasks
Subjects worked with the spreadsheet program QubeCalc (see 2.1.4). Both the simple and the complex task consisted of 6 subtasks. Subjects received the tasks in the form of a ready-made data file and two paper sheets containing task instructions. The tasks and data files were the same as those described in section 3.3.2. The files contained part of an administration of a sports club (see appendix 7B).

In the *simple* task, subjects had to:
- open the relevant datafile
- enter new data
- erase data in a single cell
- change the number of decimals in a column of data,
- insert a column
- save the file

In the *complex* task, subjects had to:
- open the relevant datafile
- change the perspective
- calculate an average number on three different pages in the spreadsheet
- change the perspective back to the original perspective
- copy a block of data to a different position on the same page
- save the file

Manuals

Two manual versions were used in the experiment: a version which contained both procedural and declarative information, and a version which contained procedural information only. The first manual version was the same as the manual which was used in the first study (see 3.2.2), apart from a few minor modifications and improvements at the detail level. The procedural-only version was constructed on the same basis. The declarative text blocks were left out, and two procedural text blocks were combined on one page, so that there were two text blocks on one page in both manual versions, as represented in a diagram in figure 4.1.

Figure 4.1

Grouping of the information types in two manual versions

Proc 1	Proc 2
Decl 1	Decl 2

Procedural + Declarative

Proc 1	Proc 3
Proc 2	Proc 4

Procedural only

Two procedural blocks were only put on one page if they matched the same general category. The spreadsheet manipulations were divided over the following categories: general QubeCalc manipulations, file manipulations, cell manipulations, manipulations on blocks of cells, manipulations on the three-dimensional worksheet, manipulations on rows, columns and pages, manipulations on graphs and calculations. Only in the category *QubeCalc-manipulations*, the number of procedural text blocks in a category was not even. As a result there was one page with only one text block in that category; the next category was started on the following page. The rest of the manual with procedural information only contained two
procedural text blocks per page. Extracts from both manual types can be found in appendices 1A and 1B.

Interim task

The interim task was a complex puzzle to distract subjects from their QubeCalc tasks (see section 2.2.2 and appendix 2). Subjects had to carry out two tasks on a four-function calculator. The interim task took them between 20 and 30 minutes.

Reasoning test and questionnaire

The test was included to measure insight into the spreadsheet system and tasks. Details about the construction of this test task are presented in section 2.2.2.

The test consisted of one part that the subject had to carry out alone and another interactive part, in which the subject cooperated with the experimenter. In the part that subjects had to perform by themselves, they were provided with a subtask of the type that they had also carried out in the first part of the experiment: calculating averages. The context and the file however were now different. This part served as the measure for delayed task performance.

In the interactive part, the experimenter carried out a spreadsheet task (see appendix 7D) that was similar to the tasks the subject had carried out before. The experimenter worked according to a pre-defined scenario that the subject was not aware of at the time. This scenario was the same for all subjects. The subjects had to signal errors that were made intentionally by the experimenter, they had to signal inefficient solutions initiated intentionally by the experimenter and they answered questions about the spreadsheet and the task. The signals and answers were given scores.

The questionnaire contained 12 questions about the spreadsheet. All the answers could have been found in the manual that subjects used in the first part, but only in the manual with both procedural and declarative information. Subjects who had had the manual version with procedural information could only know the answers if they had discovered them themselves in the first part of the experiment.

4.2.3   Procedure

The first part of the experiment was similar to the procedure that was already described in section 3.2.3. Subjects participated individually. During the introduction to the experiment, they were assigned to a user situation and to one of the manual types. Subjects were not aware of these categories. After the introduction, they carried out a simple and a complex task in QubeCalc. This part of the experiment took approximately one hour.

When the subjects indicated that they had finished both tasks, they were asked to carry out the interim task at another table in the room, away from the computers. QubeCalc was shut down and the manual was closed. Subjects were engaged in the interim task for at least 20 minutes.

Once the interim task was finished, the subjects entered the third phase of the experiment: the test, which had to be completed without the manual. Finally, subjects had to complete the questionnaire. Neither the spreadsheet nor the manual could be used while the questionnaire was being completed: subjects had to work from their memory.

Subjects were engaged in the experiment for two hours and were paid DFL. 30.

4.2.4 Subjects

Fifty-six subjects participated in the experiment. The data of 7 subjects were eliminated from the data analysis, either because they had not taken their jobs seriously or because they had skipped relevant subtasks. Thirty-nine subjects out of the 49 that were left were men, 10 were women. The students were second and third-year students from the University of Twente. Their average age was 21.7 years.

4.3 Results

4.3.1 Initial task performance

Initial task performance was operationalized in four different variables: performance time, the number of incorrect subtasks, the number of inefficiently performed subtasks and the number of attempts needed to complete a subtask. The total time subjects spent on reading the information in the manual was added to the analysis, as it was relevant to check whether or not subjects with the P-manual, which contains only half of the information, spent less time using the information.

The initial performance data were analyzed by means of a four-way ANOVA, with the factors *task complexity, user situation, manual version* and *task order*. The factor task complexity contained repeated measurements. The data are presented in table 4.1.

Table 4.1
Initial task performance: means for two manual versions (procedural only; procedural plus declarative), the simple and the complex task and three user situations

	Performance time (sec)	# Incorrect subtasks	# Inefficient subtasks	# Attempts	Total using time (sec)
Tutorial (n=16)					
Simple task					
Proc. only	722	0.1	1.1	8.4	410
Proc+Decl	658	0.1	1.5	9.4	411
Complex task					
Proc. only	2159	0.3	1.3	38.6	1411
Proc+Decl	2086	1.0	0.7	27.4	1370
Intermediate (n=15)					
Simple task					
Proc. only	400	0.1	1.0	9.0	148
Proc+Decl	334	0.4	0.7	7.5	151
Complex task					
Proc. only	1655	1.9	1.9	39.1	952
Proc+Decl	1752	0.3	0.9	30.0	1115
Reference (n=17)					
Simple task					
Proc. only	190	0.4	0.6	7.6	22
Proc+Decl	202	0.3	0.7	7.9	28
Complex task					
Proc. only	1939	0.5	0.5	50.4	787
Proc+Decl	1923	0.7	1.0	48.6	878

Both task complexity and user situation significantly affected the *initial performance time* $(F(1,36) = 190.85, p < .001; F(2,36) = 4.61, p < .05)$. The complex task required more time than the simple task. Tukey's HSD posthoc test revealed that subjects in the tutorial situation needed more time to complete their tasks than users in the other two situations. There were no main effects of manual version $(F(1,36) < 1)$ on performance time. No interaction effects were found either.

There was a main effect of task complexity on *the number of incorrectly performed subtasks* $(F(1,36) = 16.11, p < .001)$. In general, more subtasks were performed incorrectly in the complex task than in the simple task. No main effects of manual version or user situation on the number of incorrect subtasks were found $(F(1,36) < 1 ; F(2,36) < 1)$.

Situation and manual version had an interaction effect on the number of incorrect subtasks $(F(2,36) = 3.39, p < .05)$, indicating that the possible effects of manual version on the number of incorrectly performed subtasks differ for the user situations. Separate univariate analyses confirm this interpretation. Manual version does not affect the number of incorrect subtasks in the tutorial and the reference situation ($F(1,12) = 1.31$, $p = .28$; $F(1,13) < 1$). In the intermediate situation however, the subjects who had used the P-manual carried out significantly more subtasks incorrectly than their colleagues with the PD-manual ($F(1,11) = 14.97, p < .01$).

This two-way interaction is qualified by a significant three-way interaction of user situation, manual version and task complexity ($F(2,36) = 8.35, p < .01$). The intermediate situation is the only situation that shows an interaction between manual version and task complexity: the difference between the two manual versions in the intermediate situation only occurs in the complex task ($F(1,14) = 15.00, p < .01$) and not in the simple task ($F(1,14) < 1$).

No significant differences were found with respect to *the number of inefficiently performed subtasks*. There were no main effects of task complexity ($F(1,36) = 3.98$, $p = .06$), user situation ($F(2,36) = 1.66$, $p = .20$) or manual version ($F(1,36) < 1$). No interactions were found either.

Task complexity affected the *number of attempts* subjects needed to complete their subtasks ($F(1,36) = 78.79, p < .001$). In the complex task, more attempts were needed than in the simple task. There was also a main effect of user situation on the number of attempts ($F(2,36) = 3.34, p < .05$), although a One-way ANOVA does not yield a significant result and Tukey's HSD test does not show significant differences between any of the three user situations.

An interaction effect of user situation and task complexity ($F(2,36) = 3.54, p < .05$) indicates that the effect of task complexity depends on the user situation. Separate analyses show that task complexity affects the number of attempts in the tutorial situation ($F(1,15) = 4.76$, $p < .05$), there is a trend towards significance in the intermediate situation ($F(1,14) = 4.19$, $p = .06$), but the effects of complexity disappear in the reference situation ($F(1,16) = 1.66, p = .22$).

The *total information using time* differed significantly for the user situations ($F(2,36) = 14.03, p < .001$). Tukey's HSD showed that subjects in the tutorial situation spent more time using the manual than subjects in the other two situations. Task complexity also affected the total using time ($F(1,36) = 150.24, p < .001$): subjects spent more time using the manual in the complex task than they did in the simple task. Manual version had no effect whatsoever on the total using time of the information ($F(1,36) < 1$). This is surprising, as the P-manual only contained half of the text of the PD-manual. No interactions between the variables were found.

4.3.2 Delayed task performance

All subjects but one performed the calculation task correctly in one way or another and thus ended up with the correct result. The delayed task performance variables performance time and number of attempts were analyzed by means of a threeway ANOVA, with user situation, manual version and the order of the complex and simple task in the first part of the experiment as factors. The categorical variable of efficiency (efficient/inefficient) was analyzed by chi-square tests. The data are presented in table 4.2.

Table 4.2

Delayed task performance in three user situations and two manual versions: performance time, number of attempts and frequency of efficient task performance (percentages in brackets)

	Performance time (sec)	# Attempts	Efficiency +		Efficiency -	
Tutorial (n=17)						
Proc. only	347	5.4	0	*(0)*	9	*(100)*
Proc+Decl	140	2.5	4	*(50)*	4	*(50)*
Intermediate (n=15)						
Proc. only	239	6.3	2	*(29)*	5	*(71)*
Proc+Decl	170	3.0	5	*(63)*	3	*(38)*
Reference (n=17)						
Proc. only	131	2.9	6	*(75)*	2	*(25)*
Proc+Decl	87	2.3	5	*(56)*	4	*(44)*
All situations (n=49)						
Proc. only	239	4.8	8	*(33)*	16	*(67)*
Proc+Decl	131	2.6	14	*(56)*	11	*(44)*

There is a main effect of manual version on the *performance times* $(F(1,36) = 5.72, p < .05)$ and on the *number of attempts* subjects needed to perform the task $(F(1,36) = 9.34, p < .01)$. Subjects who had used the P-manual needed more time and more attempts to complete the task, than subjects who had used the PD-manual in the first part of the experiment. There was no significant contingency between manual version and efficiency of delayed task performance $(\chi^2 = 2.54, df = 1, p = .11)$.

There is also a main effect of user situation on the performance time $(F(2,36) = 4.11, p < .05)$. Tukey's HSD test reveals that subjects in the tutorial situation needed more time to complete the task than subjects in the reference situation. User situation did not affect the number of attempts during delayed task performance $(F(2,36) = 2.59, p = .09)$ and there is no significant contingency between user situation and the efficiency of task performance either $(\chi^2 = 5.85, df = 2, p = .05)$, although there is an obvious trend toward significance in the latter case.

No interactions between the variables were found. The chi-square tests used to analyze the efficiency variable were not used for different levels of the manual version or the user situation variables as the expected frequencies were too low.

4.3.3   Reasoning tasks

The data which represent the subjects' performance on the reasoning tasks are presented in table 4.3. They have been analyzed by means of MANOVA-tests with three between-subjects factors (user situation, manual version and the order of the simple and the complex task in the first part of the experiment) and four dependent variables that constituted the test.

Table 4.3
Effects of declarative information on reasoning

	Efficiency (4 items)	Error handling (4 items)	Explaining (5 items)	Applied insight (4 items)
Tutorial (n=17)				
Proc. only	0.7	3.0	3.2	1.9
Proc+Decl	1.3	2.9	3.1	2.4
Intermediate (n=15)				
Proc. only	1.7	2.9	2.4	1.3
Proc+Decl	2.4	2.9	3.9	2.0
Reference (n=17)				
Proc. only	2.5	3.4	4.0	1.9
Proc+Decl	3.2	3.4	4.1	2.7
All situations (n=49)				
Proc. only	1.6	3.1	3.3	1.7
Proc+Decl	2.3	3.0	3.7	2.4

Manual version had a multivariate effect on quality of reasoning (Wilks' $\lambda = .74$, $F(4,33) = 2.84$, $p < .05$). Subjects who used the manual with both procedural and declarative information did better on the reasoning test than subjects who used the P-manual. Separate analyses showed that manual version yielded univariate effects on efficiency and applied insight, but not on error handling and explaining (*efficiency*: $F(1,36) = 5.19$, $p < .05$; *applied insight*: $F(1,36) = 4.22$, $p < .05$; *error handling*: $F(1,36) < 1$; *explaining*: $F(1,36) = 2.28$, $p < .14$) .

There was also an effect of user situation on quality of reasoning (Wilks' λ = .45, $F(8,66) = 4.08$, $p < .01$). User situation was found to have univariate effects on efficiency and explaining, but not on applied insight and error handling (*efficiency*: $F(2,36) = 13.44$, $p < .001$; *explaining*: $F(2,36) = 4.35$, $p < .05$; *applied insight*: $F(2,36) = 1.92$, $p = .16$; *error handling*: $F(2,36) < 1$). Tukey's HSD tests revealed that subjects in the tutorial situation differed significantly from subjects in both the intermediate and the reference situation with respect to efficiency. With respect to the scores on the explaining items, the only significant difference was found between subjects in the intermediate and the reference situations. There were no interactions between any of the variables.

4.3.4   Factual knowledge

The number of errors on the questionnaire was the dependent variable that represented factual knowledge. The mean numbers of errors are presented in table 4.4.

Table 4.4

*Factual knowledge: mean number of errors on the 12-item
questionnaire in three user situations*

	# Errors in questionnaire
Tutorial (n=17)	
Proc. only	5.4
Proc+Decl	4.9
Intermediate (n=15)	
Proc. only	5.3
Proc+Decl	3.6
Reference (n=17)	
Proc. only	4.6
Proc+Decl	3.8
All situations(n=49)	
Proc. only	5.1
Proc+Decl	4.1

There was a main effect of manual version on the number of errors on the questionnaire ($F(1,37) = 5.31, p < .05$). Subjects who had used the manual with procedural information only made more errors than subjects who had used the manual with both procedural and declarative information.

There were no main effects of user situation on the number of errors in the questionnaire ($F(2,37) = 1.06, p = .36$). No interactions were found either.

4.3.5   Effects of task order

Task order hardly ever had an effect on the dependent variables. It had no significant effects on, or did not interact with any other variable for delayed task performance, the reasoning test or the factual knowledge questionnaire. Task order had a few effects on initial task performance, but only on the number of incorrectly performed tasks, the number of attempts and the total information using times (see table 4.5)..

There was only one main effect of task order on the number of attempts that subjects needed to complete the subtasks during initial task performance ($F(1,36) = 6.34, p < .05$). Subjects who carried out the simple task first needed more attempts to complete the subtasks than subjects who carried out the complex task first. Task order did not interact with other variables for the number of attempts. It had no further main effects either.

Task order interacted significantly with task complexity for the total information using time ($F(1,36) = 5.62$, $p < .05$): task order only had an effect in the simple task. Subjects who did the simple task first spent more time using information in the *simple* task than subjects who did the complex task first ($F(1,46) = 5.90$, $p < .05$). In contrast, task order did not affect the amount of time spent on using information in the *complex* task ($F(1,47) < 1$).

Finally, there was a three-way interaction of task order, manual version and task complexity for the number of incorrectly performed tasks ($F(1,36) = 6.19$, $p < .05$). Separate univariate analyses revealed that the effect of task complexity on the number of incorrectly performed subtasks depends on both manual version and task order: it is only significant when the complex task is done first and when subjects used the manual with procedural information only ($F(1,10) = 6.10$, $p < .05$). In all other combinations of task order and manual version, there is no difference between the simple and the complex task with respect to the number of incorrectly performed subtasks.

These task order effects are in agreement with the effects of task order on information use (section 3.2.5) and with the expectations: the complex task is relatively less complex when it is carried out second and the simple task is relatively more difficult when it comes first.

Table 4.5
Effects of task order on initial task performance for two manual versions and simple and complex tasks

	# Incorrect subtasks	# Attempts	Total using time (sec)
Simple task first			
Simple task			
Proc. only	.23	9.0	299
Proc+Decl	.21	8.9	239
Complex task			
Proc. only	.62	46.1	1020
Proc+Decl	.86	44.0	1048
Complex task first			
Simple task			
Proc. only	.18	7.6	93
Proc+Decl	.36	7.3	99
Complex task			
Proc. only	1.09	38.6	1128
Proc+Decl	.40	25.5	1191

4.3.6 Summary

Effects of declarative information
- Subjects who used both procedural and declarative information did not carry out their initial tasks better or faster than subjects who used procedural information only, with one exception: the intermediate users performed significantly more subtasks incorrectly when they used the manual without declarative information during the complex task.
- Subjects who received both procedural and declarative information spent as much time using the manual as subjects who received procedural information only.
- Subjects with the manual containing both information types performed better on the delayed tasks than subjects without declarative information: they were faster and needed fewer attempts.
- Subjects who received both procedural and declarative information performed better on the reasoning test than subjects who received procedural information only: in particular, subjects who had used declarative information knew better how procedures could be performed more efficiently and they were better at applying their insight, for instance in inventing strategies to solve a new problem.
- Subjects who had used declarative information scored better on the factual knowledge questionnaire than subjects who had only used procedural information.
- The differences between the manual versions did not depend on any of the other variables.

Differences between the user situations
- Subjects in the tutorial situation needed more time to complete their initial tasks than users in the other two situations. For the delayed task performance time, the only significant difference was the one between the tutorial and the reference situation: again, subjects in the tutorial situation needed more time.
- Subjects in the tutorial situation scored lower on the efficiency items in the reasoning task, than subjects in the intermediate and the reference situations. Subjects in the reference situation had higher scores for the explaining items in the reasoning task than subjects in the intermediate situation.
- The user situations did not differ with respect to factual knowledge.

Effects of task complexity
- More time was needed to complete the complex task than the simple task (initial task performance).

- More subtasks were performed incorrectly in the complex task than in the simple task.
- Except for the reference subjects, subjects needed more attempts to carry out the complex task than to carry out the simple task.

4.4   Discussion and conclusions

The effects of user situation and task complexity on task performance, reasoning and knowledge are similar to the effects of these variables on information selection and use. The effects of task complexity confirm that the complex task is more complex than the simple task. The effects of user situation confirm that users in the tutorial situation have less prior knowledge and that they may take more time on an assignment than users in the other situations. This experiment also shows that subjects in the reference situation perform significantly better than subjects in the intermediate situation with respect to the explaining items of the reasoning task. This is probably also due to a larger amount of prior knowledge in the reference situation.

The main focus in this chapter is on the effects of declarative information. In all user situations, the presence of declarative information in the manual appears to have no effects on initial task performance, but in accordance with the hypotheses, it has a positive effect on delayed task performance, reasoning and factual knowledge.

The lack of effects of declarative information on initial task performance[23] indicates that it would not be necessary to include declarative information in a manual if the subject's task were strictly incidental and if correctness, speed and efficiency were the only criteria to be met. On the other hand: subjects who use declarative information are not harmed by doing so. They spend the same amount of time using the manual as subjects who have only procedural information at their disposal. Thus, subjects who only had procedural information used those procedures longer, but they still did not perform better. Moreover, in the delayed task performance, the reasoning task and the questionnaire, they performed significantly worse.

If subjects have declarative information at their disposal, they use it. But, although they use the information, they do not benefit from it until they are confronted with the software for a second time. The question is: why do they not benefit immediately from using declarative information, and why do they benefit from the information when they work with the software for the second time, after a delay?

An explanation may be found in theories of mental model building. Users start working with software on the basis of some preliminary mental model (Norman, 1983). At the outset, this model may still be very inadequate and incomplete. The user's mental model is further developed during the phase of initial task performance. The combination of interacting with the software and using information in the manual provides the user with building blocks for developing the mental model.

During initial task performance, users are mainly interested in doing things, in carrying out their tasks. They are primarily building a model that is equivalent to what Young (1983) calls a task/action mapping model (see 4.1). Procedural information is sufficient for reaching that goal: users who have only procedural information perform equally well as the other subjects. Users who also have declarative information at their disposal sometimes also have reasons to select declarative information, but this does not help them to reach their initial goals. This is also in agreement with Young's claim that declarative information, which belongs to a surrogate model, does not help a performance-oriented user.

The finding that declarative information causes better performance on the *delayed* task can be explained by assuming that during delayed task performance, users benefit from the part of their mental model that is similar to the theoretical notion of a surrogate model. Users who used declarative information during initial task performance received more or better building blocks to develop their mental model that way. They use their knowledge of the working of the software to remember or infer the procedures they need to complete the repeated task. This explanation is in agreement with the conclusions by Kieras & Bovair (1984), who also found that subjects' retention of procedures was better when they had used declarative information that enabled them to infer procedures.

The results of the reasoning task also confirm Young's claims that a surrogate model supports reasoning: subjects who use declarative information, and who can thus build a surrogate model, perform better on a reasoning task. However, they did not perform better on all aspects of reasoning that were predicted: there were no univariate effects on *explaining* and *error handling*. This may be due to the specific declarative information blocks that the subjects selected from the click & read manual: perhaps the blocks that were relevant for the *explaining* items were not used. As the declarative information blocks contained different subtypes of declarative information, this could not be checked. In chapter 5, a subsequent experiment will be reported that gives some more insight into the specific subtypes of declarative information that are selected and used in the click & read manual. In the case of the *error handling* items, the lack of effect may also be due to the possibility that error handling is more of a procedural task than a reasoning task. Error handling consists of detection, identifying the background of the error, and recovery. In fact, the only real reasoning task that may be supported by declarative information is identifying the error background. Therefore, the three components of error handling will be analyzed separately in subsequent experiments (see chapter 5).

Finally, declarative information also positively affected factual knowledge. Although subjects probably do not use the manual with the intention to learn or to know facts, their factual knowledge nevertheless increases when they use declarative information. This possibly helps them in the second-time performance of a task and also in the reasoning task.

In summary, procedural information seems to support the development of a task/action mapping model, and declarative information seems to support the development of a surrogate model. Young only discusses surrogate models and task/action models as discrete options, but it is highly plausible that users have a task/action model and a surrogate model integrated in one mental model. A task/action mapping model may be the starting point for all users which enables them to take actions. The development of an *additional* part of the mental model, similar to Young's notion of a surrogate model, is an added value.

Of course, this experiment does not show how the mental model is exactly built. It is for instance not certain whether the task/action part is developed first, and the surrogate part afterwards, or whether the procedural and the declarative parts of the mental model are developed more or less at the same time.

This experiment does however demonstrate, that the presence of declarative information in a manual can be an important instrument in the phase of mental model building: the absence of declarative information seems to create models which lack important elements. These missing elements cause worse performance on the delayed task, the reasoning test and the factual knowledge questionnaire. Apparently, users who do not receive declarative information are not self-supportive enough to build similar models to the users who do use declarative information, at least not in the same time-span.

Thus, the inclusion of declarative information in a software manual seems far from useless: it is used spontaneously by users who have a free choice; those users are not harmed by using declarative information in any way; the users profit from using declarative information when they work with the software again on later occasions, and they become better at reasoning about their tasks. It looks as if leaving out declarative information is not the crucial factor contributing to the success of the Minimal Manual (e.g. Carroll, 1990; Carroll et al., 1987-1988). On the contrary: according to the research results presented in this and in the preceeding chapter, it would be better to include declarative information in the manual.

Chapter 5
The arrangement of procedural and declarative information

Not only the pure presence of declarative information may be of influence in the selection, use and effects of information types. Text-internal variables, such as the structure, style or visual presentation of the information types, may have their own effects.

In the next experiment, the arrangement of procedural and declarative information in the manual is varied, as a first step toward including text-internal variables in the experiments. The effects of these different information arrangements on information selection, information use, task performance, reasoning and knowledge will be reported.

5.1   Introduction

5.1.1   The need for including text-internal variables

In the preceeding experiments, information use and the effects of declarative information were investigated in the context of text-external variables such as user situation and task complexity. The only text-internal factor included in the design was the procedural or declarative content in its prototypical form. This variable appeared to affect information selection, information use, (delayed) task performance, reasoning and knowledge.

It has already been shown that other text-internal factors, such as the structure of information, its syntactic form or the visual presentation of information affect task performance and mental plans in an instructional context (e.g. Hartley, 1980; Dixon, 1987; Hoeken, Mom & Maes, 1994). Text-internal factors should also be investigated in order to gain a full understanding of what characteristics of text and context affect information use, performance and knowledge of software users. Including these variables in the study also serves a direct practical interest, as the text-internal variables can be manipulated by technical writers. For practitioners it may be relevant to know which manipulations of information structure, style or visual presentation are necessary to make a manual more effective and more usable. In this study, the scope of investigation will be restricted to a structural variable: the arrangement of procedural and declarative information.

5.1.2   Effects of the arrangement of procedural and declarative information

Information arrangement is a very broad concept in itself. In general, it can be taken as the parts of which a text consists, defined by content or function, and the relation between those parts. The scope of this study is limited to the arrangement of the procedural and declarative information items.

The arrangement of procedural and declarative information can be manipulated in several ways. One variable is the order in which the information types occur in the text: does it make a difference whether procedural information or declarative information is presented first? A second variable is the arrangement of the information types on the pages: does it make a difference whether procedural and declarative information are presented separately or mixed? Both structural variables may affect the selection and use of information, and they may also affect task performance, reasoning and knowledge.

The order of procedural and declarative information
The order of procedural and declarative information may affect the results with respect to information selection and use. Information that is presented at the top of a page is likely to attract more attention and is thus likely to be selected more often than information at the bottom of a page. However, this hypothesis does not take into account the influence of other factors that may affect the user's information needs, such as the user's background and assignment and the problems he encounters in carrying out the task.

If information order were the only variable affecting information selection and use, then the information at the top of the page, or at the beginning of a chapter or module, would probably be selected most and used longest. The information at the bottom would only be used if the information at the top was not sufficient. This would be an alternative explanation of some results reported in chapter 3. Effects of information order on task performance, reasoning and knowledge may be related to this emphasis on information: the information type that is at the top of the page may be viewed as more important. Therefore it may be applied or remembered differently than it would be if it was positioned at the bottom of a page.

It is however more probable that the influence of information order interferes with other factors: which information do users *want* first on the basis of their prior knowledge, their tasks and their assignments? This need for information may overrule the effects of information order. If the research into the Minimal Manual (e.g. Carroll, 1990a) is taken as a starting point, users in a tutorial situation are primarily interested in procedural information. They do not use the manual to get to *know* things, but to carry out real, relevant tasks and they look for concrete support for those tasks. They search the manual to find the relevant procedural information and skip the information that they don't need. On this basis, one would expect that it does not really matter whether procedural information is presented at the top or at the bottom: it will be selected and used anyway. However, if information at the top of a page does get more attention, then it is better to present procedural information at the top, for this will facilitate the users' search actions.

Some arguments for the claim that declarative information should be presented first may be derived from Anderson's (1983) ACT* theory of skill learning. According to this theory, the first stage of learning a new skill is a declarative stage. The term *declarative* is used in a different sense in this context: it means that learners acquire all knowledge very consciously and step-by-step, based on oral or written instructions. They rely on available knowledge for what they have to do. The mental representation underlying this phase may consist of a representation of the initial system state and a representation of the goal to be achieved, but also a declarative representation of the strategy to solve the problem. This strategy cannot be proceduralized until the learner has actually performed the task. The more often the task is performed, the more it will become a routine task. Once it is a routine, the knowledge is called procedural: it does not have to be retrieved consciously from the declarative memory anymore.

The declarative stage of skill learning requires a manual to contain procedural as well as declarative information. Starting from the ACT* theory, Charney & Reder (1987) proposed three components of initial skill learning:

(1)   learning novel concepts and the functionality of new procedures
(2)   learning how to execute procedures
(3)   learning in which (real-world) situations a procedure can be applied; remembering what procedure to execute in a given situation

Charney & Reder have proposed several types of elaboration in a manual for facilitating these three components. The first and the third component relate to declarative information, the second component to procedural information.

Although these theories do not make predictions about the best order in which users should select and process different information types, a tentative hypothesis could be formulated on the basis of these theories, stating that skill learners should also look for declarative information, in addition to and possibly even *before* they start looking for procedural information.

Another question that remains is whether or not these different expectations for learners apply to users in other situations. Users with more experience, or users who are in a hurry and do not have the intention to learn, may profit from a different information order than learners. In chapter 3, a possible indication for this difference was found in replication 2, where subjects in the reference situation were the only subjects to select procedural and declarative information equally as often as a first click.

The next experiment should bring clarity into the question of to what extent does the order of presenting procedural and declarative information affect the selection and use of information types, and to what extent does it affect task performance, reasoning and knowledge for users with different backgrounds and assignments.

Separating or mixing procedural and declarative information
Procedural and declarative information can be arranged in several ways. One of the design choices is the one to either separate or mix the information types. In a separated approach, all the procedural information for each user task is put in one text block and all the declarative information in another, each with separate headings. In a mixed approach, smaller sections of procedural and declarative information are combined and mixed into one large information block. Horn (1985) is an advocate of the separate approach. In his Information Mapping® approach, he defines information maps and information blocks: sections of different information types, which are all presented in different ways. The goal is to support the reader, to enable easy searching and interpretation. Smith & Goodman (1984) on the other hand presented their experimental instructions in a mixed way. Their assumption was that explanatory information would enhance the reading and interpretation of the connected procedures.

When information types are presented separately, it is easy for the user to select and skip information, and to determine the moment of switching to another information block, especially if procedural and declarative information support activities that are perceived as distinct activities by the user (*doing* is different from *knowing* and therefore, *reading to do* is different from *reading to learn* or *reading to know*. (Sticht, 1977; 1985)). It leaves the users the possibility of using the manual for a separate, declarative goal, provided that the different blocks are easily recognizable.

A manual in which the information types are mixed may give the user more guidance. A procedure may for instance be interrupted by a declarative information item, at the moment when it is relevant for the user. This may be handy, but on the other hand, it is not easy to search for a declarative item when the user is not interested in the *procedure* to which the item belongs, nor is it easy to ignore and skip a declarative item that pops up in the middle of a procedure.

However, if reading to learn and reading to do are not completely distinct tasks (Redish, 1988) and if declarative information is used as an integral part of a procedural task, to directly support the procedure, the separated approach may be less helpful. Users have to switch from one text block to another, and this switching can lead to distraction or to problems in finding back the place where the procedure was left off. In this respect, presenting the information types in a mixed way has the advantage of having declarative information immediately available at a relevant moment in a procedure. Switching from one text block to another is not necessary then.

The arrangement of procedural and declarative information may thus affect the selection and use of the information. A separated arrangement may for instance lead to a less frequent selection and shorter reading time of the declarative blocks. If users start with doing something and they are able to carry out the procedure, they may not look for further information because there is no need to do so, because they do not encounter the information automatically and because the declarative information block is large in comparison with the declarative chunks in a mixed approach, and thus not accessed readily.

Mixing the information on the other hand may lead to more frequent selections of declarative information, because the users encounter the declarative items in the middle of a procedure, when they are relevant and because the declarative items are small and thus accessible. The using time for declarative information may also be longer because more blocks are selected, although on the other hand it is equally possible that users immediately return to the procedure if the declarative item is not relevant enough. In the latter case, the declarative items will still be selected often, but the using time will be shorter than in the separated approach.

Separating versus mixing the information types may also affect task performance and reasoning, but it is not obvious whether this influence is positive or negative. In the separated text arrangement, subjects have to either actively select information, or they have to put a lot of effort into solving problems without selecting (extra) information. These extra activities may affect their achievements either positively, because they have put more time and effort into it, or negatively, either because the extra task of searching for information has distracted them from the software task or because they did not look for additional information. Subjects with the mixed manual do not need to search for declarative information once they are engaged in a procedure. This may help them to process information they would not otherwise have used, but they may on the other hand also feel interrupted by the declarative information, which may have negative results on the performance of the procedure.

5.1.3   Hypertext

Separating or mixing procedural and declarative information, or varying the order are by far not the only possible design choices with respect to information arrangement. Especially when the presentation of the manual is not restricted to paper, more drastic alternatives to the paper structure become possible.

Online manuals are an attractive alternative to the large amount of paper user documentation which often accompanies a software system. They can either be installed together with the system, or used from CD-Rom or Internet. These online manuals often have the structure of a hypertext: in this context, a hypertext is a document, consisting of subdocuments that are linked by keywords or images. These keywords or images are called links. When users of a hypertext click on a link, they are taken to the subdocument that the link refers to. All subdocuments are thus connected in a structure that is usually non-linear, contrary to most paper documents. In a hypertext manual, a subdocument about calculating an average may be one click away from a text about saving files, whereas this connection may be more difficult to establish in a paper manual.

In order to compare the variations in information arrangement to a totally different information structure, a hypertext was included in the experiment as well. The selection and use of procedural and declarative information and the effects of these information types in the Hypertext on performance, reasoning and knowledge were compared to the same variables in the three other manuals (the PD-manual, the DP-manual and the MX-manual).

The click & read method lends itself very well to present hypertext, and the QubeCalc manual that was used before could be converted to hypertext fairly easily without having to change the content or form of the text: it was essential to use the same contents, headings and formulations as in the other manuals to be able to make a good comparison with respect to information use and effects.

Other research questions concerning the Hypertext-manual
Besides the research questions concerning information use and performance, the data were also used to answer a specific, explorative question about the use of hypertext: how do users navigate through the hypertext if they have a choice of four navigation instruments? In the experimental hypertext, which will be described in detail in 5.2.2, subjects could use links inside the text, links that were listed separately underneath the text, an index (combination of hierarchical overview and alphabetically ordered items), and a so-called backtrack, that took the subjects back along the path of information blocks that they had formerly selected.

Wright & Lickorish (1990) describe an experiment in which they compared an index-option to navigation options on a text page in two hypertexts: a book-like document, containing several linear informative texts on houseplants, and a document with a matrix structure containing tabular information about the prices of various products in five fictitious shops. Subjects, who worked with only one of the two navigation systems, had to answer different kinds of questions about the information in the hypertexts and they were asked if their preference was for either page navigation or index navigation. Wright & Lickorish found that readers preferred an index for the book-like hypertext, but for the other hypertext, the links on the page were preferred and gave better results on the questions. They conclude that index navigation may facilitate tasks for which users need an overview of the structure in the document: when users are uncertain where to find certain information, this overview facilitates navigation. On the other hand, if users have to carry out a task that makes high demands on their working memory, an index away from the text display further increases this load, whereas page navigation facilitates movements to corresponding points in the text.

On the basis of the findings by Wright & Lickorish, the following hypotheses can be formulated with respect to navigation in the QubeCalc hypertext-manual:

- Users prefer an index when they are uncertain about where to find information and when they want an overview of the whole document. In the experimental tasks, there is an index at the start of every new subtask. Thus, subjects are expected to start new subtasks with the index navigation option.
- In complex subtasks (which impose a high working memory load), subjects are expected to use page navigation (links in or underneath the text) instead of the index. Accordingly, they will not use the backtrack-button here either, as this may also make memory demands. In simple subtasks, this preference for page navigation will not occur.

The relation between *linking style* and *information type* will be studied. Does a possible preference for linking style depend on the information type of the selected information? Do subjects for instance select procedural information from the index most of the time, and declarative information via external links?

It should however be kept in mind that the experiment has a more or less explorative nature when it comes to testing these hypotheses. The criteria imposed by the other, more important research questions do not always make for an optimal hypertext, as will be explained in 5.2.2.

5.2   Experiment 3

5.2.1   Design

The influence of arrangement variables on information selection and information use was investigated using a mixed design. The three independent variables were information type, user situation and manual version. Task complexity was no longer included as a separate variable in the design.

Information type was a within-subjects variable. Each manual contained both procedural and declarative information. Subjects were free to select whichever information type they wanted. User situation was a between-subjects variable. Subjects were assigned to a user situation which correspondenced to their prior knowledge and experience: the tutorial situation, the intermediate situation or the reference situation. Manual version was a between- subjects variable too. Four different manual versions were investigated (see 5.2.2): the PD-manual (information types separated: procedural information at the top and declarative at the bottom), the DP-manual (information types separated: declarative information at the top and procedural at the bottom), the Mix-manual (information types mixed; order varies) and a Hypertext-variant. These four versions were randomly given to the three user situations.

The effects of information arrangement on task performance and reasoning were investigated by means of a 3 x 4 factorial design with user situation and manual version as between-subjects factors.

The dependent variables for information selection, information use and different performance aspects did not differ from the measures already used in the former experiments. The number of clicks, the number of first clicks and the using time represented information selection and use. Performance time, the number of attempts to complete a subtask, the number of incorrectly performed subtasks and the number of inefficiently performed subtasks represented initial task performance. Performance time, the number of attempts and the frequency of inefficiently performed tasks were the dependent measures for delayed task performance. The scores on different items of the reasoning test were the dependent measures for reasoning and finally, the scores on the 12-item questionnaire represented factual knowledge (see sections 2.2 and 4.1.2 for a more elaborate discussion of the dependent variables).

5.2.2   Materials

Software and tasks
Again, subjects had to work with the spreadsheet QubeCalc. Contrary to the former experiments, subjects only had to perform one task now. The distinction between a simple and a complex task was no longer made. Subjects worked with a ready-made data file and an assignment which was presented to them on paper.

The new task consisted of 8 subtasks; all subtasks were derived from either the original simple or the original complex tasks. The context was the same as in the former complex task: subjects had to edit the administration file of a sports club (see appendix 7C). In this task, subjects had to:
- open the data file
- change the number of decimal places of a set of numbers
- insert a column
- change the perspective
- calculate average expenses on different pages
- change the perspective back to the original
- copy a block of information to a different page in the spreadsheet
- save the file

Manuals
There were four different versions of the manual. Three of them had the appearance of a printed book, just like the manuals in the former two experiments. The fourth manual had a hypertext structure and presentation.

All four manuals contained exactly the same information in an identical syntactic form. The criteria for content and form of procedural and declarative information were the same as those in the former two experiments (see 2.1). Headings were also the same in all versions. The four manuals are described below. Examples can be found in appendix 1.

The PD (Procedural-Declarative)-manual was used in both previous experiments. Each page in the manual covers one basic task, for which procedural and declarative information is presented in two separate blocks. Procedural information is always at the top of the page, declarative information at the bottom.

The procedural text block contains procedural information necessary to carry out the user task indicated in the heading at the top of the page. This is sometimes a short and simple procedure and sometimes a complex procedure with many embedded conditions and actions. The declarative text block contains different subtypes of declarative information that are all related to the relevant user task. The headings above the information blocks are representative for their contents. All subtopics are represented in the heading above the declarative information block.

The click & read presentation of the manual allows the manual user to read one block at a time. The other blocks are visible but blurred. The headings of both blocks are always sharp and well readable.

The DP(Declarative-Procedural)-manual is almost identical to the PD-manual, with the only difference being the order of procedural and declarative information blocks on a page. Procedural and declarative information are still presented in separate blocks, but the order is reversed: declarative information is always presented at the top of the page and procedural at the bottom. The headings above the information blocks and the click & read presentation method are also identical to the PD-manual.

In *the Mix-manual*, procedural information blocks are interrupted by sections of the former declarative information block; subtopics are now presented as smaller declarative blocks which can be clicked separately. The relevant part of the original heading from the PD-manual is placed above these new declarative blocks. The formulation of these headings is identical to the formulation in the other manuals, as demonstrated in appendix 1C.

The procedural information is now also divided into parts, but these parts do *not* have their own headings. The number of parts depends on the number of declarative items that are inserted. The complete procedure is sharpened when a subject clicks on one of its parts. Thus, the number of clickable declarative blocks increases, whereas the number of clickable procedural blocks stays the same. This means that the numbers of clicks should be interpreted very carefully for the Mix-manual: more declarative blocks will probably also lead to more declarative clicks in comparison to the PD- and DP-manuals. The advantage of this approach however is that it will yield information about the specific declarative items that users select and use. In the previous experiments, it was not possible to see which of the subtypes of declarative information in one block were selected and used most.

The click & read method was adapted in such a way that the manual user could sharpen either the complete procedural block by clicking on one of the procedural parts, or a single declarative block by clicking on that particular part. Contrary to the original click & read, all text blocks on a page, procedural and declarative, remained visible *and* clickable when a text block was clicked and sharpened: the *Return to full page* step was eliminated. For reasons of comparison, this adapted click & read method was not only implemented in the

Mix-manual, but also in the PD- and the DP-manuals. The adaptation of the click & read method is discussed in a more elaborate way in section 2.3.3.3.

The procedural and declarative blocks in the Mix-manual were arranged according to the following heuristics:

-   Declarative information that was relevant at a specific point in the procedure was placed immediately before or after the corresponding point.

Example
Explanations of terminology, the location of keys or screen items and warnings interrupted the procedural block immediately after the related terms in the procedural block, or immediately before a risky action.

-   If the declarative information was related to the whole procedure and it could be relevant as introductory information, then it was presented *before* the procedure.

Example
Information about the functionality of an option (*What's the use of the format-option?*), and general definitions that were related to the complete task (*What is the WorkQube?*) were placed before the procedural block.

-   If the declarative information was related to the whole procedure, and it was not information of an introductory type, then it was placed after the last step of the procedure.

Example
Related software functions were placed after a procedure.

Contrary to the other three manuals, *the Hypertext-manual* does not have a page layout. It is a collection of all the procedural and declarative text blocks, which are presented on screen one at a time as a single block when they are selected. The procedural blocks are the same as those in the three other manuals. The declarative blocks are the smaller declarative blocks that are also part of the Mix-manual.

From one information block, the users can "jump" directly to other information blocks in the manual. They can do so in four ways: by clicking on links in the text (Internal links), by clicking on links underneath the text (External links), by clicking on a *Back*-button, which takes them to the information block they selected before, and by clicking on an *Index* button, which takes them to an alphabetically organized index from which they can select a procedural or a declarative block directly.

In the experimental Hypertext-manual, there are only verbal links. There are two Internal links *in the text* of each information block: one link to procedural information and one link to declarative information. The Internal links are recognizable for the user because the words that constitute the link are underlined. The underlined words are as far as possible representative for the procedural or declarative block they refer to. However, as the actual text cannot be changed for reasons of comparison with the other manuals, the links are sometimes less representative than they could be.

This problem does not occur for the External links *underneath the text*. These are formulated in exactly the same way as the headings in the Mix-manual and thus reflect exactly what they refer to. There is always an even number of External links: one half refers to procedural blocks and the other half to declarative blocks. The two Internal links are always represented as External links, too. The exact number of links underneath the text varies from two to eight. They are made recognizable by both underlining and italicizing them.

The Index button takes the user to an index which is subdivided into the same categories as the Content page of the other three manuals: cell operations, block operations, Workqube operations, etc. Within these categories, the titles, which again are the same as the headings and the titles in the Content page of the other manuals, are arranged alphabetically. If subjects click on an Index title, they are taken directly to the selected information block.

The Back button takes subjects back to the information block they clicked prior to the block that is visible on screen. Subjects can go back in this way to the very first block they selected. The route back is exactly the same route as the one the user originally clicked. In advanced hypertext systems, a block that is selected more than once can for instance be skipped on second occurrence in the backward route (see Nielsen, 1995). This is not the case in this Hypertext.

The blurring procedure in the click & read method is not applied in the Hypertext-manual, as the user sees only one information block at a time. The headings of the other information blocks are the links the user can click on and jump to.

Interim task

The interim task was the same 20-30 minute distractor task as was used in experiment 2 (see appendix 2). The task consisted of two parts: subjects had to solve a problem with a four function calculator and they had to predict the outcome of series of keypresses in a well-reasoned way without being able to use the calculator.

Test and questionnaire

The test was identical to the test that was included in the second experiment (see appendix 7D for the assignment and section 2.2.2 for background information), except for a few small changes. An extra item for *efficiency* was added, and error handling was now spread over three categories: error detection, identifying error background and error recovery. In the second experiment it was felt that the category of *error handling* was not specific enough. Moreover, it was suspected that identifying error backgrounds required other cognitive actions than error detection and recovery. Detection and recovery may be related to procedural knowledge, whereas identifying error backgrounds may be supported by declarative information.

The questionnaire was a paper form with twelve questions about QubeCalc facts. It was the same questionnaire as was used in experiment 2, with minor changes.

5.2.3   Procedure

The procedure of experiment 3 was very similar to the procedure of experiment 2 (section 4.2.3). After an introduction, the subjects were assigned to a user situation that matched their profile. They were presented with the instructions for the experiment and they could practise working with the click & read method. Subjects were randomly assigned to a manual version.

In the first part of the experiment, subjects carried out one QubeCalc task, consisting of 8 subtasks. They could select information in the manual on the screen next to them. The manual was the only help facility available.

When subjects indicated that they had finished the assignment, the second part started: the interim task. They took a seat at a table on the other side of the room and solved the calculator puzzle there.

The delayed task, then the reasoning test and finally the questionnaire were completed during the third part of the experiment. The manual was closed during that time. First, the subjects carried out one task all by themselves, without the help of the experimenter. This task was similar to one of the more complex tasks they had already performed in phase one, but the context and data were different. In the reasoning test, the subjects had to assist and correct the experimenter, who carried out a QubeCalc task similar to the task that the subjects had carried out in the first part. Different data were used now, however. The subjects also answered questions about the task: they were for instance asked for explanations, predictions and error diagnoses. The experimenter followed a strict scenario with respect to the performance of the task, the questions asked and the subjects' independent tasks. The order of test elements was identical for all subjects. As far as subjects' answers and reactions could be predicted, the experimenter reacted in a standard way.

Finally, the subjects completed the factual knowledge questionnaire. A number of subjects did not however complete the questionnaire, because the other parts of the experiment had taken too much time and the experimental schedule did not allow for too much time overrun. The experiment took almost two hours. Subjects were paid DFL. 20.

5.2.4   Subjects

Ninety-five subjects participated in this experiment. The data of 8 subjects were removed from the analyses because one or more subtasks had not been carried out. Of the resulting 87 subjects, 19 subjects were women and 68 were men. Their average age was 22.4 years. All subjects were students from the University of Twente and other schools for higher education in the region.

5.3   Results

The results are presented in three categories: information selection, information use and information effects on task performance, reasoning and factual knowledge. The data concerning information selection and information use were analyzed by means of a three-way ANOVA, with the factors information type, user situation and manual version. The factor information type contained repeated measurements.

Two-way analyses of variance with manual version and situation as factors were used to analyze initial and delayed task performance and factual knowledge. Frequency measurements in delayed task performance were analyzed by means of chi-square tests. The reasoning test was analyzed by means of multivariate analysis of variance. Finally, Tukey's HSD tests at the 5% level were used for posthoc comparisons.

5.3.1   Effects of arrangement on information selection

The results for information selection (mean number of procedural and declarative clicks) are presented in table 5.1. The means of the Mix and the Hypertext manuals should be interpreted with reserve: the number of declarative blocks was larger than the number of procedural text blocks in these manuals (and thus also larger than in the PD- and DP-manuals). The number of declarative subitems corresponding to one procedural item varied from 2 to 5. The numbers of procedural and declarative blocks in the Mix and the Hypertext were the same, however.

Table 5.1

Information selection: mean numbers of procedural and declarative clicks in three user situations and four manual versions and the percentages of the total number of clicks

	Procedural	(%)	Declarative	(%)	Total
Tutorial (n=27)					
Proc-Decl	26.4	*60.5*	18.4	*39.5*	44.8
Decl-Proc	20.1	*46.6*	21.6	*53.4*	41.7
Mix	28.5	*45.8*	33.5	*54.2*	62.0
Hypertext	24.9	*49.2*	25.9	*50.8*	50.7
Intermediate (n=28)					
Proc-Decl	19.5	*59.9*	13.3	*40.1*	32.8
Decl-Proc	15.0	*50.8*	14.9	*49.2*	29.9
Mix	18.6	*39.2*	26.6	*60.8*	45.3
Hypertext	11.0	*37.0*	20.2	*63.0*	31.2
Reference (n=32)					
Proc-Decl	14.6	*59.0*	10.4	*41.0*	25.0
Decl-Proc	12.9	*50.1*	12.4	*49.9*	25.3
Mix	7.9	*43.2*	11.0	*56.8*	18.9
Hypertext	12.4	*38.4*	20.4	*61.6*	32.9
All situations (n=87)					
Proc-Decl	20.0	*59.8*	13.9	*40.2*	33.9
Decl-Proc	16.0	*49.2*	16.2	*50.8*	32.2
Mix	17.4	*42.4*	22.8	*57.6*	40.2
Hypertext	16.0	*41.4*	22.1	*58.6*	38.1

There was no main effect of manual version on the number of clicks ($F(3,75)$ = 1.78, $p = .16$): in all manuals, subjects selected information equally often. This is remarkable, as the Mix-manual and the Hypertext contain much more blocks to click on.

A main effect of information type indicated that there are more declarative than procedural clicks ($F(1,75) = 4.53$, $p < .05$). This may be partly due to the fact that the Hypertext manual and the Mix-manual have more declarative than procedural blocks, contrary to the other two manuals, which have equal numbers of procedural and declarative blocks. Table 5.1 shows clearly that subjects select more declarative than procedural information in both the Mix and the Hypertext manual. The information order in the DP-manual seems to have the effect that almost equal numbers of declarative and procedural blocks are selected. Only in the PD-manual, procedural information is selected more often.

An interaction effect of manual version and information type confirms this ($F(3,75) = 18.19$, $p < .001$). Separate univariate analyses indeed show that in both the Mix manual and the Hypertext, declarative information is selected significantly more often than procedural information (*Mix*: $F(1,21) = 18.43$, $p = .001$; *Hypertext*: $F(1,21) = 9.30$, $p < .01$). The larger number of declarative blocks in these manuals may make this effect more or less trivial, although one would also expect a main effect of manual version on the number of clicks if this larger number is the reason for the effect. The reason could thus also be attributed to the characteristics of the Mix- and the Hypertext-manuals. In the DP-manual, procedural and declarative information are selected equally often ($F(1,21) <1$) and in the PD-manual, procedural information is selected more often than declarative information ($F(1,20) = 52.08$, $p < .001$).

There was a main effect of user situation on the number of clicks ($F(2,75) = 18.99$, $p < .001$). Tukey's HSD test indicates that subjects in the tutorial situation select more information blocks than subjects in the reference and the intermediate situation. There were no interactions of user situation with any of the other variables. No threeway-interaction was found either.

As the declarative blocks from the PD-manual and the DP-manual were divided into several sub-items in the Mix-manual and the Hypertext-manual, it was now possible to map the exact declarative items that subjects look for. In order to get an indication of the most frequently selected items, all items that were selected on average 3 times or more were listed. Separate overviews were made for the three user situations and the manuals.

In general, the declarative items concerning the most difficult subtasks were used most frequently: items about calculating and items about the perspectives in QubeCalc. It is remarkable that the top ten (the ten information blocks selected most frequently) in the three situations were almost the same. Tutorial users select the widest range of different declarative blocks, reference users select the smallest range of different blocks. The most important result in the context of this study was however that all subtypes of declarative information were selected: no preference for specific subtypes could be distilled from the overviews.

In table 5.2, the second measure of information selection is presented: the number of first clicks, or, in other words, the number of occasions when the first click in a subtask was procedural or declarative. Subjects did not always select information in *all* subtasks: the total number of first clicks is equal to the total number of subtasks that the subjects selected any information in. Thus, the maximum total number of first clicks is 8. The number of first clicks on procedural and declarative information indicates what information subjects tend to begin with when they start selecting information.

Table 5.2
Information selection: the mean number of procedural or declarative first clicks in a subtask in three user situations and four manual versions

	Procedural	Declarative	Sign.	Total
Tutorial (n=27)				
Proc-Decl	5.9	0.9	**	6.8
Decl-Proc	1.4	4.6	*	6.0
Mix	3.8	2.7	ns	6.5
Hypertext	3.1	3.1	ns	6.2
Intermediate (n=28)				
Proc-Decl	4.3	1.7	*	6.0
Decl-Proc	1.6	3.4	*	5.0
Mix	1.6	3.9	**	5.5
Hypertext	2.3	2.7	ns	5.0
Reference (n=32)				
Proc-Decl	3.4	1.6	tr	5.0
Decl-Proc	2.4	2.9	ns	5.3
Mix	1.9	2.5	ns	4.5
Hypertext	1.3	3.4	*	4.7
All situations (n=87)				
Proc-Decl	4.5	1.4	***	5.9
Decl-Proc	1.8	3.6	**	5.4
Mix	2.3	3.1	ns	5.4
Hypertext	2.2	3.1	ns	5.3

Note
*: $p < .05$ / **: $p < .01$ / ***: $p < .001$ / ns: not significant / tr: trend ($p < .10$)

There was no main effect of information type on the number of first clicks ($F(1,75) < 1$). Apparently, the first click in a subtask was equally as often procedural as declarative. No main effect of manual version on the number of first clicks was found either ($F(3,75) = 1.05$, $p = .38$), indicating that subjects with different manuals select information in an equal number of subtasks. However, the interaction between information type and manual version is again significant ($F(3,75) = 18.05$, $p < .001$), just like it was for the number of clicks. Separate analyses (one-way ANOVAs) reveal that whether or not information type has an effect on the number of first clicks depends on the manual version. Information type did not have an effect in the Mix or the Hypertext manual: subjects who used these manuals selected equal amounts of procedural and declarative information as a first click in a subtask (*Mix:* $F(1,21) = 2.03$, $p = .17$; *Hypertext:* $F(1,21) = 2.46$, $p = .13$). In contrast, the effect of information type was significant in both the PD and the DP-manual (*PD:* $F(1,20) = 33.03$, $p < .001$; *DP:* $F(1,21) = 11.91$, $p < .01$). The effect of information type here, however, was the reverse: subjects with the PD-manual selected more procedural than declarative information as a first click, but subjects with the DP-manual selected more declarative than procedural information as a first click. It seems that the first click directly depends on the first information block on a page: in the PD-manual, procedural information was consistently at the top, in the DP-manual declarative information was always at the top, and in the other two manuals, the first block on the page was sometimes procedural and sometimes declarative.

The two-way interaction of information type and manual is qualified by a significant three-way interaction of user situation, manual version and information type ($F(6,75) = 3.13$, $p < .01$), indicating that the interaction differs across the user situations. The equal preference for procedural and declarative information in the overall results for the Mix and the Hypertext manuals does not occur in all the user situations. Subjects in the intermediate situation select more declarative first clicks in the Mix-manual, and subjects in the reference situation prefer declarative information for their first clicks in the Hypertext manual.

Also, subjects in the reference situation deviate from the overall situation in the PD and the DP manuals. In the PD manual, they seem to prefer procedural information to declarative information as first clicks, but contrary to the other two situations, the effect fails to reach significance ($F(1,7) = 5.12$, $p = .06$). In the DP manual the deviation is stronger: subjects in the reference situation appear to have no preference at all for their first click in a subtask, whereas the other two situations select significantly more declarative first clicks.

There was also a main effect of user situation on the (total) number of first clicks ($F(2,75) = 13.69$, $p < .001$). Tukey's HSD test shows that subjects in the tutorial situation perform more first clicks than subjects in the intermediate and reference situations, or, in other words, they use the manual in a greater variety of subtasks than subjects in the other two situations.

5.3.2   Effects of arrangement on information use

The effects of different information arrangements on the using time are presented in table 5.3.

Table 5.3

Mean using time (in seconds) of procedural and declarative information in three user situations and four manual versions, and the percentages of procedural and declarative time relative to the total information using time

	Procedural	(%)	Declarative	(%)	Total
Tutorial (n=27)					
Proc-Decl	1798	70.7	732	29.3	2530
Decl-Proc	1367	66.4	637	33.6	2004
Mix	1646	70.3	655	29.7	2300
Hypertext	1314	70.0	526	30.0	1840
Intermediate (n=28)					
Proc-Decl	1185	68.8	526	31.2	1710
Decl-Proc	866	58.6	607	41.4	1473
Mix	1112	64.3	580	35.7	1692
Hypertext	699	63.3	401	36.7	1100
Reference (n=32)					
Proc-Decl	680	57.8	493	42.3	1173
Decl-Proc	847	64.6	397	35.4	1244
Mix	413	48.4	511	51.6	924
Hypertext	801	54.4	607	45.6	1408
All situations (n=87)					
Proc-Decl	1197	65.2	582	34.8	1779
Decl-Proc	1019	63.0	550	37.0	1569
Mix	1004	60.1	575	39.9	1579
Hypertext	936	61.8	525	38.2	1461

A main effect of information type on the using time ($F(1,75) = 87.29, p < .001$) shows that overall, procedural information is used longer than declarative information.

There is no main effect of manual version on the total using time ($F(3,75) = 1.64, p = .19$): subjects with different manuals spent equal amounts of time using information.

Contrary to the results for information selection, there was no interaction between information type and manual version ($F(3,75) < 1$). Thus, the same main effect of information type occurs in all four manuals: procedural information is used longer than declarative information, in spite of the fact that more declarative than procedural information was selected in the DP manual and equal amounts of procedural and declarative were selected in the Mix and the Hypertext manuals.

There is a main effect of user situation on the using time ($F(2,75) = 25.69, p < .001$). Tukey's HSD posthoc test shows that the subjects in the tutorial group use the information in the manual longer than subjects in both other user situations.

Also, user situation interacts with information type ($F(2,75) = 14.91, p < .001$). This interaction effect indicates that the difference for the user situations depends on the information type. Similar to the results of previous experiments, separate analyses show that the using time of procedural information differs for the user situations ($F(2,84) = 24.53, p < .001$) whereas the using time of declarative information did not differ ($F(2,84) = 2.09, p = .13$). Tukey's HSD test shows that subjects in the tutorial situation spent more time using procedural information than subjects in the other two user situations.

The means in table 5.3 may give rise to the expectation that user situation interacts with manual version: the using time seems to differ depending on the manual version . There is only a trend towards significance for this interaction, however ($F(6,75) = 2.07, p = .07$). No further interactions were found.

5.3.3   Effects of arrangement on task performance, reasoning and knowledge

The results with respect to information effects are again presented in four categories: initial task performance, delayed task performance, reasoning and factual knowledge.

Initial task performance
The means for the initial task performance measurements are presented in table 5.4.

Table 5.4
Effects of different manual versions on initial task performance in three user situations

	Performance time (secs)	# Incorrect subtasks	# Inefficient subtasks	# Attempts
Tutorial (n=27)				
Proc-Decl	3355	1.3	3.3	39.6
Decl-Proc	3113	1.0	3.1	51.3
Mix	3020	1.2	3.2	37.5
Hypertext	2637	0.6	2.4	31.0
Intermediate (n=28)				
Proc-Decl	2474	0.2	2.8	36.5
Decl-Proc	2405	1.1	2.8	45.3
Mix	2653	0.4	2.9	49.5
Hypertext	1586	0.0	2.5	32.2
Reference (n=32)				
Proc-Decl	1885	0.3	2.3	38.5
Decl-Proc	2176	0.1	2.0	37.3
Mix	1601	0.3	2.0	34.5
Hypertext	2424	0.2	2.1	49.1
All situations (n=87)				
Proc-Decl	2544	0.6	2.8	38.3
Decl-Proc	2557	0.8	2.6	44.6
Mix	2371	0.6	2.6	40.8
Hypertext	2263	0.3	2.3	38.7

Manual version does not affect any of the four measures of initial task performance (*performance time*: $F(3,75) = 1.41$, $p = .25$; *number of incorrect subtasks*: $F(3,75) = 1.75$, $p = .16$; *number of inefficient subtasks*: $F(3,75) < 1$; *number of attempts*: $F(3,75) < 1$).

There are main effects of user situation on the performance time ($F(2,75) = 18.59$, $p < .001$), on the number of incorrectly performed subtasks ($F(2,75) = 9.20$, $p < .001$) and on the number of inefficiently performed subtasks ($F(2,75) = 7.28$, $p < .01$). Tukey's HSD tests show that subjects in the tutorial situation need more time and carry out more subtasks incorrectly than subjects in the other two user situations. Subjects in both the tutorial and intermediate situation perform more tasks inefficiently than subjects in the reference situation. The number of attempts is not affected by the user situation ($F(2,75) < 1$).

For the performance time, an interaction effect of manual version and user situation indicates that the difference in performance time for the manuals depends on the user situation ($F(6,75) = 3.30$, $p < .01$). Separate analyses show that there is no difference in performance time for the four manuals in the tutorial situation ($F(3,23) = 1.77$, $p = .18$). In the reference situation, there is a trend towards a significant difference for the manual versions ($F(3,28) = 2.63, p = .07$). The means in table 5.4 indicate that the subjects in the reference situation perform fastest with the Mix-manual. The performance time also show a trend towards significancy for the manual versions in the intermediate situation ($F(3,24) = 2.87, p = .06$). Tukey's HSD posthoc tests reveal that the difference between the Mix-manual and the Hypertext is significant at the 5% level in the intermediate situation. Thus, subjects in the intermediate situation perform faster with the Hypertext than with the Mix-manual. The PD- and the DP-manuals did not differ significantly from the other manual versions.

Delayed task performance
The results for the task that subjects carried out in phase three of the experiment are spread over three measures: the performance time in seconds, the number of attempts and the frequency of subjects performing the task inefficiently. The means are presented in table 5.5.

Table 5.5
Effects of different manual versions on delayed task performance in three user situations: mean performance time, mean number of attempts needed to complete the task and frequencies of (in)efficient task performance

	Performance time (sec)	# Attempts	Efficiency +	-
Tutorial (n=27)				
Proc-Decl	246	4.9	0	7
Decl-Proc	164	2.9	1	6
Mix	194	2.5	2	4
Hypertext	187	3.4	4	3
Intermediate (n=28)				
Proc-Decl	156	3.0	3	3
Decl-Proc	202	3.9	3	5
Mix	110	2.1	5	3
Hypertext	133	2.8	3	3
Reference (n=32)				
Proc-Decl	170	4.9	5	3
Decl-Proc	140	3.1	3	4
Mix	142	2.4	5	3
Hypertext	201	4.0	3	6
All situations (n=87)				
Proc-Decl	192	4.3	8	13
Decl-Proc	170	3.3	7	15
Mix	144	2.3	12	10
Hypertext	178	3.5	10	12

Manual version did not affect the performance time, nor the number of attempts needed to complete the task ($F(3,75) < 1$; $F(3,75) = 1.76$, $p = .16$). Neither was there a contingency between manual version and efficiency of task performance ($\chi^2 = 2.58$, $df = 3$, $p = .46$).

No main effect of user situation was found either on the performance time ($F(2,75) = 1.51$, $p = .23$), the number of attempts ($F(2,75) < 1$), or efficiency of task performance ($\chi^2 = 4.42$, $df = 2$, $p = .11$). Finally, no interactions between user situation and manual version were found.

Nine out of 87 subjects did not manage to get an adequate result in this task: seven subjects from the tutorial and two from the intermediate situation. Their time and attempts were initially included in the calculations. To check if this has a major influence on the results, test statistics were repeated for a dataset from which these nine subjects had been eliminated. The results did not change. Manual version still had no effects on performance time ($F(3,66) < 1$), the number of attempts ($F(3,66) < 1$) or efficiency ($\chi^2 = 3.56$, $df = 3$, $p = .31$). The same still applies to user situation (*time* ($F(2,66) < 1$) ; *attempts* ($F(2,66) = 1.25$, $p = .29$); *efficiency* ($\chi^2 = 1.75$ $df = 2$, $p = .41$). No interactions were found here either.

Reasoning
The results of the reasoning test are presented in table 5.6.

Table 5.6

Effects of different manual versions on reasoning in three user situations: mean number of correct items

	Efficiency	Error detection	Error background	Error recovery	Explaining	Applied insight
	(6 items)	(3 items)	(3 items)	(3 items)	(5 items)	(4 items)
Tutorial (n=27)						
Proc-Decl	0.7	1.7	1.4	2.4	2.7	1.7
Decl-Proc	1.3	2.0	1.7	2.2	3.4	2.0
Mix	1.2	2.3	2.3	2.7	2.1	1.5
Hypertext	1.3	2.4	2.4	2.9	3.7	2.3
Intermediate (n=28)						
Proc-Decl	1.5	2.0	2.2	2.8	3.3	1.8
Decl-Proc	2.1	2.3	2.7	3.0	2.8	1.9
Mix	1.6	2.1	2.4	2.9	2.9	2.0
Hypertext	2.5	2.2	2.5	3.0	3.8	2.5
Reference (n=32)						
Proc-Decl	2.8	2.6	2.8	3.0	4.6	2.5
Decl-Proc	3.1	2.1	2.4	2.7	4.0	3.0
Mix	3.9	2.4	2.8	3.0	3.6	1.9
Hypertext	3.7	2.2	2.8	3.0	3.6	2.2
All situations (n=87)						
Proc-Decl	1.7	2.1	2.1	2.8	3.6	2.1
Decl-Proc	2.2	2.2	2.3	2.7	3.4	2.3
Mix	2.3	2.3	2.5	2.9	3.0	1.8
Hypertext	2.6	2.3	2.6	3.0	3.7	2.3

Manual version had no effects on the performance of the reasoning test (Wilks' $\lambda = .72$, $F(18,192) = 1.34$, $p = .17$). Different ways of structuring information apparently do not cause differences with respect to the subjects' performance on the reasoning task.

A main effect of user situation on the reasoning test shows that the user situations do differ (Wilks' $\lambda = .48$, $F(12,136) = 5.06$, $p < .001$). Separate univariate analyses reveal that there were significant differences between the user situations for all the variables on the test except for error detection (*efficiency*: $F(2,73) = 25.14$, $p < .001$; *identifying error background*: $(F(2,73) = 9.58$, $p < .001$; *error recovery*: $(F(2,73) = 6.53$, $p < .01$; *applied insight*: $(F(2,73) = 4.19$, $p < .05$; *explaining*: $(F(2,73) = 6.64$, $p = .01$). Tukey's HSD showed for all variables that subjects in the reference situation performed significantly better than subjects in the tutorial situation. The subjects' scores in the intermediate situation were always somewhere in between. For identifying error background and recovery, they differed from the tutorial situation and for explaining, they differed from the reference situation. On the efficiency variable, all three situations differed significantly from each other.

No interactions were found between manual version and user situation (Wilks' $\lambda = .59$, $F(36,301) = 1.08$, $p = .36$), which means that the difference between the user situations does not depend on the manual version that the subjects used.

Factual knowledge

Factual knowledge is measured by means of a questionnaire. Only 52 out of 87 subjects actually completed the questionnaire; the other subjects did not have enough time left to do so. As a result, the number of subjects is very small in some of the cells, and therefore the following results should be interpreted very cautiously. The mean number of errors on the questionnaire is presented in table 5.7.

Table 5.7
Factual knowledge: mean number of errors on the 12-item questionnaire in three user situations

	N	# Errors in questionnaire
Tutorial		
Proc-Decl	2	7.0
Decl-Proc	3	5.7
Mix	4	5.5
Hypertext	5	5.6
Intermediate		
Proc-Decl	3	6.3
Decl-Proc	6	4.3
Mix	4	5.8
Hypertext	5	4.2
Reference		
Proc-Decl	6	2.8
Decl-Proc	4	2.8
Mix	6	3.3
Hypertext	4	4.8
All situations		
Proc-Decl	11	4.6
Decl-Proc	13	4.2
Mix	14	4.6
Hypertext	14	4.9

There is no main effect of manual version on the number of errors in the questionnaire $(F(3,40) < 1)$: subjects with different manuals made equal numbers of errors.

A main effect of user situation on the number of errors $(F(2,40) = 7.53, p < .01)$ indicates that different user situations do differ with respect to the number of errors on the questionnaire. Tukey's HSD test shows that subjects in the tutorial situation and subjects in the intermediate situation both made more mistakes than subjects in the reference group.

Finally, no interaction was found between manual version and user situation $(F(6,40) = 1.06, p = .40)$.

5.3.4   Navigation in the Hypertext-manual

To analyze the research questions concerning the hypertext, two-way and three-way analyses of variance were used with the factors linking style, task complexity, information type and user situation. The factors linking style, task complexity and information type contained repeated measurements.

First, the data were analyzed to see if subjects in the different user situations have a general preference for a certain type of link in combination with an information type. A three-way analysis of variance was used with the factors linking style, information type and user situation. The mean numbers of chosen linking styles are presented in table 5.8.

Table 5.8

Mean number of chosen links, divided by linking style and information type, in three user situations

	n	Index button p	d	Back button p	d	Internal button p	d	External button p	d
Tutorial	7	8.1	8.9	5.6	4.6	3.1	4.3	10.3	11.0
Intermediate	6	4.2	5.7	0.9	3.7	1.3	2.5	6.7	9.0
Reference	9	3.6	6.8	1.1	1.9	1.7	3.1	6.4	9.1
All situations	22	5.2	7.1	2.5	3.2	2.1	3.3	7.7	9.7

p = link to procedural information
d = link to declarative information

A significant main effect of linking style ($F(3,57) = 25.17, p < .001$) shows that overall, the subjects indeed had a preference. Paired t-tests reveal that the External links were chosen more often than the Index ($t = 2.80$, $df = 21$, $p < .05$). The Index and the External links were both more popular than Internal links ($t = 8.32$, $df = 21$, $p < .001$; $t = 7.42$, $df = 21$, $p < .001$) and the Back-track ($t = 4.15$, $df = 21$, $p < .001$; $t = 6.41$, $df = 21$, $p < .001$). The Internal links and the Back button were chosen equally often ($t = 0.23$, $df = 21$, $p = .82$).

This preference for certain linking styles did not depend on the information type that was selected: the interaction between information type and linking style was not significant ($F(3,57) < 1$). There was no significant interaction either between the type of link and the user situation ($F(6,57) < 1$), indicating that the preference for a certain type of link does not differ for the user situations.

As was to be expected, there was a main effect of user situation ($F(2,19) = 8.34$, $p < .01$), which only confirms what was already reported in the previous sections about information selection: the user situations differ with respect to the number of clicks. Tukey's test reveals that subjects in the tutorial situation click more often than subjects in the other two situations. Similarly, the significant main effect that was found for information type is not surprising either ($F(1,19) = 10.03, p < .01$): procedural information is selected more often than declarative information. No further interactions were found.

To see if task complexity affected these preferences, the numbers of different link types were also counted for two simple subtasks and two complex subtasks. A three-way analysis of variance was used with the factors task complexity, user situation and linking style. The means are presented in table 5.9.

Table 5.9

Mean number of chosen links in two simple and two complex subtasks in three user situations

	Index button	Back button	Internal link	External link
Tutorial (n=7)				
Simple	5.7	1.1	1.1	3.9
Complex	6.0	7.3	5.4	12.0
Intermediate (n=6)				
Simple	0.8	0.2	0.3	0.8
Complex	5.5	4.0	3.3	12.8
Reference (n=9)				
Simple	1.6	0.2	0.8	2.3
Complex	6.0	2.0	4.1	10.0
All situations (n=22)				
Simple	2.7	0.5	0.8	2.5
Complex	5.9	4.2	4.3	11.4

Main effects were found of task complexity on the number of links ($F(1,19) = 36.97$, $p < .001$) and of user situation on the number of links ($F(2,19) = 3.95$, $p < .05$): subjects select more links in the complex task, and the tutorial subjects choose more links than subjects in the reference situation. (The intermediate situation does not differ from the other two).

Again, a main effect of linking style is found ($F(3,57) = 18.03$, $p < .001$). Overall, External links are used more often than any other types of linking (more than Index: $t = 3.21$, $df = 21$, $p < .01$; more than Internal links: $t = 5.78$, $df = 21$, $p < .001$; and more than the Back button: $t = 5.83$, $df = 21$, $p < .001$). Furthermore, the Index button is used more often than the Internal links and the Back-button ($t = 4.56$, $df = 21$, $p < .001$; $t = 2.89$, $df = 21$, $p < .01$). Internal links and the Back button were used equally often ($t = 0.32$, $df = 21$, $p = .75$).

A two-way interaction between task complexity and linking style ($F(3,57) = 10.70$, $p < .001$) is qualified by a trend towards a three-way interaction between user situation, task complexity and linking style $F(6,57) = 2.15$, $p = .06$). Separate analyses for the simple and the complex task show that in both tasks, there is a main effect of linking style (*simple task*: $F(3,57) = 10.27$, $p < .001$; *complex task*: $F(3,57) = 15.62$, $p < .001$). In the simple task, both the index and the external links are used more often than internal links ($t = 3.45$, $df = 21$, $p < .01$; $t = 2.86$, $df = 21$, $p < .01$) and more often than the backtrack ($t = 3.74$, $df = 21$, $p < .01$; $t = 3.89$, $df = 21$, $p < .01$). The index option does not differ from the external links, and the internal links do not differ from the backtrack. In the complex task, external links are used more often than any other type of link (more often than *index*: $t = 4.01$, $df = 21$, $p < .01$; than *internal links*: $t = 5.19$, $df = 21$, $p < .001$; and than the *backtrack*: $t = 4.87$, $df = 21$, $p < .001$). Also, the index is used more often than the internal links ($t = 2.16$, $df = 21$, $p < .05$).

However, in the complex task, this preference does not depend on the user situation ($F(6,57) < 1$), but in the simple task, it does ($F(6,57) = 3.14$, $p < .05$). A separate analysis reveals that the tutorial situation is the only user situation that shows a significant difference for the linking styles in the simple task $F(3,18) = 10.11$, $p < .001$). The index option is selected more often than internal links and the backtrack ($t = 4.12$, $df = 6$, $p < .01$; $t = 3.28$, $df = 6$, $p < .05$) , and external links are selected more often than the backtrack, too ($t = 4.21$, $df = 6$, $p < .01$).
User situation does not interact with linking style $F(6,57) < 1$, nor with task complexity $F(2,19) < 1$.

The results concerning the preference for different styles of linking at the beginning of a subtask are presented in table 5.10. A two-way analysis of variance was applied with the factors linking style and user situation.

Table 5.10
Mean number of different link types for the first click in a (repeated) subtask

	n	From Index	Back	Internal	External
Tutorial	7	8.0	0.9	0.3	0.6
Intermediate	6	6.5	0.5	0.2	0.2
Reference	9	6.3	0.3	0.2	0.4
All situations	22	6.9	0.6	0.2	0.4

A main effect of user situation indicates that the total amount of (first) links selected in a subtask differed over the situations ($F(2,19) = 4.10$, $p < .05$). Tukey's test reveals that subjects in the tutorial group select links in more subtasks than the subjects in both other groups.

There was also a main effect of linking style on the first clicks ($F(4,76) = 32.49$, $p < .001$). The only significant difference occurred for the index-option and the other navigation instruments. The index was always used more often (*external links*: $t = 12.12$, $df = 21$, $p < .001$; *internal links*: $t = 13.47$, $df = 21$, $p < .001$; *backtrack*: $t = 11.71$, $df = 21$, $p < .001$). The interaction between user situation and linking style was not significant ($F(8,76) = 1.05$, $p = .40$).

5.3.5   Summary

- When procedural information was at the top of a page, more procedural than declarative information blocks were selected. When declarative information was positioned at the top of the page, the information types were selected equally often.
- The information type which was at the top of a page was likely to be selected first. Only the reference users did not follow this pattern.
- In all the manual types, procedural information was used significantly longer than declarative information, in spite of the selection orders. A trend towards an interaction effect of manual and user situation indicated that the effects of manual version on the using time may differ over the situations.
- Manual version did not affect any task performance, reasoning or factual knowledge measure, with one exception: in the intermediate situation, subjects had a faster initial task performance time with the Hypertext than with the Mix-manual, and in the reference situation a trend indicated that the initial task performance time was fastest with the Mix-manual.
- Subjects selected all subtypes of declarative information.
- The user situations differed in the same way as they did in the previous experiments: subjects in the tutorial situation selected more information, used the information longer and selected information in a wider variety of subtasks than subjects in the other two situations. Also, subjects in the tutorial situation performed worse in the initial task and on the reasoning task. Subjects in the tutorial and intermediate situations made more errors on the questionnaire than subjects in the reference situation.
- Subjects had a preference for certain link types in the Hypertext-manual. They generally selected the index option and the external links more often than the internal links and the backtrack. Their preference for certain linking styles did not depend on the information type they selected, but it did depend on the combination of task complexity and user situation: in the complex task, external links were preferred to any other type of link, irrespective of the user situation. In the simple task, subjects in the tutorial situation had a preference for external links, but especially for the index. The index was also preferred as a first link in a new subtask by subjects in all situations.

5.4   Discussion and conclusions

5.4.1   Effects of arrangement

Information arrangement can affect which information is selected first, and it determines which type of information is selected more often. Depending on the user situation, there is a difference between the manuals with respect to the initial performance time.

These are the only effects that the different manual versions have. They do not affect the using time of information, delayed task performance, reasoning or factual knowledge. Even the hypertext, which differs rather drastically from the structure of the other manuals, does not seem to have considerably different effects than the other manuals.

Information order
The information type at the top of a page is likely to be selected first. Information order also affects which information type is selected most: when procedural information is at the top of a page, more procedural than declarative information blocks are selected. When declarative information is at the top page position, the information types are selected equally as often, although one would expect that more declarative information would be selected in that case. These results point to a conflict between a preference for procedural content which is induced by the user's background and task, and a text-driven preference to have the information at the top.

In contrast, no such conflict can be found in the using time, which is not influenced at all by the order of the information. Subjects appear to spend more time using procedural information, even in the DP-manual. Apparently, information order affects the initial information selection, but the using time shows that a task-induced need for information overrules this effect in the long run. And as it turns out, procedural information is needed more than declarative information.

Thus, there appears to be a contradiction in the DP-manual: the selection of declarative information is larger, whereas procedural information is used longer. As the ratio of the using time of procedural to declarative information was shown to be consistently 60% - 40% in all manuals and throughout all the experiments, one may wonder whether or not the information selection in the DP-manual is efficient. Overall, subjects with the DP-manual click about 10% more declarative information than subjects who used the PD-manual, but they spend equal percentages of time using the information types and there are no significant differences in the information effects. The total using time and number of clicks do not differ for the manuals.

This can mean three things. The first explanation is the occurrence of a large number of declarative *misclicks* in the DP-manual: blocks that were selected just because the page layout induced the information selection. If subjects recognize a misclick, it will soon be replaced by a new click and the using time of declarative information per block will drop. If this latter explanation is true, the number of misclicks in the DP-manual should be higher than that in the PD-manual.

To test this assumption, the dataset was altered. All clicks that were shorter than three seconds were not counted as clicks. On the basis of the clicks that were left over, a new datafile was generated and analyzed. The results showed, however, that although the average number of misclicks was slightly higher in the DP-manual (0.73), the difference for the PD-manual (0.48) was not significant ($F(1,42) < 1$).

The second explanation may be that subjects may not really select 10% *additional* declarative information blocks, but instead they may re-read the *same* information blocks more often than subjects in the PD-manual, for instance because they start with declarative information, then come to the conclusion that they need procedural information first, and then go back to the declarative block when they think it is necessary in the middle of, or after the procedure. However, this appears not to be the case, as the data in table 5.11 show.

Table 5.11
*Mean number of times every selected information block was
used in two manuals and three user situations*

	Proc	Decl
Tutorial		
PD	1.9	1.8
DP	1.8	2.0
Intermediate		
PD	1.9	1.8
DP	1.6	1.6
Reference		
PD	1.7	1.5
DP	1.5	1.5
All situations		
PD	1.8	1.7
DP	1.6	1.7

The information blocks were used between 1.5 and 2.0 times on average. There were no significant differences in this respect for the two information types ($F(1,36) = 1.25$, $p = .27$) nor for the two manuals ($F(1,36) < 1$). There was a trend towards a difference for the user situations ($F(2,72) = 1.25$, $p = .08$): the means indicate that the subjects in the tutorial situation tend to re-use the information blocks more often. A trend towards an interaction of manual version and information types ($F(1,36) = 3.40$, $p = .07$) might be the only indication that the declarative information blocks are re-used more often in the DP-manual than in the PD-manual. However, separate tests do not confirm this: there is no difference for the manual versions with respect to the number of times that the declarative blocks are re-used. ($F(1,41) < 1$), nor for the procedural blocks ($F(1,41) = 1.80$, $p = .19$). Paired t-tests show that in the PD-manual, procedural blocks are re-used more often than declarative blocks ($t = 2.64$, $df = 20$, $p < .05$), whereas this difference does not occur in the DP-manual ($t = 0.44$, $df = 20$, $p = .66$).

Thus, it would appear that subjects really process 10% more declarative information in the same amount of time. If this is true, then it is still not certain if it helps them in any way: subjects with the DP-manual did not perform better or worse on any of the effect measurements in this experiment. If no other effects of this 10% additional declarative information blocks are overlooked, then these subjects probably use more declarative information than is strictly necessary for better performance and reasoning.

For all explanations it can be argued that information selection in the DP-manual is not efficient enough, but, on the other hand, this does not seem to have any negative effects. There is one possible negative effect that has not been investigated in this experiment: inefficient information selection may annoy the subjects, and that may in turn lead to a negative appreciation of the manual and a lower motivation to continue using it.

Separated or mixed?
No important effects of separating or mixing of information type were found in this experiment. The Mix-manual on the one hand and the PD- and DP-manuals on the other hand did not differ significantly on any of the dependent measures, except for information selection: in the Mix-manual, subjects selected more declarative than procedural information, contrary to the PD-manual and the DP-manual. Given the larger number of declarative blocks in the Mix-manual, this is however not very surprising. The effect is not due to the specific Mix-feature of the declarative blocks being right at the relevant places in the procedure, for then there would have been a difference with the Hypertext, which does not have this feature.

The Mix-manual yielded remarkable results in the initial task performance time for the reference users: they seemed to perform very fast with the Mix-manual. There was only a trend towards a difference however with the other manuals.

Information use and information effects with the Hypertext manual
Surprisingly, the Hypertext manual did not lead to differences with respect to information use either. Just like in the Mix-manual, subjects selected more declarative than procedural information, but again this is probably mainly due to the larger number of declarative blocks. Hypertext does not cause subjects to use procedural and declarative information any longer or shorter than the other manuals. Probably, the need for information caused by other factors such as the user's background or the problems that are encountered in the task, has more impact on the eventual time spent on using the information than the way in which the information is structured in the document, no matter how extreme the structural changes.

Only subjects in the intermediate situation had some benefit from the hypertext: their initial performance time with the Hypertext manual was better than that with the Mix-manual.

User situations
From the results in this experiment, the same overall picture arises as in the other two experiments with respect to the three user situations. In general, tutorial users seem to select more information than users in the intermediate or the reference situation, they use it longer, they select information in a wider variety of subtasks and they perform worse on initial task performance, the reasoning test and the questionnaire. Also, subjects in different user situations again spend different percentages of time on procedural and declarative information: subjects in the tutorial situation come close to the ratio of 70% procedural to 30% declarative, whereas the subjects in the reference situation spend close to 50% of their time on procedural and 50% on declarative information.

5.4.2   Navigation in hypertext-manuals

The hypotheses about a preference for navigation instruments, which were formulated on the basis of the experiment by Wright & Lickorish (1990), are confirmed: subjects use both index and page navigation, but they do so in different situations. At the start of a new (sub)task, when users are not certain where to go in the manual and need an overview, they prefer an index. When the task is complex, users prefer page navigation in the form of external links. However, the results yield some additonal information.

The preference for certain linking styles in general does not depend on the type of information that is selected, nor on the user situation. The factors affecting the choice of navigation style in general are apparently constrained by characteristics of the task itself.

Another additional result is the finding that users with a lot of experience who do not have a learning intention do not have a preference for certain linking styles in simple tasks, contrary to users in a tutorial context, who generally prefer the index option or external links. This may be a result of experience in combination with hurry (subjects got the assignment to work fast): the simple task is simple enough for these users to carry it out without selecting much information anyway. The total amount of information that they use may be too small to show any preference for linking styles.

It is remarkable that external links are used frequently, but internal links far less often, although they are both instruments for page navigation. There may be at least three explanations for this difference. First, it may simply result from the fact that there are only two internal links and usually more than two external links. However, the numbers do not really seem to count: there is for instance only one Back-button and one Index-button; the Backtrack is not used more or less than the Internal links, and the Index is used much more frequently. The choices are not equivalent for the users; they have four options to go somewhere else, and they choose between those four options first. The next step is to make a choice between the items presented.

Secondly, the preference for the external links may be due to the higher quality of the reference. The underlined words in the Internal links are often just a vague indication for the information that the user looks for, whereas the external links are the same as the headings in the book-like text, and are much more indicative for the content of the information that the user will jump to. Searching for the right place to go is probably faster and easier in the external links.

Thirdly, clicking information in the text may be annoying for the users, as they have to interrupt the reading process. That may not be harmful as long as the click yields nothing more than a pop-up window with a short definition, but in the case of this experiment, subjects were taken to a new information block that required new concentration, and that could thus distract the user from the earlier information block. Probably, the second and the third explanation together are responsible for the infrequent use of internal links.

The backtrack was not very popular either. Possibly, it was too difficult to remember the previous steps and thus keep track of the path, but probably subjects want to be certain about where to go, and then the other navigation instruments are more attractive. The Backtrack may only be adequate in situations in which the subject needs information that he remembers having seen before. This may be different from a backtrack like that used by Internet-browsers such as Netscape, where the size of the information space is much larger and the alternative navigation instruments for the backtrack not always usable. The infrequent use of the backtrack may be an indication that subjects in this experiment did not often re-read information.

Chapter 6
Conclusions

In this final chapter, the general conclusions are summarized. In section 6.2, some practical recommendations are formulated on the basis of the results and conclusions. The advantages and limitations of the click & read method are discussed in a separate section (6.3), and section 6.4 concludes with some directions for future research.

6.1   General conclusions

Five general conclusions from this study are discussed below.

1 Procedural information is preferred to declarative information, but declarative information is selected and used to a fairly high degree and has positive effects on delayed task performance, reasoning and knowledge.

Contrary to what could be expected on the basis of observations by the Minimalists (e.g. Carroll, 1990a), users in all situations do not skip declarative information. On the contrary, they select it rather frequently, and they spend quite some time using it. Moreover, declarative information proved to be useful, as the user's insight, knowledge and performance on future tasks is better than that for users who cannot use declarative information. This conclusion is in agreement with the conclusion by Kieras & Bovair (1984), who found that declarative information about system components and the power flow of a system enhances inferences about procedures. The declarative information that was used in the experimental manuals in this study was not similar to information about system components and power flow, however, but the declarative information did allow for inferences about procedures.

By following procedures, inferring procedures, processing declarative information and interacting with the software, users probably build a more elaborate and more adequate mental model than users without declarative information. However, users do not immediately benefit from this mental model, the first time they work with the software. They benefit from the mental model at a later stage, during repeated and (new) tasks that require reasoning skills. Moreover, they are supported by more factual knowledge.

2   *User situations differ with respect to the amount of selected information and the time users spend using information. Users in a tutorial situation select more information items than users in a reference situation and sometimes more than users in an intermediate situation. Users in a tutorial situation also spend more time using procedural information than users in a reference situation, but these time differences do not occur for using declarative information.*

The three user situations can therefore not be generalized with respect to information use. The only measure that systematically does *not* differ is the using time for declarative information, which suggests that the use of declarative information is independent of the user situation. The control experiment in chapter 3 revealed that probably the combination of experience and assignment causes the differences.

A problem in the interpretation of the differences for the user situation is the interpretation of the intermediate situation. It is not always obvious how the intermediate situation relates to the other two user situations. Sometimes it differs from the tutorial situation, but often, it does not differ from any of the other two situations. The mean number of selected items or the using time is usually half way between that of the tutorial and the reference situations. Thus, it is difficult to tell whether the intermediate users act more like tutorial or more like reference users.

Looking at the results of this study, one may wonder whether or not the intermediate situation should be investigated further, or whether it should be ignored in future studies. There are a couple of reasons for paying more attention to this situation.

If the intermediate situation would have been very similar to either the reference or the tutorial situation, there would be enough reason to assume that the separate status of the intermediate situation should not be continued. However, the intermediate situation did differ from the tutorial situation in several instances. These differences may be an indication of the possibility that users in an intermediate situation find themselves in a different phase of developing skills and knowledge than tutorial users. And, even though there are no significant differences for users in an intermediate situation and users with even more experience and a strictly incidental task, the mean scores of the intermediate and the reference situations are sometimes far apart. Thus, the intermediate situation might still be relevant.

A more practical reason for including this "in-between" situation in future studies is the size of this group of users. Computer skills and knowledge are more and more common. An increasing number of people knows how to work with various types of software. The dichotomy of novices and experts may become too simple, as the largest group of users find themselves at a level of experience that is somewhere in between the novice and expert levels. Moreover, the assignment where users are in a hurry and are aware at the same time that the assignment will occur more often in the future, is probably an assignment which occurs frequently in professional situations.

Studying users at an intermediate level of experience with different types of task may yield more information about the development of knowledge and skills and the effects of information in a manual on this development. This may enable a description to be formulated of the process that users go through when they develop from novice to expert user. Studying the type of assignment in the intermediate situation in more depth will possibly yield information about incidental learning. Users who want to achieve a goal fast, but who at the same time know that they have to do a similar task tomorrow, may be more prone to incidental learning than users with other assignments. This aspect of the user situation may also be relevant with respect to the results obtained in this study.

3   *Task complexity causes users to select both procedural and declarative information more often and it causes them to use both information types longer: users select more information in general and spend more time on the information when the task is complex. Only users in a reference situation with a complex task spend as much time using procedural information as they do using declarative information.*

The finding that complex tasks cause more information to be selected and used than simple tasks is in itself trivial, but the finding that there is no overall shift in the proportions of procedural and declarative information is new: one might expect that complex tasks require relatively more declarative information. The reference situation is the only situation where this phenomenon occurs, however, which may be due to reference users having a greater capability for processing declarative information.

4   *The arrangement of procedural and declarative information in the manual only affects the (initial) selection of information. Different arrangements do not affect how long the information types are used, nor do they have consequences for task performance, reasoning and knowledge.*

This conclusion about the arrangement of procedural and declarative information means that different text structures do not cause users to spread their time differently over the information types. At first, they still take the organization of the information as their guide, which results in effects on (initial) information selection, but soon other factors in the task and the context take the lead in determining what is relevant information. Thus, the arrangement of the information types may only serve to a certain extent as a writer's guide to information use in manuals. It determines how much information of each type is selected and what information is selected first, but that has no consequences for the time spent on the information types, nor on performance or knowledge.

5 *In hypertext manuals, an index and external links appear to be the most important navigation instruments. An index is especially important at the beginning of a new task, and external links are especially important in complex tasks. Internal links and a backtrack option are used infrequently. Procedural and declarative information is not selected by means of different navigation styles.*

The preference for external links and indexes, which was found in experiment 3, is in agreement with previous research by Wright & Lickorish (1990), which pointed to the importance of the presence of navigation options on the document page when the tasks made high demands on the user's working memory, and the importance of indexes when users needed an overview of where they could find information. Still, this finding should be interpreted with some caution, as the experimental design and materials were not optimal for answering the hypertext questions.

6.2   Practical implications

On the basis of this study, some recommendations can be formulated for designing manuals. The recommendations are not very detailed: several follow-ups of this study would be required to make the recommendations specific and concrete enough to include them in a handbook for technical writers. Instead, they should be interpreted as general guidelines which can be applied in various ways.

Including declarative information
The most important recommendation is to include declarative information in software manuals. The experiments revealed that declarative information in software manuals is used spontaneously and that declarative information is useful when users have to work with the software more than once. Moreover, using declarative information does not seem to take extra time. However, in

order to serve as a practical guideline, two additional questions should be answered: *what* exactly is the declarative information that should be included, and *how* should declarative information be included?

Which declarative information should be included?
This study does not offer a clear answer to the first question. It is not yet certain whether all the subtypes of declarative information that have been included in the experimental manuals, such as description items, terminology items and functionality items (see section 1.1.3 for a complete overview), have the same positive effects on delayed task performance, reasoning and knowledge. What is known now is that the positive effects occur when the different subtypes of declarative information can *all* be used. However: it might well be that only a small selection of the subtypes is responsible for the effects of declarative information. Future experiments will have to reveal which exact subtypes are responsible and why.

How should declarative information be included?
More research would also be needed to give a clear-cut answer to the question of *how* declarative information should be presented. In this study, one characteristic of the presentation may have been very important: procedural and declarative information could always be easily distinguished by the users. The information types were marked in various different ways: procedural and declarative information were presented in separate blocks, these blocks had different headings, and the syntactic forms of procedural and declarative text were different. Even in the Mix-manual, which was included in the third experiment (chapter 5), the information types could be distinguished in this way. It is well possible that this differentiation between the information types was at least partly responsible for the results: it was made possible for users to make their own choice, they were not confronted with unexpected information. They could choose *when* they needed procedures and *when* they needed declarative information. As a result, they were not annoyed by information they did not want, and they were ready to process the information they selected.

A manual in which the information types are *not* distinguished has not been investigated in this study. Therefore, the recommendation for making the distinction visible is a tentative recommendation, but it is not only based on the observation that it worked in this study. Ramey (1988) also explicitly advises technical writers to visually mark different information types: step-by-step procedures should be differentiated clearly from descriptions. A series of usability studies showed that users want to be able to reliably skip either of these information types. Furthermore, Mack et al. (1983) describe users who skipped or executed declarative information from a wordy traditional instruction manual. Their observations may also be due to the manual design giving users a hard time selecting the information that they want.

There are several ways to enable users to distinguish between the information types. The methods that were used in the experiments can be applied: different text blocks, different headings that are representative for the procedural or declarative contents, and different syntactic form features. Another way of distinguishing between information types was presented by Robert Horn (1982;1985): the Information Mapping ® approach, in which the information is divided into several short modular units called *blocks*. A set of blocks with a similar purpose is grouped into a larger unit, a *map*. Horn for instance mentions *Procedure maps*, *Concept maps* and *Fact maps* as different types of basic maps.

The order of presenting procedural and declarative information or the different arrangements in which the information types can be mixed do not seem to matter: they do not cause any differences in using time, performance, reasoning or knowledge. If there is another good reason to make users select certain information first, then this important information should be put at the top of the page.

Declarative information for all user types
Many handbooks advise technical writers to take different user types into account when designing a manual (e.g. Brockmann, 1990). However, this is difficult to achieve in practice: many commercial manuals are intended to be informative for users with different levels of experience and for users with different assignments. Or, the manuals should be designed to suit the largest or average group of users, which often consists of intermediate users.

Fortunately, the recommendation to include declarative information in manuals applies to all user types. Although users with different prior experience and different assignments also differ with respect to information use and performance, all types of users benefit from declarative information. They all use substantial amounts of declarative information, and declarative information always causes better results on delayed task performance, reasoning and knowledge.

6.3   An evaluation of the click & read method

The click & read method, which was used to measure information selection and information use in the three experiments, proved to be well suitable for measuring information use in manuals. It appears to be a better method for this type of research questions than the three more traditional methods that were discussed in chapter 2 (reading time, eye movement registration and thinking aloud). However, the click & read method also has some limitations which prevent the techniquefrom being applied to all types of research questions. Several aspects of the method can still be improved.

Advantages of the click & read method
The most obvious advantage of the click & read method, in comparison to other methods, is the combination of freedom of information selection with a precise recording of the relevant data. The reading process is left intact, the experimenter does not have to interfere, the subject does not feel as if he is being observed, while the selection moments and times are recorded by the computers. The logfiles and the (optional) video data enable the experimenter to trace back every single moment in the manual reading process or the problem solving process after the experimental session is over.

A potential risk at the outset was the risk that subjects may not get used to the click & read-way of selecting information. If turning to a second screen and clicking blurred information blocks had been a very strange procedure to subjects, it would have distracted them from their spreadsheet tasks. The recorded selection moments and times would not be valid anymore. However, in pilot tests as well as in all three experiments, subjects experienced the method as a natural way of looking things up. A couple of observations support this claim.

First, subjects in the pilot tests and in the first experiment were explicitly asked if they had felt disrupted by the click & read-way of looking up information. None of them answered this question affirmatively. In all three experiments, a number of subjects indicated spontaneously that this way of using a manual was handy, and that it was too bad that they could not afford two computers at home. The only criticism that subjects sometimes expressed concerned the size of the letters on the screen. Although they could read the texts well, they thought a larger typeface would be more comfortable.

Furthermore, approximately half of the subjects did not realize that the experiment was about manuals until the experiment was over and the research goals were explained to them. That is a good indication in favour of the claim that the method does not attract the subjects' attention once they are engaged in the software tasks. This can mean one of two things: either the software tasks are so complex so that they require a lot of concentration, or the click & read method seems a natural way of reading. The latter explanation is more probable, because task complexity was varied, and subjects experienced the method in a similar way in both the simple and complex tasks. Moreover, if the click & read method did not seem natural to subjects, they would be distracted by it while trying to focus on the complex software tasks, and this type of distraction did not occur either.

The observation that the click & read method offered a fairly natural environment to the subjects may be attributed to the fact that people have become used to graphic user interfaces: in the period between 1993 and 1995, when the experiments were conducted, the Windows operating system, online help facilities, online documentation and looking up information on Internet became more and more common, also for students. Thus, clicking with a mouse for help and searching headings for the right help topics were already established skills.

Finally, a pleasant additional advantage of the click & read method is its stability: it never crashed and never yielded other computer problems.

The need for further improvements

Its advantages make the click & read method a very useful supplement to other methods, but that does not alter the fact that the method would need further improvements in future research. The most obvious improvements are directly connected with improvements of the hardware and they can undoubtedly be realized with the rapid progress of hardware techniques. The two most eye-catching problems in this respect are the quality of the screen texts and the laborious preparation of the materials.

Using a 21" screen instead of a 17" screen is the most necessary adjustment to solve a major part of the problems. Two sheets of A4-paper fit exactly next to each other on a 21" screen, so the scanned pictures would not have to be resized anymore. The size of the letters would be exactly the same as it is on the printed pages, and moreover, the quality is better if it does not have to be resized (resizing makes the text also slightly less sharp). The 21" screen would thus kill two birds with one stone: the screen text quality would improve, and less time would be needed for the editing process in PhotoStyler.

The 21" screen would even open a possibility for another refinement: instead of actually clicking on the selected text blocks, subjects could just move the mouse over the information, just like they would do by finger pointing in a book. When the mouse pointer is on the selected block of information, the information could be sharpened, and the time and block name are written to the logfiles. This possibility could not yet be implemented in the experiments because the information on the 17" screen is still too small, and the adaption of the typefaces to resolve the problem in experiment 3 (see chapter 5) causes the information to jump after each mouse movement. Moreover, this refinement would need a much faster computer, because the mouse would move over many blocks, so that a lot of data would have to be transferred at high speed. This refinement would cause a need for redefining the using time of the information, as it is not probable that every block of information that the mouse moves over is actually read.

With respect to the problem of time-consuming preparations, the 21" screen also offers an indirect solution. Because the pictures take up more space and more memory if they are no longer resized, a more powerful computer would be necessary, and that of course also has a positive influence on the time needed for the preparations.

Limitations of the click & read method

The click & read method also has limitations that would be more difficult to solve than the technical problems mentioned above:

- It does not measure exact reading time, but information using time.
- The preparations for the click & read method require technical knowledge and more than basic programming skills.

Measuring reading time can yield different information or answer different questions than measuring using time. Even for the current research questions, reading time could have been relevant. A hypothesis might for instance be that information characteristics have different effects on reading time than they have on using time.

The only way to measure reading time now is to check the videotapes and read from the video clock how many seconds subjects actually watch the screen: a method that is much more prone to errors and much less precise than the measuring of using time. The click & read method could also be adapted in such a way that subjects would have to hold the mouse button down until they have read the selected information. This strategy was seriously considered at the outset, but it was not implemented because of the fear that this would be too inconvenient for the subjects, who often turn from one screen to the other while having their hands on the keyboard at the same time, being engaged in carrying out the software tasks. The method was intended to approach a natural situation as closely as possible, and that is not possible if reading time is to be measured in this way. A more principal objection is the fear that measuring reading time by holding down the mouse button could also cause users to read differently: they may try to remember more in order to avoid constant switches from the keyboard to the manual.

A second limitation of the click & read method is the fact that it requires some advanced technical skills to write or adapt it to a new situation. If the method has to be programmed from scratch, advanced programming skills are necessary for writing the code. Adapting the programming code and creating or adapting the interface are relatively simple tasks, but they still require a learning stage. Unfortunately, the click & read method is not a ready-made program that can be distributed on a diskette and applied to any text.

6.4   Directions for future research

In this final section, ideas for future research are presented. These ideas vary from refinements of the current operationalizations and conclusions, to more general ideas for investigating the theoretical assumptions that were made in the explanation of the results.

Possible follow-ups for these experiments
The experiments in this study yielded precise figures about the selection and use of information in software manuals, but no information was obtained about users' *motivations* to select certain information types at certain moments. This information could be inferred from a close analysis of the logfiles and the videotapes, as the logfiles show the exact moments when declarative information was used in the task performance process. This analysis could reveal in what (problem) situations declarative information is selected.

Another way to find that out would be to conduct an additional experiment in which a combination of the click & read method and the thinking aloud method are used, as the thinking aloud method is particularly suited for recording information about the users' motivations.

In this study, procedural and declarative information were always presented in their standard syntactic forms. All signals that users can get to distinguish between the information types were provided. The question remains how important those signals are for users. If procedural information had been presented in a declarative form (prose, longer sentences, no imperatives), would the same results have been obtained? The syntactic form of the information types would have to be varied to investigate this. This would require a new adaption of the click & read method. When this is investigated, it may also be relevant to try to record reading time besides using time. Wright & Wilcox (1978) distinguished three components of using time: reading, planning and applying. They found that form characteristics only influenced the reading phase, but not the planning and applying phases. Similar effects may occur when different arrangements or different syntactic forms of procedural and declarative information are investigated.

A third question that remains is the question of what specific declarative information is relevant for users. Declarative information has positive effects on delayed task performance, reasoning and knowledge, but *which* specific subtypes of information cause these effects? A new classification should be made of subtypes of declarative information, which differs from the text-based classification in chapter 1. This text-based classification was not indicative of the reasons why declarative information is selected and why it is useful. Perhaps the subtypes of declarative information should be classified in terms of the functions that those subtypes can fulfil for users in relation to the functions of procedural information. Then comparative tests should indicate which subtypes of declarative information cause which effects.

The arrangement of procedural and declarative information can direct users with respect to the order in which they select information and the amount of information they select, but as there are hardly any effects on using time, performance and reasoning, the only good reason for manipulating the structure of the information types would be task inherent: if a specific task requires reading certain information first, then it may help to put this information first. Further research could nuance this claim. The user's *appreciation* of different text structures may for instance be a good argument for choosing a specific structure. The discussions with subjects after the experiment gave rise to the expectation that the Mix-manual was appreciated less than the other manuals. This may for instance have a negative effect on the motivation to read the manual. Appreciation of the text was not a variable in this experiment, however. It should be included in future studies into the effects of text-internal variables.

Other topics on the research agenda
In the experiments in this study, paper manuals were imitated. The reason why the study started from paper manuals is a very practical one: lots of paper manuals are still produced and many software users still have paper manuals to help them, even though on-line manuals are becoming increasingly popular. Regarding this starting point, a suggestion for further research might be to investigate similar research questions for on-line manuals. This suggestion may indeed seem relevant if the results are generalized to on-line help systems that only present quick and very brief guidelines for completing certain tasks. However, there is also a reason to assume that there would be no differences with the paper manuals presented by means of the click & read method . In this study, different factors appeared to influence information needs and selection behaviour, such as task complexity, user situation and the information type itself. Those factors are also relevant in the process of using on-line manuals.

The development of the users' mental models is a topic that definitely needs more research. The positive effects of declarative information on delayed task performance, reasoning and knowledge were explained in terms of the user's mental model of the software and the task. The user starts with some preliminary mental model, and then both the interaction with the software and the processing of the information in the manual help the user to expand the model. The experiments in this study have shown that the interaction with the software alone, combined with procedural information, was not enough to build a mental model that adequately supports delayed task performance and reasoning tasks. It was therefore assumed that users who were able to use declarative information could build a more elaborate and adequate mental model than users who were not able to use declarative information during initial task performance. What we still do not know, however, is *how* procedural and declarative information in a manual is incorporated in the user's mental model, how these building blocks make for a "better" mental model and how they relate to the information that is deduced from the interaction with the software. The results of the current experiments suggest that users need external information to acquire declarative knowledge. Is that true, or can users still also infer declarative knowledge from procedures and the performance of their tasks?

A closely related question asks how manuals can support the development from novice users to expert users. The results in this study suggest that tutorial users need relatively more procedural information than other users, and they also read a wider variety of different topics. Reference users on the other hand hardly need any information when they have to carry out a very simple task, and they use relatively more declarative information when they carry out a complex task. The study does not show where these differences come from. What are the differences between the mental models of novice and expert software users that explain why they have different information needs? They often use the same information during initial task performance. Do they incorporate these information items differently into their mental models? How do the mental models develop from a novice's model to an expert's model? Answers to these questions may contribute to a better understanding of the reasons *why* declarative information in manuals is used and why it can be so useful.

Afterword

In the introduction to this book, an example was presented of a manual in which the author claimed that the first part of the manual would not contain explanations about underlying theoretical concepts, but only "practical skills". The author's explicit intention was to include no theoretical explanations in the beginning of the manual, but only procedures. Still, in spite of this intention, several theoretical explanations in the form of prose sections were actually included in those first parts.

After this study, we still don't know why the author included this declarative information in spite of his intentions, but we do know now that it was not a bad idea to do so. This study has revealed that all types of users *want* to use declarative information and that declarative information can also be very useful to them. The author of the Excel/Visual Basic manual did the right thing by including the explanations he must have thought indispensable. Not his decision, but the idea that declarative information should be eliminated from manuals must be reconsidered.

Notes

1   The knowledge to which these articles refer is presented to subjects in the form of written instructions or pictures. With respect to the distinction made between the information types, there is a close relation between information represented in a user's memory and information in a document that is offered to users. Investigations of procedural and declarative knowledge usually start from the assumption that the information that is presented to subjects in written form will later be the same as the information represented in the subjects' memories or mental models, although this assumption may not be reasonable (see for instance Churchill, 1992, p.4).

2   The terms *procedural elaboration* or *conceptual elaboration*, which are used by Charney et al., may be extra confusing, as they can be interpreted in two ways:
    a.   *Procedural* and *conceptual* refer to the information in the elaboration itself
    b.   *Procedural* and *conceptual* refer to the information that is elaborated upon
    In their articles, Charney et al. use the first interpretation: they are concerned with the information in the elaboration itself (see Reder et al., 1986, p.71; Charney et al., 1988, pp. 54-55)

3   The definitions of procedural and declarative in this study should be interpreted as a proposal; an attempt to describe as explicitly as possible how the information types were operationalized in this study. The variety of definitions that have been used before indicate that it is probably difficult to reach a consensus on the definitions of procedural and declarative information.

4   The *context* in which such sentences are placed may also partly determine the identification as procedural or declarative. If the examples [3] and [4] are placed in a larger declarative block that is marked as a block with explanations, they will less easily be interpreted as procedural items. If they are combined with explicit procedures, it is more likely that they will also be used as procedural information.

5   A recent overview of the design principles of the Minimal Manual is presented in Van der Meij & Carroll (1995).

6   Smith & Goodman's use of the term *schema* is more or less similar to the concept of a *mental model* of the system and the task, although the relation between written instructions and knowledge has been made more explicit in their theory.

7   To exclude the possibility that this information order will have an effect on the selection and use of procedural information, it would be better to vary the information order on the pages. However, with the separate procedural and declarative block, this seemed very unnatural and a more or less chaotic approach. Therefore, this information order was originally chosen, in the knowledge that the reverse order (procedural at the bottom, declarative at the top) would be tested in

experiment 3 (see section 2.1.3 about the arrangement of procedural and declarative information).

8   Statistic analysis indicates that there is no significant difference between the number of procedural and declarative lines ($t = 1.37$, $df = 22$, $p = .19$), nor between the number of procedural and declarative sentences ($t = 0.34$, $df = 22$, $p = .74$) in the 23 pages of the manual. The number of words is larger in the declarative parts than in the procedural parts ($t = 3.58$, $df = 22$, $p < .01$). This is not surprising, as long sentences are inherent to the syntactic form characteristics of declarative text.

9   Unfortunately, the address mentioned in the QubeCalc files was no longer valid. An attempt to remit the required money in 1993 to the developers in San Jose failed.

10 Experience (prior knowledge) and situational aspects (assignments) were combined. In a later phase of the project, an additional experiment was conducted to examine the relative influence of these two factors. The underlying assumption was tested that information use is only affected by a combination of experience and situational aspects The results of this experiment will be discussed in 3.5.2.

11 *Keylog* is developed by Jacco Brok, who currently works with Ericsson. At the time he worked with the department of Ergonomics at the University of Twente. Lars Boelen adapted Keylog to the current needs.

12 Thus, *efficiency* in this study is not defined in terms of the number of keystrokes or the number of errors.

13 In delayed task performance, subjects did not have any manuals at their disposal, so for this situation, task performance time was performance time only.

14 I am very indebted to Lars Boelen, with whom I jointly developed the click & read method. Lars was a network operator at the University of Twente at the time. He is currently working with a large Dutch computer company. He was specifically responsible for all the programming work during the development.

15 For reasons of conciseness, a click on procedural information will be called a *procedural click* and a click on declarative information a *declarative click*.

16 This order of information was consistent throughout the manual. As this consistent information order may bias the results, the influence of information order is measured in the third experiment (see chapter 5).

17 Analysis of variance was appropriate as the assumption of homogeneity of the variances was not violated, except for a small subset of measures in the simple task. However, analysis of variance has been reported to be robust against moderate violations against the assumptions (Cohen, 1977, pp. 273-274).

18   Tukey's tests were always preceeded by one-way ANOVAs with user situation as an independent variable.

19   The percentages in the table cannot automatically be concluded from the absolute means that are mentioned in the table. Percentages were only calculated if subjects had selected information, or, in other words, when the denominator (the total number of clicks) was not zero. Therefore, the mean perentages are based on a slightly lower number of subjects than the absolute numbers. In experiment 1, 4 out of 51 subjects did not select any information in the simple task. In the complex task, all subjects selected information.

20   The percentages in the table cannot automatically be concluded from the absolute means that are mentioned in the table. Percentages were only calculated if subjects had selected information, or, in other words, when the denominator (the total number of clicks) was not zero. Therefore, the mean perentages are based on a slightly lower number of subjects than the absolute numbers. In experiment 1, 4 out of 51 subjects did not select any information in the simple task. In the complex task, all subjects selected information.

21   Just like in the previous tables, the percentages only reflect the pattern of the subjects who did indeed select information. When the subjects had not selected any information at all, the absolute number of clicks was set to 0. These zeros are accounted for in the calculation of the absolute average numbers, but the corresponding percentages cannot be calculated. In replication 1, only 3 out of 9 subjects in the reference situation needed to select any information in the simple task. Thus, the extreme percentages of the simple task in the reference situation are only based on 3 subjects and should be interpreted with reserve. This problem did not occur in the tutorial situation, where all seven subjects selected information and in the intermediate situation, where 6 out of 8 subjects selected information. It may be attributed to the sharper contrast between the simple and the complex task with respect to complexity.

22   The control experiment was conducted by Mark Kamphuis. It was conducted after all experiments in this and the following chapters were finished.

23   The only effect that manual version has on initial task performance occurred in the intermediate situation and the complex task: subjects with the P-manual performed more subtasks incorrectly. It is however not clear what the explanation for this isolated result should be.

References

Alexander, P.A., Schallert, D.L., & Hare, V.C. (1991). Coming to terms: How researchers in learning and literacy talk about knowledge. *Review of Educational Research, 61,* 315-343.

Anderson, J.R. (1983). *The architecture of cognition.* Cambridge, MA: Harvard University Press.

Bayman, P., & Mayer, R.E. (1984). Instructional manipulation of users' mental models for electronic calculators. *International journal of man-machine studies, 20,* 189-199.

Brockmann, R.J. (1990). *Writing better computer user documentation: from paper to hypertext (Version 2.0).* New York: Wiley & Sons.

Carroll, J.M. (1990a). *The Nurnberg Funnel: Designing minimalist instruction for practical computer skill.* Cambridge, MA: MIT Press.

Carroll, J.M. (1990b). An overview of minimalist instruction. *Proceedings of the 23rd Hawaii International Conference on System Science (HICSS-23),* 210-219. Washington: IEEE.

Carroll, J.M., Mack, R.L., Lewis, C.H., Grischowsky, N.L., & Robertson, S.R. (1988). Exploring exploring a word processor. In S. Doheny-Farina (Ed), *Effective documentation: What we have learned from research* (pp. 73-102). Cambridge, MA: MIT Press.

Carroll , J.M., & Van der Meij, H. (1996). Ten misconceptions about minimalism. *IEEE transactions on professional communication, 39,* 72-87.

Carroll, J.M., Smith-Kerker, P.L., Ford, J.R., & Mazur-Rimetz, S.A. (1987-1988). The Minimal Manual. *Human Computer Interaction, 3,* 123-153.

Carroll, J.M., Smith-Kerker, P.L., Ford, J.R., & Mazur, S.A.(1986). *The Minimal Manual.* (IBM Research report 11637). San Jose: IBM Research Division.

Charney, D., Reder, L.M., & Wells, G. (1988). Studies of elaboration in instructional text. In S. Doheny-Farina (Ed), *Effective documentation: What we have learned from research* (pp. 47-72). Cambridge, MA: MIT Press.

Charney, D.H., & Reder, L.M. (1987). Initial skill learning: an analysis of how elaborations can facilitate the three components. In P. Morris (Ed.), *Modelling cognition* (pp. 135-165). New York: Wiley & Sons.

Churchill, E.F. (1992). The formation of mental models: Are 'device instructions' the source? In G.C. van der Veer, M.J. Tauber, S. Bagnara, & M. Antalovits (Eds.), *Human-Computer Interaction: Tasks and organization - Proceedings of the 6th European conference on Cognitive Ergonomics (ECCE 6)*, 3-16. Roma: CUD

Cohen, J. (1977). *Statistical power analysis for the behavioral sciences (Revised Ed.)*. New York: Academic Press.

Dixon, P. (1987). Actions and procedural directions. In R.S. Tomlin (Ed.), *Coherence and grounding in discourse* (pp. 69-89). Amsterdam: John Benjamins.

Donin, J., Bracewell, R.J., Frederiksen, C.H., & Dillinger, M. (1992). Students' strategies for writing instructions: Organizing conceptual information in text. *Written Communication, 9*, 209-236.

Duffy, T.M., Mehlenbacher, B., & Palmer, J. (1989). The evaluation of online help systems: A conceptual model. In E. Barrett (Ed.), *The society of text: Hypertext, hypermedia, and the social construction of information* (pp. 362-387). Cambridge, MA: MIT Press.

Ericsson, K.A. (1988). Concurrent verbal reports on text comprehension: A review. *Text, 8*, 295-325.

Foss, D.J., Smith-Kerker, P.L., & Rosson, M.B. (1987). On comprehending a computer manual: analysis of variables affecting performance. *International Journal of Man-Machine Studies, 26*, 277-300.

Guthrie, J.T., Bannett, S., & Weber, S. (1991). Processing procedural documents: A cognitive model for following instructions. *Educational Psychology Review, 3*, 249-265.

Hartley, J. (1980). Space and structure in instructional text. In J. Hartley (Ed.), *The psychology of written communication*. London: Kogan page.

Hartley, J. (1994). *Designing instructional text (Third edition)*. London: Kopan Page.

Hoeken, H., Mom, M., & Maes, F. (1994). Translating hierarchical instructions into linear text: Depth-first versus breadth-first approaches. In M. Steehouder, C. Jansen, P. van der Poort, & R. Verheijen (Eds.), *The quality of technical documentation* (pp. 99-113). Amsterdam/Atlanta: Rodopi

Horn, R.E. (1982). Structured writing and text design. In D.H. Jonassen (Ed.), *The technology of text: Principles for structuring, designing and displaying text* (pp. 341-367). Englewood Cliffs, NJ: Educational Technology Publications.

Horn, R.E. (1985). Results with structured writing using the Information Mapping Writing service standards. In T.M. Duffy, & R. Waller (Eds.), *Designing usable texts* (pp. 179-211). Orlando, FL: Academic Press.

Jacobson, R. (1995). *Microsoft Excel/Visual Basic step by step*. Redmond, WA: Microsoft Press.

Jansen, C.J.M., & Steehouder, M.F. (1989). *Taalverkeersproblemen tussen overheid en burger. Een onderzoek naar verbeteringsmogelijkheden voor voorlichtingsteksten en formulieren* [Communication problems between government and citizens]. The Hague: SDU.

Just, M.A. & Carpenter, P.A. (1980). A theory of reading: From eye-fixations to comprehension. *Psychological Review, 87*, 329-354.

Kern, R.P. (1985). Modelling users and their use of technical manuals. In T.M. Duffy & R. Waller (Eds.), *Designing usable texts* (pp. 341-371). Orlando, FL: Academic Press.

Kieras, D.E., & Bovair, S. (1984). The role of a mental model in learning to operate a device. *Cognitive Science, 8*, 255-273.

Knowles, C. (1988). Can Cognitive Complexity Theory (CCT) produce an adequate measure of system usability? In Jones, D.M., & Winder, R.

(Eds.), *Proceedings of the fourth conference of the British Computer Society*, 291-307.

Lazonder, A.W., & Van der Meij, H. (1993). The minimal manual: Is less really more? *International journal of man-machine studies, 39*, 729-752.

Mack, R.L., Lewis, C. H., & Carroll, J.M. (1983). Learning to use word processors: Problems and prospects. *ACM Transactions on office information systems, 1*, 254-271.

Mirel, B. (1991). Critical review of experimental research on the usability of hard copy documentation. *IEEE transactions on professional communication, 34*, 109-122.

Nielsen, J. (1995). *Multimedia and hypertext: The Internet and beyond.* Boston, MA: AP Professional.

Norman, D.A. (1983). Some observations on mental models. In D. Gentner, & A.L. Stevens (Eds.), *Mental models*. Hillsdale, NJ: LEA

Nystrand, M. (1986). *The structure of written communication.* Orlando, FL: Academic Press.

Ramey, J. (1988). How people use computer documentation: Implications for book design. In S. Doheny-Farina (Ed.), *Effective documentation: What we have learned from research* (pp. 143-157). Cambridge, MA: MIT Press.

Reder, L.M., Charney, D.H., & Morgan, K.I. (1986). The role of elaborations in learning a skill from instructional text. *Memory & Cognition, 14*, 64-78.

Redish, J.C. (1988). Reading to learn to do. *Technical Writing Teacher, 15*, 223-233.

Sasse, M.A. (1991). How to t(r)ap users' mental models. In Tauber, M.J., & Ackermann, D. (Eds.), *Mental models and human-computer interaction 2.* Amsterdam: Elsevier.

Schriver, K.A. (1984). Revising computer documentation for comprehension: ten exercises in protocol-aided revision. *Technical Report, 14*, Pittsburgh, PA: Communications Design Center.

Schumacher, G.M., & Waller, R. (1985). Testing design alternatives: a comparison of procedures. In T.M. Duffy, & R. Waller (Eds.), *Designing usable texts* (pp. 341-371). Orlando, FL: Academic Press.

Shneiderman, B. (1987). *Designing the user interface: Strategies for effective human-computer interaction.* Reading, MA: Addison-Wesley.

Smith, E.E., & L. Goodman (1984). Understanding written instructions: the role of an explanatory schema. *Cognition and Instruction, 1,* 359-396.

Steehouder, M.F. (1994). The quality of access: Helping users find information in documentation. In Steehouder, M., Jansen, C., van der Poort, P., & Verheijen, R. (Eds.), *The quality of technical documentation* (pp. 131-144). Amsterdam/Atlanta: Rodopi.

Sticht, T. (1977). Comprehending reading at work. In M.A. Just, & P.A. Carpenter (Eds.), *Cognitive processes in comprehension* (pp. 221-246). Hillsdale, NJ: Erlbaum.

Sticht, T. (1985). Understanding readers and their uses of texts. In T.M. Duffy, & R. Waller (Eds.), *Designing usable texts* (pp. 315-339). Orlando, FL: Academic Press.

Ummelen, N. (1994). Procedural and declarative information: a closer examination of the distinction. In Steehouder, M., Jansen, C., van der Poort, P., & Verheijen, R. (Eds.), *The quality of technical documentation* (pp. 115-131). Amsterdam/Atlanta: Rodopi.

Van der Meij, H., & Carroll, J.M. (1995). Principles and heuristics for designing minimalist instruction. *Technical Communication, 2,* 243-262.

Virtanen, T. (1992). Issues of text typology: Narrative- a basic type of text? *Text, 12,* 293-310.

Werlich, E. (1979). *Typologie der Texte* [Typology of texts]. Heidelberg: Quelle & Meyer.

Wright, P. (1988). Issues of content and presentation in document design. In M. Helander (Ed.), *Handbook of human-computer interaction* (pp. 629-652). North-Holland: Elsevier Science.

Wright, P. (1989). The need for theories of NOT reading: some psychological aspects of the human-computer interface. In H. Bouma (Ed.), *Working models of human perception* (pp. 319-340). London: Academic Press.

Wright, P., Creighton, P., & Threlfall, S.M. (1982). Some factors determining when instructions will be read. *Ergonomics, 25*, 225-237.

Wright, P., & Lickorish, A. (1990). An empirical comparison of two navigation systems for two hypertexts. In R. McAleese, & C. Green (Eds.), *Hypertext: State of the art* (pp. 84-93). Oxford: Intellect Limited.

Wright, P., & Wilcox, P. (1978). Following instructions: an exploratory trisection of imperatives. In W.J.M. Levelt, & Flores d'Arcais (Eds.), *Studies in the perception of language* (pp. 129-153). New York: Wiley and Sons.

Young, R.M. (1981). The machine inside the machine: users' models of pocket calculators. *International Journal of Man-Machine Studies, 15*, 51-85.

Young, R.M. (1983). Surrogates and mappings: two kinds of conceptual models for interactive devices. In D. Gentner, & A.L. Stevens (Eds.), *Mental models*. Hillsdale, NJ: LEA

Appendix 1   *Extracts from experimental manuals*

1A PD-manual

QubeCalc

Moving the cursor

*If you want to move the cursor over a distance of only **1 or a few cells**:*

Press the arrow keys as often as is necessary.   The cursor moves one cell at a time.

*If you want to move the cursor **directly to a certain cell**:*

1. Press F5.   The question: "Go to which cell? [x;y;z]" appears.

2. Type the cell coordinates of the cell where you want to place the cursor, separated by spaces, and press Enter.   The cursor moves directly to the new cell.

*If you want to move the cursor **to another page**:*

Press PgUp.   The cursor moves to the next page.
Press PgDn.   The cursor moves to the previous page.

*If you want to move the cursor **to the last cell of the page**:*

Press End.

*If you want to move the cursor **to the first cell of the page**:*

Press Home.

What is a cursor?; Of which components do cell references consist?; Size of the worksheet

What is a cursor?

The cursor in QubeCalc can take different shapes. Usually it appears in the shape of a small block in a cell, to indicate that this is the active cell. In the menus, the cursor is a small block which marks the active menu-item. When data are being changed, the cursor appears as a blinking dash on the status line. The cursor responds to several keys. The arrow-keys always work, but when the cursor has to be moved over longer distances, or when a new cursor position is known exactly, QubeCalc has more efficient commands for cursor movements.

Of which components do cell references consist?

Sometimes, cell references are required in order to move the cursor. QubeCalc makes a distinction between absolute and relative cell references. In formulas, this distinction may be important, but for the current purpose, it is not relevant. For direct cursor movements, 3 cell coordinates for the destination cell are sufficient.

Cell references exist of an X-, a Y-, and a Z-coordinate which are separated in QubeCalc by semi-colons. The screen shows which coordinates are the X-, Y-, and Z-coordinates. In the standard perspective (perspective A, see elsewhere in this manual), the X-coordinate reflects the column number, the Y-coordinate the row number and the Z-coordinate the page number.

Size of the worksheet

The X-, Y-, and Z- coordinates can take a value of up to 63. That means that there is a maximum of 63 columns, 63 rows and 63 pages in a WorkQube. Thus, the last cursor position on the last page is (63,63,63).

1B P-manual

QubeCalc

Moving the cursor

*If you want to move the cursor over a distance of only **1 or a few cells**:*
Press the arrow keys as often as is necessary.　　The cursor moves one cell at a time.

*If you want to move the cursor **directly to a certain cell**:*
1.　Press F5.　　　　　　　　　　　　　　　　The question: "Go to which cell? [x;y;z]" appears.

2.　Type the cell coordinates of the cell where you want to place the cursor, separated by spaces, and press Enter.　　　　　　　　　The cursor moves directly to the new cell.

*If you want to move the cursor **to another page**:*
Press PgUp.　　　　　　　　　　　　　　　The cursor moves to the next page.
Press PgDn.　　　　　　　　　　　　　　　The cursor moves to the previous page.

*If you want to move the cursor **to the last cell of the page**:*
Press End.

*If you want to move the cursor **to the first cell of the page**:*
Press Home.

Choosing in a menu

If you see a different menu to the one you are looking for:
1. Press Escape　　　　　　　　　　　　　The irrelevant menu disappears from the screen.

If there is no menu and you want to make a choice from a certain menu:

Method 1:
1. Finish any data-entry actions by pressing Enter or Escape.
2. Press /.　　　　　　　　　　　　　　　The Main Menu appears on screen.
3. Go to the menu-option you need by pressing the arrow-keys, and press Enter.　　　　　A submenu appears on screen.
4. Go to the menu-item of your choice by pressing the arrow-keys and press Enter.　　Either a new submenu appears on screen, or the command is being executed.

Method 2:
1. Finish any data-entry actions by pressing Enter or Escape.
2. Press /.　　　　　　　　　　　　　　　The Main Menu appears on screen.
3. Type the first letter of the menu-item of your choice.　A submenu appears on screen.
4. Again type the first letter of the menu-item of your choice.
　　　　　　　　　　　　　　　　　　　Either a new submenu appears on screen, or the command is being executed.

1C Mix-manual

QubeCalc

What is a cursor?

The cursor in QubeCalc can take different shapes. Usually it appears in the shape of a small block in a cell, to indicate that this is the active cell. In the menus, the cursor is a small block which marks the active menu-item. When data are being changed, the cursor appears as a blinking dash on the status line. The cursor responds to several keys. The arrow-keys always work, but when the cursor has to be moved over longer distances, or when a new cursor position is known exactly, QubeCalc has more efficient commands for cursor movements.

Moving the cursor

*If you want to move the cursor over a distance of only **1 or a few cells:***
    Press the arrow keys as often as is necessary.   The cursor moves one cell at a time.

*If you want to move the cursor **directly to a certain cell**:*
1. Press F5.   The question: "Go to which cell? [x;y;z]" appears.

2. Type the cell coordinates of the cell where you want to place the cursor, separated by spaces, and press Enter.
    The cursor moves directly to the new cell.

Of which components do cell references consist?

Sometimes, cell references are required in order to move the cursor. QubeCalc makes a distinction between absolute and relative cell references. In formulas, this distinction may be important, but for the current purpose, it is not relevant. For direct cursor movements, 3 cell coordinates for the destination cell are sufficient.

Cell references exist of an X-, a Y-, and a Z-coordinate which are separated in QubeCalc by semi-colons. The screen shows which coordinates are the X-, Y-, and Z-coordinates. In the standard perspective (perspective A, see elsewhere in this manual), the X-coordinate reflects the column number, the Y-coordinate the row number and the Z-coordinate the page number.

*If you want to move the cursor **to another page:***
    Press PgUp.   The cursor moves to the next page.
    Press PgDn.   The cursor moves to the previous page.

*If you want to move the cursor **to the last cell of the page**:*
    Press End.

Size of the worksheet

The X-, Y-, and Z- coordinates can take a value of up to 63. That means that there is a maximum of 63 columns, 63 rows and 63 pages in a WorkQube. Thus, the last cursor position on the last page is (63,63,63).

*If you want to move the cursor **to the first cell of the page**:*
    Press Home.

1D Two sections from the Hypertext-manual (presented on separate screens)

QubeCalc

Moving the cursor

*If you want to move the cursor over a distance of only **1 or a few cells**:*
Press the arrow keys as often as is necessary.   The cursor moves one cell at a time.

*If you want to move the cursor **directly to a certain cell**:*

1. Press F5.   The question: "Go to which cell?
                                              [x;y;z]" appears.
2. *Type* the *cell coordinates* of the cell where you want to place the cursor, separated
   by spaces, and press Enter.   The cursor moves directly to the new
                                              cell.

*If you want to move the cursor **to another page**:*
Press PgUp.   The cursor moves to the next page.
Press PgDn.   The cursor moves to the previous
                                              page.
*If you want to move the cursor **to the last cell of the page**:*
Press End.

*If you want to move the cursor **to the first cell of the page**:*
Press Home.

Size of the worksheet   *Loading a file*

Entering data in a cell   *Of which components do cell references consist?*

Choosing from a menu   *What is a cursor?*

QubeCalc

Of which components do cell references consist?

Sometimes, cell references are required in order to *move the cursor*. QubeCalc makes a
distinction between absolute and relative cell references. In formulas, this distinction may
be important, but for the current purpose, it is not relevant. For direct cursor movements, 3
cell coordinates for the destination cell are sufficient.
Cell references exist of an X-, a Y-, and a Z-coordinate which are separated in QubeCalc
by semi-colons. *The screen shows* which coordinates are the X-, Y-, and Z-coordinates. In
the standard perspective (perspective A, see elsewhere in this manual), the X-coordinate
reflects the column number, the Y-coordinate the row number and the Z-coordinate the
page number.

Cell references in calculations   *Calculating with formulas*

The six perspectives   *Moving the cursor*

The screen and the status line   *Changing the perspective*

Appendix 2   *The interim task*

The interim task was based on experimental research by Bayman & Mayer (1988) and by Young (1983), who studied mental models by using the concept of a four function calculator: a simple calculator with only the functions "+", "-", "/" and "x" function. Four function calculators work in a specific way that does not always match the algorithms that people normally use to make simple calculations. People have to fully understand the internal working of the calculator in order to be able to use all the options the calculator offers. Four function calculators for instance enable the function n^2 in a shorter way than most people would calculate it.

	What most people do	Four function calculator
You want to calculate 4^2	4 x 4 =	4 x =
You want to calculate $((4^2)^2)^2$	4 x 4 = x 16 = x 256 =	4 x = x = x =

Two tasks were constructed to let subjects work with a four function calculator. They had to understand the internal working of the calculator in order to be able to perform the tasks. Subjects could find information about the working of the calculator and about the tasks that can be performed with it on paper with instructions attached to a whiteboard in front of them. They were allowed to use this information whenever they thought it was necessary.

In the first task, subjects had to use the calculator to calculate the 24th "number of Fibonacci". Fibonacci was an Italian mathematician whose name is connected with a certain chain of numbers in which each number is the sum of its two predecessors. The chain starts as follows: 1   1   2   3   5   8.....
"2" Is the third number of Fibonacci, "5" is the fifth number of Fibonacci, and subjects had to calculate the 24th number of Fibonacci. They were not allowed to use pen and paper, so they had to use the calculator. The memory functions of the calculator were disabled, and subjects were not allowed to write down intermediate answers either.
The procedure "1 + = + = + = + =......." (24 times the sequence "+ =" in total) eventually led to the correct answer.

In the second task, subjects were not allowed to actually use the calculator. They had to predict the contents of the calculator display in calculations of which the input was given on a sheet of paper (see example). For every input item, the corresponding display contents had to be predicted. Also they had to explain why they thought the predicted outcome was correct. Predicting the correct outcome was only possible if they understood the working of the calculator's internal memory.

Example:
Input   10   /   =
Display   ...   .

Appendix 3   *Factual knowledge questionnaire*

Questions about QubeCalc

1   Explain how the menu structure in QubeCalc is built up.

2   Why does the Graph menu contain the options A, B and C?

3   Which information can you find on the status line?

4   a   How does QubeCalc recognize different types of input data?

    b   Explain the differences between the data types that can be used in QubeCalc.

5   How many characters fit into one cell?

6   What is the difference between working with blocks in QubeCalc and working with blocks in many other programs?

7   When do you use relative cell references?

8   In which ways can the / key be interpreted by QubeCalc?

9   What is "Datafill?"

10 What happens when you:

    * enter more figures than can fit into one cell?

    * enter more letters than can fit into one cell?

Appendix 4 *Illustrations of click & read screens*

4A The click & read method: a page with blurred text blocks from the QubeCalc manual (Section 2.3.3)

On screen, the headings were sharp and well legible. When subjects clicked on the blurred text blocks, these blocks were enlarged and sharpened (see Appendix 4B).

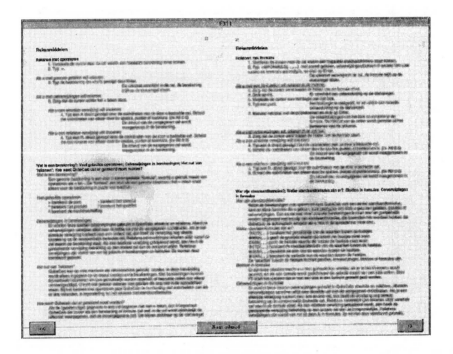

4B   *The click & read method: blurred page with one selected text block (Section 2.3.3.1)*

The text block has been enlarged and sharpened after a mouse click. The subject has to click *Terug naar pagina* (Back to full page) first to make a new selection.

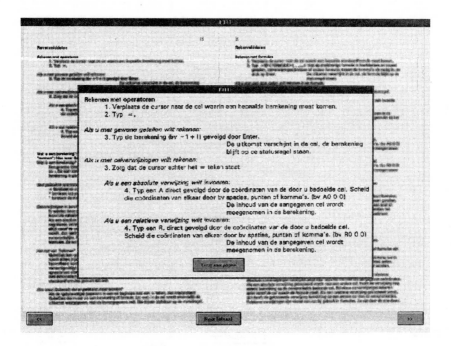

4C The improved click & read method (Section 2.3.3.3)

The text block to the upper left has been clicked. On screen, it is now sharp and well legible. The other text blocks are still blurred, except for the headings. They can be clicked directly from this position.

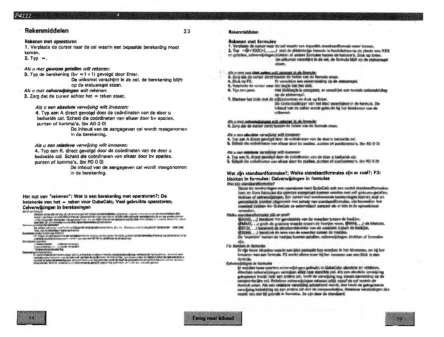

Appendix 5   *Examples of logfiles and processed logfiles*

5A   Integrated logfiles

```
13:02:44 '='        13:03:23 Space      13:03:49 '1'        13:05:11 "F4101
13:02:45 'R'        13:03:24 '+'        13:03:49 '3'        13:05:27 Up
13:02:53 '1'        13:03:24 Space      13:03:49 Space      13:05:28 Up
13:02:54 Space      13:03:26 'R'        13:03:50 '0'        13:05:28 Up
13:02:54 '3'        13:03:27 '1'        13:03:53 Enter      13:05:28 Up
13:02:55 Space      13:03:28 Space      13:03:58 '/'        13:05:28 Up
13:02:55 '0'        13:03:28 '9'        13:03:59 Enter      13:05:28 Up
13:02:56 Space      13:03:29 Space      13:04:00 Right      13:05:29 Up
13:02:58 '+'        13:03:29 '0'        13:04:00 Right      13:05:29 Up
13:02:58 Space      13:03:29 Space      13:04:00 Right      13:05:29 Up
13:03:06 'R'        13:03:31 '+'        13:04:00 Right      13:05:29 Up
13:03:10 '1'        13:03:31 Space      13:04:17 Enter      13:05:29 Up
13:03:10 Space      13:03:32 'R'        13:04:19 Right      13:05:29 Up
13:03:11 '5'        13:03:33 '1'        13:04:19 Right      13:05:29 Up
13:03:11 Space      13:03:35 Space      13:04:19 Right      13:05:30 Up
13:03:12 '0'        13:03:37 '1'        13:04:20 Right      13:05:30 Up
13:03:12 Space      13:03:37 '1'        13:04:22 Enter      13:05:30 Up
13:03:15 '+'        13:03:38 Space      13:04:55 "Klik"     13:05:31 Left
13:03:15 Space      13:03:40 '0'        13:04:55 "F305"     13:05:49 '/'
13:03:17 'R'        13:03:40 Space      13:04:59 "Klik"     13:05:55 Right
13:03:18 '1'        13:03:41 '+'        13:05:00 "Inhoud"   13:05:56 Right
13:03:19 Space      13:03:42 Space      13:05:07 "Klik"     13:05:56 Right
13:03:19 '7'        13:03:45 'R'        13:05:09 "F310"     13:05:58 Enter
13:03:21 Space      13:03:47 '1'        13:05:11 "Klik
13:03:22 '0'        13:03:47 Space
```

5B   The result of processing phase 1: Summarizing arrow keys and character strings

```
13:02:44   13:03:50  =R1~3~0~+~R1~5~0~+~R1~7~0~+~R1~9~0~+~R1~11~0~+~R1~13~0
           13:03:53  Enter
13:03:58   13:03:58  /
           13:03:59  Enter
13:04:00   13:04:00  4 x Rechts   (4,0)
           13:04:17  Enter
13:04:19   13:04:20  4 x Rechts   (4,0)
           13:04:22  Enter
           13:04:55  "F305"
           13:05:00  "Inhoud"
           13:05:09  "F310"
           13:05:11  "F4101"
13:05:27   13:05:31  1 x Links   16 x Op   (-1,16)
13:05:49   13:05:49  /
13:05:55   13:05:56  3 x Rechts   (3,0)
           13:05:58  Enter
```

5C   The result of processing phase 2: Addition of menu options

```
13:02:44   13:03:50  =R1~3~0~+~R1~5~0~+~R1~7~0~+~R1~9~0~+~R1~11~0~+~R1~13~0
           13:03:53  Enter
13:03:58   13:03:58  /
           13:03:59  Enter [ Cell ]
13:04:00   13:04:00  4 x Rechts   (4,0)
           13:04:17  Enter [ Cell Copy ]
13:04:19   13:04:20  4 x Rechts   (4,0)
           13:04:22  Enter
           13:04:55  "F305"
           13:05:00  "Inhoud"
           13:05:09  "F310"
           13:05:11  "F4101"
13:05:27   13:05:31  1 x Links   16 x Op   (-1,16)
13:05:49   13:05:49  /
13:05:55   13:05:56  3 x Rechts   (3,0)
           13:05:58  Enter [ Insert ]
```

Appendix 6   *Instructions for the experiment*

Tutorial situation

This experiment consists of two computer tasks. We would like to investigate how people solve everyday tasks with the spreadsheet QubeCalc.

In front of you, you will see a computer which is running the spreadsheet system "QubeCalc". We will ask you to **learn to work** with QubeCalc by carrying out two assignments. You have plenty of time. The assignments are not very important in themselves, but they should enable you to learn how the spreadsheet works in general: the assignments function as a guide through the tasks.

You will find a manual on the instruction screen next to you. You can leaf through the pages and make text blocks bigger and fully readable by clicking on the relevant icons with the mouse. When you have finished, you will receive a test assignment and a questionnaire about the spreadsheet. You cannot use the manual anymore in that stage.

Do you have any questions? Then you can ask them now! If the procedure is clear to you, you can start by practising mouse clicking on the manual screen. After the practise you can click "start experiment" and start with the first assignment.

Intermediate situation

This experiment consists of several computer tasks. We would like to investigate how people solve everyday tasks with the spreadsheet QubeCalc.

It is important that you concentrate on the assignments you will receive during the experiment, and that you will try to carry out those assignments **as fast and as well** as possible. You do not need to know specific details about the program. You will receive more assignments, and you will probably be able to use elements from the first assignments again in later assignments.

When you have finished your assignments, you will receive an extra assignment. You can use a manual throughout all the assignments. You will find the manual on the instruction screen next to you. You can leaf through the pages and make text blocks bigger and fully readable by clicking on the relevant icons with the mouse.

Do you have any questions? You can ask them now! If the procedure is clear to you, you can start by practising mouse clicking on the manual screen. After the practise you can click "start experiment" and start with the first assignment.

Reference situation

This experiment consists of two computer tasks. We would like to investigate how people solve everyday tasks with the spreadsheet QubeCalc.

It is important that you concentrate on the assignments you will receive during the experiment, and that you will try to carry out those assignments **as fast and as well** as possible. You do not need to know specific details about the program.

You will find a manual on the instruction screen next to you. You can leaf through the pages and make text blocks bigger and fully readable by clicking on the relevant icons with the mouse.

Do you have any questions? Then you can ask them now! If the procedure is clear to you, you can start by practising mouse clicking on the manual screen. After the practise you can click "start experiment" and start with the first assignment.

Appendix 7   *The experimental spreadsheet tasks*

7A *Experiment 1*

Simple task
You are about to work in part of an administration of a club which makes a clothes collection and organizes a clothes sale every year to line the club's purse.

After the latest collection, the stock is as follows:
414 sweaters
261 pairs of trousers
552 T-shirts
188 skirts
105 coats
262 ties

1 Open the file "Voorraad". (= "stock")
2 Delete the numbers in the "#Voorraad" column.
3 Enter the new numbers.
4 Make the numbers appear in the correct format (0 digits after the decimal point)
5 Calculate the new contents of the cells in the column "Verkoopwaarde Voorraad" (= stock value)
6 Add up the new column "Verkoopwaarde Voorraad", so that the new outcome appears in the "Total" cell underneath that column.
7 Add an empty column to the very left side of the screen, and "number" the rows containing information from A to F.
8 Save the file "Voorraad" using the same name. The old file is no longer needed.

Complex task
You are about to work in part of an administration of a club. The club keeps track of salary expenses, travelling expenses and telephone expenses per quarter. They have entered their data up to 1993. Now these data should be processed further; mean expenses should for instance be calculated, a typing error should be corrected and a graph should be created. What has to be done is described more precisely in the task instructions below.

1 Load the file "Kosten".
2 Somebody made a typing error when entering the numbers for the fourth quarter of 1993. The salary expenses should be rounded off to units of 10 cents, so the last two numbers in the cells of the second column are not correct. Change these numbers.
3 Change the perspective of the spreadsheet in such a way that the years, that are on the "page"-axis will appear on the y-axis. The different types of expenses stay on the x-axis.
4 Make a bar graph from this new perspective which displays the salary expenses for the first quarter of the three different years. Display the graph on the screen.
5 Go back to the original perspective, with the quarters on the height-axis, the expenses on the breadth-axis and the years on the depth-axis.
6 Calculate the average travelling expenses per quarter in 1993. The outcome should be displayed under the total amount of travelling expenses in 1993. Do the same thing for the years 1992 and 1991 by copying the calculation for 1993.
7 The column of "Totals" is positioned very closely to the column in front, because in this way, everything fits on one screen. It does however give an unclear view of the data. As you have finished now anyway, copy the column of totals as a block to the empty column to its right, and delete the data in the original column afterwards. Do so for 1991, 1992 and 1993.

8   Save the file "Kosten" using the same name. The old file is no longer needed.

7B Experiment 2

The introductions to the simple and the complex tasks were the same as those in appendix 8A. Therefore, only the subtasks are mentioned here.

Simple task
1   Open the file "Voorraad". (= "stock")
2   Enter the new numbers in the "#Voorraad" column.
3   There were and still are no data about collected or sold shoes. Therefore, erase the cell that contains the word "shoes" in the first column.
4   The numbers in the "#Voorraad" column do not need any decimal places. Make the numbers appear in the column without decimals.
5   Add an empty column to the very left side of the screen, and "number" the rows containing information from A to F.
6   Save the file "Voorraad" using the same name. The old file is no longer needed

Complex task
1   Open the file "Kosten".
2   Change the perspective of the spreadsheet in such a way that the years, that are on the "page"-axis (z-axis) will appear on the y-axis. The different types of expenses stay on the x-axis.
3   Calculate the average travelling expenses for the *fourth* quarters of the years 1991, 1992 and 1993. The travelling expenses can be found in column no. 4 (the third column filled with data). The outcome should be displayed under that column. Do the same thing for the *first* quarters of the three years.
4   Change the perspective back to the original perspective.
5   The column of "Totals" is positioned very closely to the column in front, because in this way, everything fits on one screen. It does however give an unclear view of the data. As you have finished now anyway, copy the column of totals as a block to the empty column to its right, and delete the data in the original column afterwards. Do so for 1991, 1992 and 1993.
6   Save the file "Kosten" using the same name. The old file is no longer needed.

7C Experiment 3

You are about to work in part of an administration of a club. The club keeps track of salary expenses, travelling expenses and telephone expenses per quarter. They have entered their data up to 1994. Now these data should be processed further; mean expenses should for instance be calculated. What has to be done is described more precisely in the task instructions below.

1   Open the file "Kosten".
2   The amounts in the column "Travelling expenses" only have one decimal place. They ought to have two decimal places. Change that for all years.
3   Change the perspective of the spreadsheet in such a way that the years, that are on the "page"-axis (z-axis) will appear on the y-axis. The different types of expenses stay on the x-axis.
4   Calculate the average travelling expenses for the *fourth* quarters of the years 1992, 1993 and 1994. The travelling expenses can be found in column no. 4 (the third column filled with data). The outcome should be displayed under that column. Do the same thing for the *first* quarters of the three years.

5   Change the perspective back to the original perspective.
6   The column of "Totals" is positioned very closely to the column in front, because in this way, everything fits on one screen. It does however give an unclear view of the data. As you have finished now anyway, insert a column there. Do so for the 1992, 1993 en 1994 data.
7   Finally, prepare the page for the 1995 data already:
    a. Copy the 1994 page to the empty page behind it.
    b. Erase all the amounts on the copy.
    c. Change the year from 1994 into 1995.
8   Save the file "Kosten" using the same name. The old file is no longer needed.

7D Reasoning task

The spreadsheet task with a brief description of the reasoning problems that had to be solved by the subjects.

General:
(The experimenter uses arrow keys until the subject indicates that the actions can be performed faster.)
(The experimenter works cell by cell until the subject indicates that working in a block is faster.)

1   Open the file "Cijfers" ("Grades").

The experimenter loads the file in a correct way.

The file "Cijfers" presents test results of 4 students for the subjects French, English and Mathematics. The students had to take two tests for each subject. The file should present the average grades per test, per student and per subject. The averages per subjects are based on the average test results.

2   Check whether or not all the grades mentioned are in the file. Enter any grades or calculations that are missing.

The subject performs this subtask all by himself - delayed task performance

3   Check whether or not all test results are rounded off to one decimal place and whether all student averages to zero decimal places. Change the format of all amounts that do not have the correct number of decimal places.

*   *The experimenter first tries to change the formats by using the Justify-option. Subjects should signal the error and indicate what the correct procedure is.*
*   *Then the correct menu-option is chosen, but it is applied in a cell-by-cell way. The subject should signal the inefficiency. If he doesn't, the experimenter continues changing one cell at a time.*
*   *Subjects were asked what would happen to the format of numbers if a certain column would be narrowed. Would the extra decimal place automatically disappear?*
*   *The experimenter then narrows the column (from width 9 to width 3). A series of asterisks appear in the column. Subjects should explain this.*

4   Now change the WorkQube in such a way that tests 1 and 2 appear on the x-axis, the students on the y-axis and the subjects on the z-axis.

* The subject should explain what this assignment actually means (test in columns, students in rows, subjects stay on the pages) In fact, only the x-axis and the y-axis are exchanged.
* The subject should tell the experimenter how this can be done (perspective).
* The current perspective is D, but the default is A. The experimenter tells the subjects that she is going to try perspective D to carry out the task. Subjects should signal that D cannot be correct. If they don't, the experimenter will indeed try perspective D and nothing will happen. Subjects are asked why nothig happens. If they give the correct answer, they are asked how they know that this is already perspective D (can be seen on screen) and whether or not they know the correct perspective to achieve the goal.

5 The formula that has been used to calculate the test averages consists of an addition that is divided by 4. That is not the best way to calculate this. There is also a formula for "Average": "avg". Change the formulas for the subject French.

* The experimenter asks why the AVG method is better.
* The experimenter asks how she should change the formula (Edit function). If the subject answers that the formula should be retyped, the experimenter retypes it.
* The experimenter types no capitals in the formula (error), and also, she puts "/4" behind the average formula.The subject should signal the two errors, explain why they are errors and tell the experimenter what the correct procedure is.

6 Make all the average grades appear on one screen.

* The experimenter asks what strategy should be followed to solve this problem. (Perspective)
* The experimenter chooses the correct perspective F, but starting from an empty row. The result is an empty page on screen. The experimenter asks the subjects if all the data are now lost, and how this can happen.

7 Save "Cijfers" (the old file is no longer needed) and leave QubeCalc.

Utrecht Studies
in Language and Communication

Series editors:

Paul van den Hoven and Wolfgang Herrlitz

The last two decades have shown a remarkable increase of research on communication and language use in specific social and cultural settings, ranging from broad and more or less heterogeneous communities to highly specialized professional organizations. This increase draws upon a manifestly growing cooperation between such diverse disciplines as text linguistics, discourse analysis, ethnography of communication, speech act theory, cognitive linguistics, educational linguistics, cognitive psychology and anthropology. Cooperative efforts from these approaches are essential in order to improve our understanding of:

- the functional quality of texts and text features in view of the specific goals and the addressees of professional and educational institutions
- the relationship between discourse and context in specific and changing social and cultural settings, including multilingual and multicultural interactions
- the cognitive basis of discourse processing in continuously changing contexts, and the skills underlying goal-directed language use in familiar as well as novel situations
- the acquisition of such flexible linguistic capacities in educational settings.

At the Center for Language and Communication of the Rijksuniversiteit Utrecht in the Netherlands, an interdisciplinary approach is being pursued directed towards developing and integrating theoretical insights in language use in specific social and cultural contexts, and in the processes, both in first and second language learning, by which people acquire the ability for such language use. The aim of the Utrecht Studies in Language and Communication is to publish results of research in this area, as well as immediately related areas.

Volume 1: **Studies of functional text quality.** Edited by Henk Pander Maat and Michaël Steehouder. Amsterdam/Atlanta, GA 1992. 186 pp.
ISBN: 90-5183-412-8   Hfl. 60,-/US-$ 37.50

Volume 2: **Tom Koole & Jan D. ten Thije: The construction of intercultural discourse.** Team discussions of educational advisers. Amsterdam/Atlanta, GA 1994. XII,267 pp.
ISBN: 90-5183-600-7   Hfl. 90,-/US-$ 56.-
This book breaks open the 'black box' of the workplace, where successful immigrants work together with their Dutch colleagues. In their intercultural team meetings the work itself consists of communication and the question is how that work is done.
The teams consist of Dutch, Turkish, Moroccan, and Surinamese educational experts whose job it is to advise schools and teachers on the form and content of language teaching.
Their meetings are structured according to *institutional* patterns, such as 'interactive planning' and 'reporting', and according to *intercultural* discourse structures. For instance, Dutch team members identify their immigrant colleagues as 'immigrant specialists' and are themselves identified as 'institutional specialists'. Further, the intercultural pattern 'thematizing and unthematizing racism' provides the team members with communicative methods to deal with the societal contradictions that exist between different cultural groups, in the Netherlands as well as elsewhere. These intercultural discourse structures concur with the institutional patterns so that, for instance, they affect the outcomes of planning discussions.
Most studies on intercultural communication focus on misunderstandings and miscommunications. This book demonstrates that also communication without miscommunication can be shown to be intercultural.

Volume 3: **Quality of technical documentation**. Edited by Michaël Steehouder, Carel Jansen, Pieter van der Poort, Ron Verheijen Amsterdam/Atlanta, GA 1994. 257 pp.
ISBN: 90-5183-627-9   Hfl. 75,-/US-$ 46.50
User manuals, reference guides, project documentation, equipment specifications and other technical documents are increasingly subjected to high quality standards. However, it is not clear whether research efforts are keeping pace with this increasing importance of documentation quality.

This volume includes studies from researchers as well as practitioners, exemplifying three approaches towards document quality.

Product-orientation, with an eye for usability in various manifestations such as tutorials, concept definitions, tools for users of documentation to find information, methods of eliciting user feedback, and cultural differences.

Process-orientation, in which the quality of technical documentation is regarded as an outgrowth of a process involving sub-steps such as storyboarding, pre-testing and use of automation tools in writing and producing documents.

Professional orientation, in which attention is focused on those who create technical documentation.

The volume will be of interest to a broad audience of writers, managers and trainers with technical and non-technical backgrounds, such as: quality managers; communication managers; technical communicators; trainers in computer usage; teachers, researchers and students of (technical) communication.

Volume 4: **Functional Communication Quality.** Edited by Luuk van Waes, Egbert Woudstra and Paul van den Hoven. Amsterdam/Atlanta, GA 1994. 219 pp.
ISBN: 90-5183-738-0   Hfl. 65,-/US-$ 40.50
In this volume researchers from American and European universities and institutes present their recent research on 'Functional Communication Quality'.

Functional refers to the purposes of the communication process. The relations between these purposes and the best way to describe them, are some of the topics discussed.

Communication refers to a complex interactive process. Relevant variables include the speech act of the participants, features of the message, chosen channel, moment, duration, frequency, environment. The participants in this process are individuals and groups as well as organizations and parts of organizations.

Quality can be described from several points of view: a technical point of view with efficiency as its goal, an operative point of view which aims for effectiveness or an aesthetic point of view.

This volume shows that a multi-perspective approach to Functional Communication Quality (FCQ) is the only way to obtain a better insight

into this area of communication studies. The papers are grouped in four different chapters, each dealing with a different perspective on the theme:
• FCQ in an organizational context;
• FCQ and research methods;
• FCQ and text analysis;
• FCQ and electronic tools.
The book also contains an overview of organizational communication research in France and Spain.
This volume will be of interest to a broad audience of researchers and students in the field of organizational communication studies and the field of writing studies, communication consultants and communication managers, professional writers and software engineers.

Volume 5: **Michel Pêcheux: Automatic Discourse Analysis.** Edited by Tony Hak and Niels Helsloot. With contributions of Simone Bonnafous, Françoise Gadet, Paul Henry, Alain Lecomte, Jacqueline Léon, Denise Maldidier, Jean-Marie Marandin and Michel Plon. Translated by David Macey. Amsterdam/Atlanta, GA 1994. viii,264 pp.
ISBN: 90-5183-645-7   Hfl. 75,-/US-$ 46.50
This volume offers the long-awaited overview of the work of the French philosopher and discourse analyst Michel Pêcheux, who was the leading figure in French discourse analysis until his death in 1983. The volume presents the first English publication of the work of Pêcheux and his co-workers on automatic discourse analysis. It is presented with extensive annotations and introductions, written by former colleagues such as Françoise Gadet, Paul Henry and Denise Maldidier.
Outside France, French discourse analysis is almost exclusively known as the form of philosophical discourse presented by such authors as Michel Foucault and Jacques Derrida. The contemporary empirical forms of French discourse analysis have not reached a wider public to the degree they deserve. Through its combination of original texts, annotations, and several introductory texts, this volume facilitates an evaluation of both results and weaknesses of French discourse analysis in general and of the work of Michel Pêcheux and his coworkers in particular.

Volume 6: **Joost Schilperoord: It's about time.** Temporal aspects of cognitive processes in text production. Amsterdam/Atlanta, GA 1996. 354 pp.
ISBN: 90-5183-947-2   Hfl. 100,-/US-$ 62.50

A central issue of cognitive studies of text production is "What goes on in people's minds when they produce a text?", "How do they plan the text?", "How do they decide in what order to express their thoughts?" In this volume, writers are followed in their footsteps during the moment-to-moment process of producing routine business letters. Their writing processes are explored in *real time* with the ultimate goal to contribute to a cognitive theory of text production. Such a theory should tell what kind of mental structures underly text production, how these structures are converted into coherent texts, and how this process is framed within real writing time.

The study starts from a large corpus of real-life text production processes. It combines methods to explore both process and product of text production. Processes are described by analyzing the pause patterns that emerge in the course of writing. Products are described by analyzing their hierarchical structure. Together, these descriptions yield several significant insights in the real time organization of cognitive processes in production.

The study can be characterized as a cognitive linguistic approach to text production. This volume will be of special interest to researchers in the field of (psycho-)-linguistics, textlinguistics and cognitive science.

Volume 7: **Nicole Ummelen: Procedural and declarative information in software manuals.** Effects on information use, task performance and knowledge. Amsterdam/Atlanta, GA 1997. 224 pp.
ISBN: 90-420-0128-3   Hfl. 75,-/US-$ 46.50

People who use software manuals want to get something *done.* Procedural information directly supports this goal, but the use of declarative information in manuals has often been under discussion. Current research gives rise to the expectation that manual users tend to skip declarative information most of the time. Also, no effects of declarative information in software manuals have yet been found.

In this study, information use and information effects in software manuals are investigated in three experiments, thereby taking different user types, different task types and different information arrangements into account. A new technique was applied: the *click&read* method. This technique enables the software user to use the manual and carry out software tasks at the same time while information selection and times are recorded automatically in logfiles.

For the first time, quantitative data are presented about the amounts of procedural and declarative information that were selected and the times that were spent using these information types. Although procedural information is selected more often and used longer, declarative information appears to be a substantial part of the information selection. Moreover, the results show that using declarative information positively affects performance on future tasks, performance on reasoning tasks and factual knowledge.

Volume 8: **Geraldine W. van Rijn-van Tongeren: Metaphors in medical texts.** Amsterdam/Atlanta, GA 1997. 186 pp.
ISBN: 90-420-0127-5   Hfl. 60,-/US-$ 37.50
This book claims that metaphors must be seen as indispensable cognitive and communicative instruments in medical science. Analysis of texts taken from recently published medical handbooks reveals what kind of metaphors are used to structure certain medical concepts and what the functions are of the metaphorical expressions in the texts.

Special attention is drawn to the idea that scientific facts do not originate from passive observation of reality. Imaginative thinking and the use of metaphors are required to make the unknown accessible to us. Yet, although metaphors are often a *sine qua non* for the genesis of a scientific fact, they may also inhibit the development of alternative views. This is due to the fact that metaphors always highlight certain aspects of a phenomenon while other aspects remain obscured. Analysis of the metaphors used in medical texts may reveal exactly which aspects are highlighted and which remain hidden and may thus help to find alternative metaphors (and possibly therapies) when current metaphors are no longer adequate.

This book should be of interest not only to linguists, translators and researchers working in the field of intercultural communication, but also to doctors and medical scientists, and those interested in the philosophy of science.